The Grounds of the Novel

The Grounds of the Novel

Daniel Wright

Stanford University Press
STANFORD, CALIFORNIA

Stanford University Press
Stanford, California

© 2024 by Daniel Wright. All rights reserved.

No part of this book may be reproduced or transmitted in any form or by any means, electronic or mechanical, including photocopying and recording, or in any information storage or retrieval system, without the prior written permission of Stanford University Press.

Printed in the United States of America on acid-free, archival-quality paper

Library of Congress Cataloging-in-Publication Data
Names: Wright, Daniel, 1983- author.
Title: The grounds of the novel / Daniel Wright.
Description: Stanford, California : Stanford University Press, 2024. | Includes bibliographical references and index.
Identifiers: LCCN 2023017221 (print) | LCCN 2023017222 (ebook) | ISBN 9781503636835 (cloth) | ISBN 9781503637559 (paperback) | ISBN 9781503637566 (epub)
Subjects: LCSH: Fiction—History and criticism—Theory, etc.
Classification: LCC PN3331 .W75 2024 (print) | LCC PN3331 (ebook) | DDC 808.3—dc23/eng/20230830
LC record available at https://lccn.loc.gov/2023017221
LC ebook record available at https://lccn.loc.gov/2023017222

Cover art: Odilon Redon, *The Eye Like a Strange Balloon Mounts Toward Infinity*, 1882

CONTENTS

PREFACE
The Truth of Earth vii

INTRODUCTION
On What There Is in the Novel 1

1 **Groundwork** 32

2 **Underground** 69

3 **The Ground Gained** 106

4 **Meeting Grounds** 136

AFTERWORD
Basement 177

Acknowledgments 187

Notes 191

Bibliography 209

Index 223

PREFACE

The Truth of Earth

I am seeking a ground upon which to know that fictions are real.

I have never sought to know whether Pegasus exists, a question that has sometimes preoccupied philosophers. There he is, I've always thought, right there where I can see him, a winged majesty, his feet just lifting off the ground.

In *Daniel Deronda* (1876), there's a horse named Primrose who falls and breaks his knees.[1] Primrose does not lift off the ground; he breaks against it. There are horses where I live, in reality, and the ground underneath them is hard and unforgiving. The horses here are bound to the ground by gravity. Even a leap is a danger.

I don't wonder much about Pegasus, but I do wonder about Primrose, who seems so much like a real horse. Primrose exists, of that much I remain certain. George Eliot conjured him. There he is, in the novel, and that is enough for me. But I seek to know about the manner or the texture of his being and the being of the ground that breaks him. Does he only borrow his reality from the horses I have seen and known, and must he pay it back? Or is Primrose's being his own, sufficient, even unto death?

The question then turns back upon Pegasus. He is mostly a horse, I must admit, but he wings away and leaves the ground behind, while Primrose buckles and falls upon the ground. Are those two grounds the same? Or does being in the realist novel, where horses don't have wings, have a particular texture, different from the textures taken by being in myth or in romance or in lyric?

I am seeking the ground upon which Primrose breaks his knees, the ground that sustains him and kills him, the ground upon which to know that he is real, the ground where I might stand and feel the thump of him as he falls.

I can only find the ground that I seek, the ground upon which Primrose breaks his knees, by reading *Daniel Deronda* closely. It is only there in that novel that it can be found.

If I want to know about being in the actual world, where actual horses run and leap and fall, I should become a metaphysician. If I want to know about being in the novel and about the ground upon which unreal horses like Primrose stand, I should become a novel-reader, or better yet, a novelist.

Metaphysicians seek grounds for being too, and sometimes with a method we might call novelistic. Walter Pater marveled at how Plato, even as he pursues the most abstract metaphysical questions (what is being?), populates his dialogues with the concrete details of everyday life, a way of grounding the strangeness of metaphysics upon familiar territory. It is the "impress of visible reality" in his dialogues that makes Plato something like a novelist: his talent at rendering ordinary life has "a touch of the peculiar fineness of Thackeray.... Plato enjoys it for its own sake, and would have been an excellent writer of fiction."[2]

"Would have been"? Pater shies away into the conditional tense, and I wonder why. Perhaps it's that while Plato does write fiction, it's only as a counterpoint, a bass line, to his metaphysics. Strangely, fiction, even in all its unreality, makes a solid ground for philosophy. Plato paints the details of his fictional world "as if on the margin of his high philosophical discourse, himself scarcely aware, as the monkish scribe set bird or flower, with so much truth of earth, in the blank spaces of his heavenly meditation."[3]

I am seeking the truth of the novel's earth.

I am seeking the ground of the novel, which is made or found in blank spaces, which fills up empty margins.

Perhaps I seek all of this because I am drawn to margins, or because I want to understand the violence of being marginalized. When people in a novel look to the ground, when narrators point our attention to that empty margin of their world, it is often because they want to get free of a constraint, because they desire to imagine being otherwise, being loosened, being between real and unreal, being unbinarized.

To draw myself toward the blankness just underneath the novel's world is difficult. Novels are so full. How can I want to empty them?

To turn in that way, to make myself turn that way, away from the people and places of the novel and toward its being, is an erotic training. I train my desires as Pater says that Plato trained his, to become "a lover of the invisible, but still a lover, and therefore, literally, a seer, of it, carrying an elaborate cultivation of the bodily senses, of eye and ear... into the world of intellectual abstractions; seeing and hearing there too, ... filling that 'hollow land' with delightful colour and form."[4]

I desire the hollow land that the world of the novel fills. I seek to hollow the novel and see what remains.

Willa Cather fantasized about it too: "How wonderful it would be," she writes of the realist novel, "if we could throw all the furniture out of the window... and leave the room as bare as the stage of a Greek theater."[5] But then how would we live and move and find our way in what Cather calls in the title of her essay "The Novel Démeublé"—only a bare ground and nothing more? Upstage and downstage we could orient ourselves, but to what end? Our survey of clear ground complete, the sigh of relief exhaled, how do we put the furniture back in its place?

I seek to know how the novel, like Plato's dialogues, gives "an illusive air of reality or substance to the mere nonentities of metaphysic hypothesis."[6] When Cather calls the novel a room, when she says that if the room were emptied it would become like an empty stage: those are metaphors of fictional being. An air of substance: that is a metaphor of fictional being too. By the art of metaphor we give the nonentities of the novel something like substance; we ground them; we make substance of an air.

In Jane Austen's *Pride and Prejudice* (1813), Elizabeth Bennet surveys the grounds of Pemberley and slowly feels herself overcome with the knowledge of her love for Mr. Darcy. Her eyes become unable to see the specific "objects" that her aunt and uncle point out to her, until finally we're told that "she distinguished no part of the scene," which is maybe a way of saying that suddenly she can only see its disorienting wholeness, details stripped away, what we'll see Hardy later on calling a "form without features," only the ground upon which she and Darcy both stand, or the empty stage upon which "the scene" is playing out.⁷

As Elizabeth's eyes cease to distinguish this from that, so that all around her becomes a scene with no parts, her mind goes out not to Darcy himself but to the spot to which he is always attached even as he moves closer or farther away: "Her thoughts were all fixed on that one spot of Pemberley House, whichever it might be, where Mr. Darcy then was."⁸

I am seeking the spot, whichever it might be, where Mr. Darcy then was, and now is.

But if I fix my thoughts on that spot, I am doing something different than Elizabeth. I cannot go to that spot as she does, and yet Austen makes sure I know that it is there. Mr. Darcy exists more vividly for me because there is a spot where he is.

Austen is so careful with her prepositions, so careful to conclude her sentence with the existential verb, "was": Elizabeth's thoughts are fixed "on" the spot, but we don't know if Mr. Darcy is on it or in it, attached to it by his feet or by his whole essence or just by language. It doesn't matter whether he's in the sitting room or the kitchen: that one spot, whichever it might be, is always where Mr. Darcy then is. The spot is where he is and therefore the spot is how he is.

I am seeking the placeholder, the blank space, the hollow land, by which Austen and Elizabeth Bennet locate Mr. Darcy with their thoughts, or maybe by which they make him real, giving him an air of substance, even when he exists only in their thoughts. Why can't he float free? Why put him on the spot?

There is the spot where Mr. Darcy is. There is the ground and Primrose breaking his knees. There is the truth of earth. *There is.* Or as Emmanuel Levinas says, "This impersonal, anonymous, yet inextinguishable 'consummation' of being, which murmurs in the depths of nothingness itself we shall designate by the term *there is.* The *there is,* inasmuch as it resists a personal form, is 'being in general.'"⁹

I seek the spots in the novel where fictional being is consummated—where the *there is* of "being in general" can no longer resist a personal form. There is. There is the spot. There is the spot, whichever it may be. There is the spot, whichever it may be, where Mr. Darcy now is.

"A presence of absence, the *there is* is beyond contradiction; it embraces and dominates the contradictory. In this sense being has no outlets."¹⁰ I seek the ground of the novel, the fictional *there is,* "a density, an atmosphere, a field" that embraces and dominates the contradiction of "real" and "unreal." When I enter the unreality of the novel, I am not exiting being, which has no outlets. I am moving in a different way, between modes or registers of being, between frameworks for talking about being.

If Pater looks to the margins of Plato's metaphysics to find the truth of earth that ornaments it, I look to the novel and find metaphysics in its margins and at its edges, planted in its earth: its spots, its ground, its groundwork, its underground, its meeting grounds.

I seek the support of the novel's ground, but I am alien to its way of being. Is it like a yoga class, when I'm told to lay on my back and feel the earth rising up to meet my breath? How difficult it is to follow that instruction truly, what efforts of careful but relaxed attention it requires, what guilty admission of how often I spurn the ground by ignoring its solidity, or assuming that its support is passive rather than active. There are those times, too, when I intellectualize, keenly aware that it's not the earth I'm lying on but a floor on the second story of a building that holds me suspended in midair. And after all, it's some more pervasive but invisible energy, the force of gravity, that only barely holds me flat. Isn't it strange, this precarious balance between pressure and ease that allows me to lie there, a whole and breathing body, without becoming crushed, and without simply floating upward, gasping for air?

I am seeking the novel's metaphors of fictional being. I am seeking the novel's air of substance. I am seeking a ground upon which to know that fictions are real.

The Grounds of the Novel

INTRODUCTION

On What There Is in the Novel

Pegasus was the beginning of this book.
W. V. O. Quine's essay "On What There Is" (1948), a field-shaping work for modern metaphysics, denies Pegasus's existence, and I've always been enraged by that denial. I can see now that I began writing this book to explore that rage and maybe to locate its source. It was connected, I vaguely knew, to the moment I first read Quine's essay as a queer philosophy major, probably twenty years old, being initiated into a field that seemed to me oppressively straight in its style of thinking, so precise and so inhospitable to the meandering lines of thought I desired more than anything. Pegasus is a metonym in Quine's essay: his nonexistence stands for the nonexistence of all Pegasus's fellow fictional beings too, and the nonexistence of the fictional worlds in which they live. I who had known fictional beings, I who had been to fictional worlds, could not follow in Quine's certainty that they don't exist, or that when we talk about existence we really must limit ourselves to actuality.

That was the beginning of this book: a young queer person wavering between philosophy and literature; a feeling that a certain mode of philosophical argument constrained the category of being in a way that made me panic, that foreclosed the paths I wanted to follow; a sense that I must defend Pegasus against Quine and his ilk; a burning, ireful conviction that if I allowed Quine to deny the existence of Pegasus, he would come for me next. If unreal beings didn't exist, then what became of me? or, at least, what became of the queer parts of me that felt both electrically real and also always existing under threat of derealization? Quine's essay was macho, aggressive, unquestioning, confident. I desired mess and not the sharpened clarity prized by philosophy. Pegasus couldn't speak back, certainly not in that kind of language, and neither could I.

But there's a twist to Quine's argument that offered even me a way in, and that allowed the essay to remain present to me all those years, something that could rankle in my mind, difficult simply to expel. While Quine argues with imposing certainty that no, fictional beings such as Pegasus do not exist, he also includes in his essay two counterarguments, each delivered by a fictional character invented as if to be given the opportunity to speak in defense of his own kind. First, the fictional philosopher McX brings out an old saw, what Quine calls "the old Platonic riddle of non-being." If Quine can deny the existence of Pegasus, there must in the first place be something called Pegasus for him to cast out into the void of non-being, and so by denying Pegasus's existence, Quine inadvertently affirms it: "Non-being must in some sense be, otherwise what is it that there is not?" Quine finds this line of argument frustrating. McX claims, Quine laments, "that I refuse to recognize certain entities." But Quine refuses the very terms of the accusation: "I maintain that there are no entities, of the kind which he alleges, *for* me to recognize."[1] McX says that Pegasus exists because "Pegasus is an idea in men's minds." Quine says that "the mental entity is not what people are talking about when they deny Pegasus," and that even McX "cannot . . . persuade himself that any region of space-time, near or remote, contains a flying horse of flesh and blood" (22). Because McX himself is a fiction, a "mental entity" like Pegasus, Quine has an advantage here. He gets to speak on behalf of "people," and to declare that "people" don't think figments of the imagination count when it comes to talking about being. But what about those of us disagreeing with Quine and pitying McX? Quine claims to speak on my behalf, and it's at this point in my reading that I become claustrophobic, wanting nothing more than to escape the conditions of existence that Quine foists upon me.

The fictional philosopher Wyman then enters the scene. Quine thinks that McX's argument is ridiculous, but he has high hopes for Wyman, whose way of thinking is "less patently misguided." Quine remains committed to getting rid of Pegasus, no matter what either of these fictional people has to say about it; it's only that Wyman's kind of argument may be "more difficult to eradicate." Wyman suggests that fictional beings such as Pegasus exist in a different way than the entities of the actual world exist. We might even use a different word, saying that while both have being, Pegasus subsists as opposed to the real horse who exists (23). While we real beings are actual and determinate, Pegasus is an "unactualized possible" (22). Nevertheless, Pegasus *is*.

Two fictional characters written into a philosophical essay partly about fictionality ask that fictional existence (i.e., their own) not only be recognized but recognized sensitively, with a close attention to its texture and its temporality. We might need a finer-grained vocabulary of actuality and possibility in order to grapple with Pegasus, or with Wyman—or so Wyman himself claims from his place in the realm of the unactualized. It strikes me as especially callous, then, when Quine brushes aside Wyman's promising argument with a sneer. Wyman's theory is unacceptable, Quine argues, because inelegant, perhaps even a threat to law and order; it generates an image of a "bloated universe," "overpopulated," "unlovely," a "slum of possibles," "a breeding ground for disorderly elements" (23). Quine's metaphor, by which admitting fictional beings into existence leads to a dangerous overpopulation, and by which the metaphysician acts as a border guard who protects the territory of "what there is" from the huddled masses of the unactualized, is strikingly moralized and politicized.[2] Quine is terrified of an uncontrollable incursion, the endlessly proliferating mass of "possible men" he suddenly sees accumulating in his doorway. "Are they the same possible man or two possible men? How do we decide? How many possible men are there in that doorway?" he asks, like someone in a gothic novel beset by ghosts (23). He thinks that Wyman's ontology implies possible beings intruding everywhere at once, overrunning the boundaries of their slum, but that is nowhere in Wyman's argument, which allows for different modes of being: Pegasus and those possible men "subsist" rather than "exist." They are just fine in their fictional world, which clearly doesn't have the same limitations as ours when it comes to space.

Who said that Pegasus wants to invade our world? Who said that all those infinite possible men want to squeeze into Quine's doorway? Following Quine's argument, these imagined threats seem ridiculous to me, and yet he takes them so seriously, understanding his duty to be the thinning of the herd of those who count as beings. We could try to "rehabilitate" Wyman's wayward metaphysics, Quine concludes, but "I feel we'd do better simply to clear Wyman's slum once and for all." We could try to police Wyman, to keep his fictional world over there, cordoned off from our actual world over here, but Quine is satisfied with nothing short of annihilation.

This book began because I read Quine's essay and felt its cruelty. But then, how can one be cruel to fictions, really? Quine has a point, I sometimes think: whether we decide that Pegasus or Wyman or any possible man exists or not is a mere philosophical exercise. Nothing is truly at stake here beyond the deciding of some questions about the proper job of metaphysics. For Quine, that job is to answer the question, "What is there?" (21). But if that factual question initially seems in Quine's account so dispassionate, then how do we get to Quine's metaphor of the disorderly slum and his anxiety about those possible men who haunt his doorway? The French philosopher Étienne Souriau, whose *Different Modes of Existence* appeared several years before the publication of Quine's essay, already recognized the cruelty of the metaphysician who would cast "beings of fiction" out of reality, describing fictional beings as those "fragile and inconsistent entities" who "have been chased, one after the other, from every controlled and conditioned cosmos."[3] And Bruno Latour alludes to Souriau's work in his similarly titled *An Inquiry into Modes of Existence* (2013), where he argues that fictional beings "possess full and complete reality in their genre, with their own type of veridiction, transcendence, and being."[4] In the line of thinking that runs from Souriau to Latour, we find a powerful alternative to Quine's exile of fictional beings, but for all their passionate defense of the fictional, their work includes no analysis of works of fiction. Novels remain for Souriau and Latour hypothetical objects. Or in other words, they still focus on the "in or out" question, except that, as opposed to Quine, they argue for the "in" camp.[5]

If I identify with Wyman's plea for recognition, it's because Quine himself makes me see what's at stake in Wyman's exclusion from being: terror, disgust, exile, control. The question of existence, even when it comes to fictional being, even when it is framed as a simple problem of sorting and listing, comes attached to moral and political positions as to who is allowed admission into jealously guarded spaces and categories, about the distribution or hoarding of a limited resource called being, and about the extension or refusal of recognition.

This book began because I began to think that if Wyman fails to defend his own being against Quine's determination to eliminate it, that's because Wyman is an intentionally impoverished fiction, designed to serve a narrow function, to speak briefly and unsatisfactorily on the "in or out" question of being before being dispatched, never able to tell us what his fictional being feels like. Does it feel empty, like living in a vacuum, or does it hum with its own kind of unaccountable fullness? Maybe philosophy wasn't the right context for thinking about the question of fictional being. Maybe instead I should look to novels themselves, not as developing a defense of fictional being against the possibility of its extermination but rather as doing their own thing, imagining being their own way, gloriously indifferent to Quine's interrogation. I think of this indifference as a mirror image of the reader's "ontological indifference," which Catherine Gallagher describes as key to the slow historical process of fictionality's coherence as a category distinct from lying. "Willingly entering the language game of fiction," she argues, "enables a psychological state of ontological indifference, a temporary disregard for the fictional conditions of the pleasurable sensation."[6] But where Gallagher's reader is secure in their reality, able to offer their reasoned and willing consent, to exchange their ontological sensitivity for pleasure only temporarily, disregarding rather than acknowledging that their real pleasure is caused by something unreal, I wonder about how the novel sometimes asserts its own ontological distinctness as a resource rather than understanding it as an embarrassment it must bribe us to forget. "Ontological indifference" in Gallagher's account names a transitory and willed forgetting, in which we accept the fictional world for a little while *as if* it were real. I suggest that in place of indifference, we might think of the novel as cultivating an innate ontological pragmatism in all of us, a faculty that helps us to navigate the adjacency and overlapping of fiction and actuality even after we leave the novel's fictional world. As Zadie Smith argues, the novel is "the place where things are true and not true simultaneously: the ultimate impossibility." But to Smith the simultaneity of "true and not true" isn't something we learn to disregard or to which we become indifferent, it's rather what makes the novel "great." Novels "free us," Smith goes on, "into an understanding that the tension between true/not true might in fact be livable."[7]

For example, as a queer person I must develop an ontological pragmatism that allows me to be queer and to feel real pleasure in my queerness without worrying at every moment, or at the beginning of every day, about whether or not "queerness" is real or fictional, a metaphysically fundamental difference or a social construct. Michel Foucault called that ontological pragmatism, that livable tension, "'reverse' discourse": the world writes a fiction for us, but a fiction that also comes to feel indispensably real, the "legitimacy" and "naturality" of which we feel compelled to defend.[8] That might be why I always understood Quine's dismissal of Wyman as obliquely connected to homophobia. It wasn't that I thought metaphysical violence or ontological marginalization were the same as actual violence and marginalization, or that the experience of being Wyman was the same as the experience of being my queer self. Rather, I thought there was a resource there, in the way that fictional being tries to resist derealization simply by insisting on its own terms (subsistence rather than existence, the unactualized rather than the nonexistent), a resource that helped me to imagine rejecting the in-or-out kind of metaphysics that arrogates to itself the authority to decide once and for all which metaphysical differences are fundamental and which are contingent.

After all, although Quine believes that the aim of ontology is to determine what there is and what there isn't, there are other viable ways of conceptualizing the philosophical investigation of being. Recently, the philosopher Jonathan Schaffer has proposed a return to Aristotle's idea that the primary task of metaphysics is not to determine what exists and what doesn't—simply "to *list the beings*"—but rather to determine "what grounds what."⁹ Schaffer points out that "Metaphysics so revived does not bother asking whether properties, meanings, and numbers exist. Of course they do! The question is whether or not they are *fundamental*" (347). The Aristotelian view takes a "permissive disinterest" in "existence questions," seeking instead the fundamental ground against which all other beings are understood as derivative (352). Schaffer offers an implicit rejoinder to Quine's "slum of possibles" by pointing out that if we follow the Aristotelian argument, "there is no longer any harm in positing an abundant roster of existents, *provided it is grounded on a sparse basis*" (353). The problem is not to figure out what does or doesn't belong on that roster but rather to order it, to find its mechanisms of support.

In the preface we saw Willa Cather wondering about something similar in relation to the grounds of the novel: Could we toss the furniture of the realist novel out of the window and find the empty stage, the sparse ground, beneath?¹⁰

That preface represents my first, circling attempt to feel with Pegasus and Primrose and Mr. Darcy, to find a ground upon which to know that they are real, and to lay the ground for my own argument by offering an initial collection of philosophical and literary examples. In this introduction, I turn more fully to philosophy and novel theory, and to a more traditional argumentative language, to lay a different kind of ground, assessing what it might really mean to take the novel's figuration of its metaphysical ground seriously, to read the novel for its metaphors of fictional being.

This is a book about how the novel imagines its own ontological grounds through figuration. In the chapters that follow, I examine four metaphors of the novelistic ground: the groundwork in Thomas Hardy, the underground in Olive Schreiner and Colson Whitehead, the ground gained in Henry James, and meeting grounds in Virginia Woolf, Zadie Smith, and Akwaeke Emezi. As we'll see, these metaphors do different things and suggest different ways of understanding the metaphysics of fictional being. The chapters of the book follow a roughly chronological order, and they are often in dialogue with one another, but they do not imply a developmental narrative: some chapters compare novels across historical periods and national contexts. Again and again, these novelists work in their different ways to make the grounds of the novel appear as insistently material, identified with the landscape, the earth, the painter's canvas, the body, even when the tenor of the metaphor is a fictional abstraction, a shadowy support at the root of a conjured world.

In the actual world, the grounds, limits, or edges that support our sense of what existence means—the fundamental Being, the Absolute, the Totality that underlies or sates or surmounts it all and yet always eludes our grasp, just above or beneath us, just to the other side of the limit of our knowing—are given. Schaffer for his part argues that the ultimate ground of our actual ontology is "the whole concrete cosmos" (361). (We hear an echo of Souriau's image of the metaphysician's "controlled and conditioned cosmos" from which the beings of fiction have been exiled. Schaffer's cosmos is much more welcoming.) It is for us to discover the grounds of our existence because we are part of the actual world these grounds ground. That discovery might never happen, might in fact be an impossibility, but only in a limited sense. We might think we're not up to the task of understanding Being itself, or of grasping the sublime object that is "the whole concrete cosmos," but it's at the very least not a logical impossibility that I would come to comprehend or at least develop a clear picture of such things. I argue that novels, however, have their own figural vocabulary for imagining the grounds, limits, edges of fictional being, and that this vocabulary is necessarily different than the philosophical one we use to investigate the ontology of our actual world. In a fictional world, ontological grounds are cleared and secured, but also sometimes obscured, by metaphor—worked, reworked, opened up, painted over, buried. While for the most part the grounds of the novel can seem a merely passive support for our interpretive work upon the text, the taken-for-granted foundation that we mostly ignore, I show how novelists imagine the ground as an active pressure, something with breath and force and life even in its heavy stasis.

On the one hand, the pressure of the ground can be a comfort, a rapprochement, the ground that I press into pressing back as if in acknowledgment. On the other hand, pressure can be a resistance or refusal, the ground that shoves or heaves or erupts. Thinking about queer relationships to grounding and ungrounding, for example, Sara Ahmed argues that "the ground into which we sink our feet is not neutral: it gives ground to some more than others."[11] That is true of the grounds imagined and figured in the novel too. I worry that I have made the novel sound like a utopian escape from Quine's narrow definition of being and his policing of ontological borders, but if his work shows us anything, it's that no theory of ontology is without its painful circumscriptions, and it has been important to me to push back against those constraints. While this book and the selection of authors I consider in it make clear my scholarly training in the field of Victorian studies, the novels of that canon cannot allow us to see the metaphysics of fictional being with anything approaching wholeness or trueness. Victorian novels push questions about the metaphysics of Blackness, queerness, and transness out of view, and after all, those were the kinds of questions that first prompted the conceptualization of this book. We glimpse these problems at best obliquely in the work of Hardy, Schreiner, James, and Woolf.

As the book progresses, I turn to Whitehead, Smith, and Emezi as well as to metaphysical work in Black studies and in trans studies, to bring into view what Nahum Chandler calls the "metaphysical infrastructure of the discourse" that has centered whiteness and grounded white supremacy for hundreds of years; and to problematize a metaphysics that, as Cáel M. Keegan puts it in the context of trans studies, "might produce the feeling that one is being made into an impossibility."[12] I engage with these fields in acknowledgment of my positionality as a white cisgender critic, and also as a queer person in solidarity with their broader aim of understanding the metaphysics of marginalized being. The work of thinkers in Black and trans studies is crucial to the development of my argument, but I also hope that my argument about the metaphysics of fictional being has something to contribute in turn to these fields' ongoing work of investigating the metaphysics of racialized, trans, and queer embodiment and identity. As I've already suggested, an attunement to the simultaneous reality and unreality of fictional being might help us to conceptualize other kinds of being that exist in the complicated tension between the actuality of lived experience and the fictionality of social construction.

Each of this book's chapters focuses on a particular metaphor for fictional being. In chapter 1, I follow the metaphor of groundwork through Thomas Hardy's fiction. Both a painterly metaphor (the canvas covered with primer before the painting begins) and an agricultural metaphor (the working of the ground before sowing), groundwork points our attention to the blank, colorless, but weirdly material and vivid ground upon or within which fictional being takes its specific shapes.

In chapter 2, I turn to the metaphor of the underground in Olive Schreiner's *The Story of an African Farm* (1883) and Colson Whitehead's *The Underground Railroad* (2016). In conversation with the work of Fred Moten on blackness as "ontology's underground," its "ante- or anti-foundation," this chapter thinks through Schreiner's and Whitehead's different approaches to the racialization of ontology's foundational darkness.[13]

Chapter 3 examines Henry James's metaphor of "the ground gained" by the novelist in his creation of a fictional world. I argue that James's desire, as expressed in his New York Edition prefaces, to return as a rereader and reviser to the world of his past fictions, hoping to locate there the traces of the unworked ground that always seems to preexist the novel itself, an object of the novelist's discovery rather than an object of his creation, is an ontological desire, a desire to get clear about how, in the context of the novel, ontological grounds can be crafted, created, broken, and reconstituted.

Chapter 4 thinks about the metaphor of the novel as a meeting ground that sustains and supports both fictional and actual realities. Through readings of Virginia Woolf, Zadie Smith, and Akwaeke Emezi, I wonder what is at stake in the novel and the theory of the novel when it comes to maintaining or dissolving dividing lines between fictional and actual being. I argue that what Emezi calls the novel's "metaphysical dysphoria" helps us to imagine dysphoria's metaphysics, and in turn a theory of being hospitable to those for whom "being" is aqueous, provisional, in-between, trans, nonbinary, nonhuman.

Finally, in a brief afterword, I look to the metaphor of the basement in both Walter Pater's unpublished essay "Diaphaneitè" and the prologue to Ralph Ellison's *Invisible Man* (1952). My objects here are Pater's "basement type," a slantwise fictional being who bides their time below, waiting to emerge to regenerate the world; and Ellison's narrator in his basement dwelling, describing what it is like to live as what Souriau might call a being of fiction, chased out of a controlled and conditioned cosmos, who nevertheless claims the being that is his right.

Insofar as the novelists I analyze in this book want to encourage us to think about the central ontological problem of fiction—

not, as I've already suggested, *whether* a fictional world exists, but rather *how* it exists and what are the shapes and textures of its existence—they turn to the poetics of metaphor. They link the commonplace philosophical metaphor of ontological grounds, in which an object such as the whole concrete cosmos is the tenor, and ground or the act of grounding is the vehicle, with literary metaphors that are paradoxically more literal, in which some unknowable object, the basis of fictional being, remains the tenor, and ground remains the vehicle, but a vehicle made tangible and textured in images of the ground, the groundwork, or the underground. I try to feel how these novelists conjure a force akin to gravity, which keeps us as we read always delicately and sometimes painfully poised upon a razor's-edge horizon between earth and sky, between the safe repose of groundedness and the vertiginous freedom of becoming ungrounded, or between the different theories of ontology appropriate to the actual and the fictional.[14]

In philosophy, discussions of ontology use images of foundations, hierarchies, grounds, and so on as what Hans Blumenberg calls "absolute metaphors," and I suggest that they work in a similar way in the novel. He defines absolute metaphors, in fact, through his own metaphor of grounding: they work to clarify "*foundational elements* of philosophical language," and therefore, as opposed to the merely rhetorical, decorative metaphors that we might think of as exemplifying "the inauthenticity of figurative speech," absolute metaphors "resist being converted back into authenticity and logicality." That's another way of saying that absolute metaphors are dead metaphors—so deeply entrenched in our philosophical language that they no longer appear to be metaphors at all. Blumenberg wants to develop a science of "metaphorology" that can "burrow down to the substructure of thought, the underground, the nutrient solution of systematic crystallizations," and he argues that absolute metaphors are the ones we would need to analyze in order to reach that absolute foundation of thought itself, because they "'answer' the supposedly naïve, in principle unanswerable questions whose relevance lies quite simply in the fact that they cannot be brushed aside, since we do not *pose* them ourselves but find them already *posed* in the ground of our existence."[15] Finally, absolute metaphors offer "a point of orientation," "they give structure to a world, representing the nonexperienceable, nonapprehensible totality of the real."[16] If absolute metaphors represent, they don't do so in the denotative or referential sense: they only orient us toward their nonapprehensible object, suggesting a structure that holds together what is always beyond experience and beyond apprehension, whether for us or for the beings of a fictional world.

It seems significant to me that in addition to his interest in the absolute metaphors that form the foundation of our philosophical language and "give structure to a world," Blumenberg was interested in the ontology of novelistic being, although he didn't draw explicit connections between these two aspects of his work. Blumenberg argues that the novel makes "a new claim of art—its claim not merely to represent *objects* of the world, or even to imitate *the* world, but to actualize *a* world. A world—nothing less—is the theme and postulate of the novel."[17] If absolute metaphors ground and "give structure to a world," and if the novel claims "to actualize a world," then it seems clear that we must think novelistic being and metaphorology together. We need to look beyond mimesis, Blumenberg suggests, to understand "the novel's thematization of reality," the way that by claiming to make a world where one didn't exist before, the novel poses what philosophers would call metametaphysical questions about the scope and nature of metaphysics itself, and about the epistemological problem of how we know about being.[18] As David Manley puts it in an overview of the field, "Metaphysics is concerned with the foundations of reality.... Metametaphysics is concerned with the foundations of metaphysics."[19] In making its "claim of art," the novel develops a strikingly different concept of reality than the one that structures our actual being. Blumenberg describes it as "a reality that can never be assured, is constantly in the process of being actualized, and continually requires some new source of confirmation." I've been following Blumenberg's thought here in picturing the grounds of the novel as provisional and incomplete, and yet somehow sufficient, and in suggesting that the novel's metametaphysical work, its status "not as a fiction of reality, but as a *fiction of the reality of realities*," relies upon the work of metaphor.[20] The novel's ongoing actualization proceeds by way of figuration, reactivating and reliteralizing the figure of the ground as it feels its way over and over again toward a secure point of orientation for the being of a nonexistent world.

I argue that the novel's elaboration of its own fictional being is not, in other words, an ontological problem to be solved but rather a genre of immanent ontological critique. In the novel, ontology is a project marked by incompletion and provisionality, resting upon blank or soft or liquid grounds, mere metaphors, rather than upon the absolute and actual foundations pursued by the philosophical investigation of ontology.[21]

And yet the choice between philosophy and literature still presents itself as nearly impossible. Confronting that dichotomy, we might feel something like what I felt reading Quine in college, or what Simone de Beauvoir felt when as a young voracious reader she tried to sort out her allegiances to philosophy and the novel as different modes of metaphysical inquiry: "After having thought out the universe through the eyes of Spinoza or Kant, I would wonder: 'How can anyone be so frivolous as to write novels?' But when I would leave Julien Sorel or Tess d'Urberville, I would think it useless to waste one's time fabricating systems. Where was truth to be found? On earth or in eternity? I felt torn apart."[22] Looking for what we've seen Pater calling "the truth of earth" leads us, weirdly, to the grounds of the novel, as opposed to the abstract and universalizing systems of so many philosophical approaches to being.

Beauvoir goes on to describe how she and her fellow existentialists eventually came around to the novel precisely because of its concreteness of description, its unfolding in time, its narration of subjective experience, all of which allow for a depiction of metaphysics as an experience rather than an activity. "Metaphysics is . . . not a system," she argues; "one does not 'do' metaphysics as one 'does' mathematics or physics," that is, according to a law-bound procedure grounded in irrefutable axioms. "In reality, 'to do' metaphysics is 'to be' metaphysical; it is to realize in oneself the metaphysical attitude, which consists in positing oneself in one's totality before the totality of the world." To be metaphysical means to grasp intuitively the problem of being; it is to posit oneself as a whole being and to see one's wholeness from the outside, as something engaged with a much bigger wholeness, the totality of the world, that exceeds the limits of one's own knowledge. Where philosophers so often confront "metaphysical reality" and desire "to elucidate its universal meaning in abstract language," with the goal of a "systematized," "timeless," "objective" theory of being, novelists are interested in "manifesting an aspect of metaphysical experience that cannot otherwise be manifested: its subjective, singular, and dramatic character," or what Beauvoir calls "the original upspringing of existence in its complete, singular, temporal truth."[23] The novel's metaphysics is idiosyncratic, provisional, uncertain, springing up from the ground rather than calmly awaiting discovery: we jump into any given novel not sure what grounds being there, and in that sense the novel can show us what it feels like "to be" metaphysical.

One aim of this book is to show how novelists do the kind of metaphysical work Beauvoir describes, and in this sense, although I often engage with the work of a heterogeneous group of philosophers and theorists (from Quine to Schaffer to Moten to Ahmed) throughout these pages as a way to sketch a larger context for certain metaphysical problems, I'm keen to prioritize the close reading of novels and theories of the novel, and to see novels as posing their own metaphysical problems, rather than taking up questions already posed by philosophers. As Beauvoir says, for the novelist, "it is not a matter of exploiting on a literary plane truths established beforehand on the philosophical plane."[24] The novel's "plane" of being might be self-sufficient, preoccupied by problems of being that would never occur to philosophers living in actuality. Even Quine understood that the case for fictional being must be made by fictional beings; it's only that he didn't know how to hear them when they speak.

Taken together, Schaffer and Blumenberg helped me to see how the absolute metaphor of grounds for being might yoke together the philosophical and novelistic conceptualizations of existence in unexpected ways. But I still wondered what it would mean to see the novel's being as self-sufficient in the ways that I've described above. Certainly I don't think that fictions are *really real*, nor do I want to venture the even stronger claim that fictional being is somehow *more real* or more complex than actual being. But I do want to take fictional being seriously and to find a vocabulary that would allow me to consider it as both continuous with and distinct from actuality.[25] The work of Souriau and Latour can take us part of the way there: thinkers who take seriously the idea that there might be room for many "modes of existence." Taking the "beings of fiction" seriously is part of the project of that kind of ontological pluralism. Two philosophers in more direct conversation with Quine—Alexius Meinong, who has often been suggested as a model for Quine's fictional Wyman, and Rudolph Carnap, who offered a powerful rejoinder to Quine only two years after the publication of his field-shaping essay—helped me to think about how a flexible approach that sees being from multiple angles, in the vocabulary of philosophy, theory, and the novel, might be crucial to the kind of ontological pragmatism I described earlier.[26] In Meinong's work we find a nonbinary conception of being that refuses a simple division of "real" and "unreal" and urges us to attend to the overlaps between seemingly incommensurate fields of inquiry. In Carnap's work we find a true ontological pragmatism that replaces what he sees as irresolvable questions about the nature of being with the idea of different frameworks for talking about being.

Meinong's essay "The Theory of Objects" (1904) laments what he calls in the title of the essay's second section "The Prejudice in Favour of the Actual" that characterizes so much work in the field of metaphysics.[27] While it might be true, he writes, that "metaphysics has to do with everything that exists," as Quine would later reiterate, there are many nonexistent objects that we can know of and talk about despite their nonexistence: "The totality of what exists . . . is infinitely small in comparison with the totality of the Objects of knowledge. This fact goes easily unnoticed," he continues, "probably because the lively interest in reality which is part of our nature tends to favor that exaggeration which finds the nonreal a mere nothing" (79). It makes sense that we humans are especially interested in reality, since it's where we live, but despite this prejudice, the nonreal is not nothing, Meinong insists, and if we conceive of metaphysics as a philosophical science of reality, we exclude an enormous number of objects from consideration. We should be alive, he says, to the unexplored "neutral zone" between carefully defined fields of philosophical inquiry. Sometimes this means looking to a gap between fields, other times it means finding areas of overlap that can then "be investigated from both sides"

(77). Nonreal objects find themselves lost in just such a neutral zone, somewhere between metaphysics and psychology, between the realms of being and nonbeing, that we illuminate in our reading and writing about unreal worlds.

Meinong's approach is essentially nonbinary: there are the concrete things that "exist" (a wooden chair, my brain, my body), and the nonreal objects that only "subsist" (a right angle, my mind, Pegasus), but then there is a "third order of being," he hypothesizes, a quality rather than a class of objects, "adjoined to existence and subsistence. . . . This sort of being must belong . . . to every Object as such" (84). This third order of being allows us to take an agnostic approach to the division between the real and the nonreal, and to conclude that it may not be as hard a division as the one Quine desires. Some quality that we call "being" extends across the boundary between the existent and the subsistent, between Quine and Pegasus. Think about the color blue, and whether it can be said to exist independently from actual blue objects, for example. Quine would respond with a decisive "no." Blue things exist, but "blueness" does not. But Meinong wonders, what if "Blue, or any other Object whatsoever, is somehow given prior to our determination of its being or non-being, in a way that does not carry any prejudice to its non-being" (84). We must train ourselves out of our prejudice in favor of actuality, so that we can see all objects with an equally reverent and nuanced attention, whatever their modes of being. Whether something is "actual" or not is beside the point, at least in those many cases where the adjudication of being (Quine's population control) is not our goal. Being belongs to all objects that can be thought, whether they exist or not. We can then see any object that presents itself to us, at least at first, as simply a "claimant to being" (85).

Meinong's image of the "claimant," and the legalistic framework it invokes, will remind us of Quine's refusal of Wyman's claim. And just as Quine responds to Wyman's concept of the "unactualized possible" with his image of the "slum of possibles" that such an ontology would create, Bertrand Russell recalls in his autobiographical essay "My Mental Development" that his theory of descriptions, with its skepticism about the existence of fictional beings, developed out of "the desire to avoid Meinong's unduly populous realm of being."[28] Meinong concludes his own essay by celebrating multitudinousness, wondering about the "specialized theories of Objects, their number scarcely to be determined" that might work, like mathematics, to investigate the strange in-between being belonging to unreal things. I would suggest that the theory of the novel could be added to that list, and indeed, in recent years, theorists of the novel have become more attuned to how the novel marks out a kind of ontological neutral zone. But such theories can still contradict each other in remarkable ways. In *The Value of the Novel*, Peter Boxall argues for the novel's "unique ability to put the relationship between art and matter, between words and the world, into a kind of motion, to work at the disappearing threshold between the world that exists and that which does not, between the world that we already know and understand and that which we have not yet encountered."[29] More recently, in *Free Indirect*, Timothy Bewes makes precisely the opposite argument as he points to the contemporary novel's "quality of not only refusing to connect the work and the world but of thinking, inhabiting, even forging the space of their disconnection."[30] My hope is to develop a theory of the novel in which both of these evaluations of the novel's ontological claims can be true simultaneously: yes, the novel imagines a "disappearing threshold" that allows for the meeting and overlapping of fictionality and actuality, as we'll see most powerfully in chapter 4; but also yes, the novel refuses to authorize its own being only by reference to the world outside of it, and in that sense it forges the kind of ontological disconnection between fictionality and actuality that Bewes imagines.

Carnap, unlike Meinong, is a skeptic about the usefulness of metaphysical arguments, aligned with what Manley calls the tradition of "strong deflationism" in metametaphysics, which holds that metaphysical debates are really "'verbal' or 'terminological' disputes" about "how to *describe* certain situations, rather than about how things really *are*."[31] In his essay "Empiricism, Semantics, and Ontology" (1950), Carnap rejects the metaphysical questions that interest Quine as essentially meaningless, aiming for impossible answers, and argues we'd be better served by thinking through the various ways we talk about being in different contexts. We might in certain situations genuinely ask about whether Pegasus exists, whereas in other situations (when sitting around a seminar table discussing Greek myths, for example), we take the fact of Pegasus's existence as a given, so obvious that it's not worth discussing at all. Carnap names these differing situations "frameworks": "If someone wishes to speak in his language about a new kind of entities, he has to introduce a system of new ways of speaking, subject to new rules; we shall call this procedure the construction of a *framework* for the new entities in question."[32] When we start to ask questions about being, we do so in relation to a particular framework, so that the question isn't simply "in or out?" but something rather more complex.

There are questions about being that are "internal" to any given framework: for example, from within the framework of "the thing world" we can ask, "Are unicorns and centaurs real or imaginary?" and we can determine the answer to that question by empirical investigation. But Carnap rules out what he calls "external questions" about "the existence *of the framework itself*," since to exist simply means "to be an element of the framework," to be something about which we have developed, at least provisionally, an agreed-upon way of speaking. Carnap's approach is pragmatist at heart. When we need to get a job done—solving a mathematical formula, interpreting a novel—we adopt the framework that allows us to do it with "efficiency," a keyword in Carnap's essay, rather than getting bogged down in metaphysical perplexities that are decidedly inefficient since essentially unresolvable.[33] If we're constantly debating whether numbers exist or not, we're never able to get to the work of doing things with numbers.

We as literary critics frequently adopt "the fictional world" as our framework, within which we don't worry about whether Dorothea or the village of Middlemarch actually exists, but rather we simply get started with our work. But what would questions "internal" to this framework look like? Carnap suggests that when we ask questions about being in the framework of the thing world, we understand ourselves to be conducting an empirical investigation, simply looking around and seeing if the thing in question exists in the thing world, a version of Quine's assertion that the central question of metaphysics is "What is there?"[34] In the framework of "the system of natural numbers," Carnap offers "Is there a prime number greater than a hundred?" as an example of an internal question; however he points out that in this case, we don't pursue an answer "by empirical investigation based on observations, but by logical analysis based on the rules for the new expressions" that this framework introduces into our language.[35] Each framework develops its own language and its own rules for dealing with questions about being, and so I wonder what questions might be "internal" to the framework "the fictional world of the novel." I've already suggested that the question "Is Dorothea Brooke real or imaginary?" doesn't fit the bill. To question her existence would be equivalent to questioning the existence of the framework as a whole.

I would argue that as readers and critics of the novel who have adopted fictional being as our framework, we ask questions about the terms and forms and shapes and structures and textures of fictional existence, not the binary "real or imaginary," "yes or no" questions that Carnap takes as his examples, and we read novels carefully in order to begin answering those questions. Is that an "empirical" investigation? Sometimes I think it is. I look at concrete examples printed in a book and take them as evidence to substantiate my claims about the structure and texture of fictional being as the novel imagines it. I might also say that I pursue a creative or even affective investigation, drawing upon my own imaginative resources to speak in a particular novel's language, to take on its vocabulary as my own, to use that merging of self and novel to tell you about the feelings that novels inspire in me. Either way, the problem of what kinds of questions about being are "internal" to this framework, and about how we would describe our method for addressing those questions, seem to me basic problems for the enterprise of literary criticism to which we are not always attuned. I have offered my own answers to these questions, but I think that Carnap's emphasis on the collaborative process of constructing a framework can be instructive here: our ways of speaking about fictional being are provisional and contestable, already solidly constructed in some places but sometimes raising perplexities when we stumble upon problems we hadn't anticipated, something like J. L. Austin's idea of ordinary language philosophy as revolving around the endlessly complex question of *"what we should say when,* and so why and what we should mean by it."[36]

If we take literary criticism in Carnap's terms as a "way of speaking" developed to describe, interpret, and manipulate the framework of the fictional world, subject to its own rules, then to adopt this way of speaking and this set of rules does not mean to believe in the actual existence of Elizabeth Bennet. We occupy what Jonathan Kramnick has described in somewhat Carnapian terms as an "ontologically plural as well as populous" world, in which the formation of disciplines simply acknowledges that different kinds of objects require different metaphysical vocabularies and different kinds of analysis.³⁷ Or as Anahid Nersessian puts it, "art doesn't have to be about real things, and criticism doesn't have to pretend that it is," because "works of art have an ontology distinct from if not wholly divided from other kinds of things in the world."³⁸ Kramnick and Nersessian both echo Carnap's argument that to employ multiple frameworks, to acknowledge the validity and uniqueness of multiple disciplines, is not to presume a multiverse of overlapping and contradictory realities. Rather, to accept a framework, Carnap argues, "means nothing more than to accept a certain form of language, in other words, to accept rules for forming statements and for testing, accepting, or rejecting them."³⁹

We are always at liberty, then, to reject the language of fictionality as nonsensical to our ears, incoherent or objectless in some way, but once we begin to take on its vocabulary, to discuss Heathcliff's motivations, for example, we cede our right to question the existence of fictional characters and worlds. Because here we are, talking about them! At that point, to wonder about their very existence is simply a useless diversion. As Leo Bersani puts it, writing in a different context about the "virtual being" of dreams and comparing them to the virtual being of cinematic fiction, "To ask about the ontological status of the virtual is to risk having virtuality disappear into the question designed to establish its 'reality' ... as if the notion of virtual being itself were nothing but a virtuality buried within realized being, an illusory potential for potentiality."⁴⁰ I want to insist upon the virtual ontology of the novelistic world as standing in a similarly paradoxical relation to the ontology of the actual, somehow primary rather than secondary—speaking its own language, pursuing its own problems, not as a dim mimesis of actuality but as a strangely independent world. We flatten and oversimplify fictional being if we explain it only in terms of, with reference to, or in opposition to actual being. Such an approach leads us again and again to the kinds of questions that interest philosophers but stop us short as literary critics: whether fictional beings exist or not; whether statements about fictional characters or worlds are "true"; whether claiming the existence of fictional characters requires us to elaborate theories of "possible worlds," and so on.[41] These are important and complex philosophical questions about the nature of fiction as it relates to or opposes or pluralizes reality, but they are *interpretive* questions only in a very limited sense.

Whether the world of a novel exists or subsists is a metaphysical question, in other words, that may be relevant in certain contexts but has no special bearing upon the work of literary interpretation. The novel claims the being that is due to it, the being that is its right. As we've already seen, however, such claims always risk refusal, the richness of fictional being spurned by an actuality that sees it only as thin, malformed, provisional, possible, disorderly. Opening his *Aesthetic Theory*, Theodor Adorno thinks of this as a modern problem, perhaps dating to the new experimentalisms that emerged on or about 1910: "It is self-evident that nothing concerning art is self-evident anymore, not its inner life, not its relation to the world, not even its right to exist."[42] It's possible to read Adorno as making a narrow and concrete claim about a social problem: whether we grant art a right to existence in a society more and more indifferent to its impact, in which art has become a more and more esoteric pursuit. But given the direction of *Aesthetic Theory* as a whole, it's clear that Adorno's claim is at least inflected by the metaphysical problem of art's being. Adorno's "not even" indicates that he sees this problem of the right to exist as fundamental, the confusion we must get clear about in the first place before we can proceed to work out our uncertainties about art's inner life and its relation to the world. But these confusions are tangled together, too, by Adorno's paratactic listing: none of these things is self-evident any longer, and so examining the inner life of the artwork is one way of finding our way back to our lost certainty about art's being.

That's the route I take in this book, in which I argue that closely analyzing the "inner life" of the novel, its language and its form—description, figuration, omniscient narration, and so on—can help us to pose questions not only about a fictional world's claim to being but also about how it grounds its being and gives that being a particular texture. On the one hand, looking at the novel itself and its own formal concepts, we could think along with Dora Zhang and Hannah Freed-Thall that "ground" is a "holding or undergirding element," "the condition of possibility for representation," a deeper version of what we usually call "setting."[43] On the other hand we could read novels closely and come to feel their peculiar groundlessness, precisely because the novel seems simply to ground itself, to emerge out of nowhere and nothing. Kevin Ohi, for example, thinks through the problem of the text's "inception" or beginning in these terms: the "self-grounding quality of literary fiction," a "groundless positing," a "fundamental groundlessness" that we "mirror" in our reading, "forms founded after they have begun," a "self-conscious fiat where texts as if call themselves into being."[44] Ohi has in mind something like the problem Adorno identifies when he says, electrified by paradox, that "by their very existence artworks postulate the existence of what does not exist and thereby come into conflict with the latter's actual nonexistence."[45] We see that an artwork exists, and we must therefore acknowledge (along with thinkers such as Meinong) that by its very nature it makes a claim to being, a claim on behalf of the existence of actually nonexistent objects. But the claim can't get fully away from the dizzying metaphysical contradictions that Adorno's sentence dramatizes or that Ohi points to in his assertion of fiction's groundless, self-positing being.

Or, as Audrey Jaffe has argued, perhaps this kind of paradox is exactly the point of realism and its formal conventions, if we follow her claim that "realism is a function of desire" in psychoanalytic terms: a desire that tips over into fantasy, its object the "real" that it can never fully possess, that might not exist in the first place, or at least not in the way that the novel wishes it would. Jaffe opposes her approach to those critics who remain "attached ... to the idea of a real behind realism."[46] We might think here of Elaine Freedgood and Cannon Schmitt, who show how the novel functions as a theory of referential language, or a "denotative" genre filled with technical detail and specialized objects, always trying to point our attention to actual things and to the world outside of the novel. But even Freedgood and Schmitt insist that the denotative function of realism is not a matter of simple correspondence between word and referent: in many cases denotation leads us down a rabbit hole, chasing related bits of knowledge, so that really "we can only gesture at the denotative, the technical, and the literal as at a constellation of meaning at which we will probably never be able to arrive," the denotative "gesture" inaugurating its own kind of fantasy of the real as endlessly linked trivia.[47]

I'm not all that afraid of infinite regress, a problem that could easily haunt this book, and that is opened up by Ohi's idea of the novel as "self-grounding" or Freedgood's more recent claim that the novel "is ruptured by its twin commitments to fictionality and reference," and therefore characterized by "a vertiginous heteroontologicality" or "ontological flexibility" that teaches us to move deftly in imaginary space and so contributes to projects of "expansion and colonization."[48] (I return to Freedgood's argument, and especially her treatment of metalepsis, in chap. 2.) Although the question "What grounds the ground?" will emerge at one or two points, I am generally content to take it as a red herring, since it represents to me the urge always to get outside of the novel in our reading of it, and a fear of staying put on the novel's ground, which can sometimes feel like quicksand but is in fact perfectly capable of supporting a fictional world and even my intrusive temporary presence there.[49] In this book, I do argue for what we might call, following Jaffe, a real behind realism. But where Jaffe finds an object of fantasy, to be reiterated again and again, ghosted forth but never realized, I find a fictional (but I argue no less "real" or "existent") ground for realism. Seeking the grounds of the novel, I find novelists using figural language to evoke provisional, incomplete, obscured, even liquid foundations "inside" of the text rather than to point outside of the novel's world to the foundations of actual being as if looking for a guarantee. Novels don't give us the feeling of standing firm in relation to a solid and graspable reality but rather the feeling of standing upon the unfamiliar ground of nonbeing. If Freedgood sees the novel as hetero-ontological, ripped apart (much like Beauvoir is) by its inability to choose between fictional and actual being, I perhaps try to see the novel's homo-ontologicality, its commitment to its own internal structures of being, when it seems to refuse or at least withdraw from reference and denotation into figuration.

The novel's ground is thrillingly alive rather than threateningly unstable. That thrill of being held in a different kind of being, standing upon a different kind of ground: I argue that that's precisely the pleasure and interest of novel reading, not a pleasure purchased by indifference to fictionality, to return to Gallagher's terms, but a pleasure sustained by the novel's satisfaction with remaining incomplete or impossible in its being.

Being incomplete is not the same as being shattered or unformed or unreal. Writing this book, I have kept in mind Ludwig Wittgenstein's own metaphor of the ground and its depths, by which he explains that all justifications for why we follow the rules of our various language-games simply must end somewhere. "Once I have exhausted the justifications," he writes, "I have reached bedrock, and my spade is turned. Then I am inclined to say: 'This is simply what I do.' (Remember that we sometimes demand explanations for the sake not of their content, but of their form. Our requirement is an architectural one; the explanation a kind of sham corbel that supports nothing.)"[50] To put this into my own language: in looking for the grounds of the novel, I believe we sometimes hit bedrock, and our spade is turned. We can conclude, this is simply what this novel does, what this novel is, how this novel works. These are the rules this novel follows in talking about fictional being. Explanations that move ever deeper, or that leap reflexively outside of the novel to look for a final metaphysical justification for the novel's fictional being are sham corbels, ornamental rather than loadbearing. Certainly we can make such explanations, and they may be as beautiful as any decorative piece of stonework, but we don't need them to hold up our edifice.

In advocating for an "internalist" approach to analyzing the novel on its own terms, I don't mean to trot out a lightly renovated New Criticism, shutting out the world in favor of an exclusive focus on the text's internal workings, its "unity" or its status as a "whole," nor am I selling a rewarmed version of the deconstructionist commonplace that "there is nothing outside of the text."[51] My claim on behalf of close reading is a claim that fictional being understands itself, and that if I wish to understand it, I should look carefully at how it imagines and describes the conditions of its existence. If I am a formalist, it is only in the sense that I pay attention to formal features of the novel, particularly figuration, because they are there to be attended to, and I have found that they help me in my reckoning with my own perplexities. I don't take form to be "ontological" in some especially material sense, as in Sandra Macpherson's definition of "form as nothing more—and nothing less—than the shape matter (whether a poem or a tree) takes."[52] I simply wouldn't know how to read for that kind of form: Is metaphor a shape that matter takes? Certainly it arises out of words positioned on paper, but that material fact doesn't take me anywhere as a reader of metaphor.

Formal features and techniques and patterns can help me to see how the novel develops its own pictures of, and questions about, fictional being, but they are not themselves a material foundation.

I follow Toril Moi in her belief, inspired by her own reading of Wittgenstein, that "literary criticism ... doesn't have what we can plausibly call competing methods," and that when we talk about our different methods, we usually mean something like "existential investments" or "thematic and political interests," or "views of what is important in literature (and life)." "In the encounter with the literary text," Moi continues, "the only 'method' that imposes itself is the willingness to look and see, to pay maximal attention to the words on the page."[53] Beyond that, we might say we hit bedrock, and our spade is turned. The justifications are exhausted. This is simply what I do.

The novel's metaphors will of course lead us to actuality if we follow them far enough, but I would suggest it's usually wrong to think of metaphor in fiction in that way. When Olive Schreiner says that existence is like a great tree with its roots underground, a metaphor I explore further in chapter 2, we understand the comparison because trees and the underground really exist in our world. But trees and the underground also exist in the fictional world elaborated by Schreiner in *The Story of an African Farm*, where her narrator and her characters live, and the point of the metaphor is not, I think, to denote actual trees and actual soil, but rather to pursue a metaphysical idea within the context of the fiction.

I don't argue in this book that novels *never* look beyond their own internal structure to an actual existence beyond their limits. As Freedgood and Schmitt help us to see in their work on the novel as a genre of denotation, Zola's description of the underground space of the coal mine in *Germinal*, loaded with rich technical detail, is quite different than Schreiner's use of the underground as a metaphorical vehicle used to illuminate the tenor of fictional being.⁵⁴ I hope, however, to show that when novels describe undergrounds, grounds, the seabed, the horizon, they often slip between the literal and the figurative. When novels denote, they are doing so not because pointing to the actual world is a necessary anchor for fictional being, but rather because novels imagine themselves as existing in an open-ended and porous relationship with actuality. I know that the world of *The Story of an African Farm* only exists in our heads as we read, but I don't know that the narrator or characters of the novel imagine their existence in that way. My readings show what it feels like to "be" metaphysical, in Beauvoir's terminology, within the novel.

ONE

Groundwork

In *Far from the Madding Crowd* (1874), Thomas Hardy's narrator describes the "obliteration by snow" of what had been our view of the landscape of Melchester Moor:

> For the first time in the season [the moor's] irregularities were forms without features; suggestive of anything, proclaiming nothing, and without more character than that of being the limit of something else—the lowest layer of a firmament of snow. From this chaotic skyful of crowding flakes the mead and moor momentarily received additional clothing, only to appear momentarily more naked thereby.... The instinctive thought was that the snow lining the heavens and that encrusting the earth would soon unite into one mass without any intervening stratum of air at all.[1]

Hardy's "forms without features" are linked to those empty phrases by which this denuded description clings to shape and outline: anything, nothing, something. We're urged to remember that form doesn't finally dissolve in this winter scene, even if it threatens to; rather, it "momentarily" loses the features that give it texture, life, and detail. Anything, nothing, something: these pronouns themselves have featureless, nonspecific antecedents. "Anything" points indifferently at a wide field of possibility in which the object we seek is any specific thing at all arising out of the void; "nothing" stands in for an absence; and "something" barely registers the presence of an object that has lost its nameable identity, out of mere forgetfulness perhaps, or out of the more total kind of erasure that Hardy's blizzard scene dramatizes, in which the best we can do is make out some hazy thing just out of reach of the eye, even just out of reach of the narrator's omniscience, as the limits, layers, and strata that organize the world are overrun.

The overwhelming whiteness blanketing Hardy's scene, turning it into a cluster of featureless forms, makes it something like a canvas covered over with primer before the painter begins anew; but in the aesthetic purposefulness of this set of white-on-white shapes, the scene is perhaps even more akin to Robert Rauschenberg's white canvases. Those early experiments in minimalism would come to critique the wild, spilling, colorful forms of abstract expressionism, and were perhaps the apotheosis of Rauschenberg's invention, as Leo Steinberg famously claimed, of the "flatbed picture plane," which "makes its symbolic allusion to hard surfaces such as tabletops, studio floors, charts, bulletin boards—any receptor surface on which objects are scattered, on which data is entered, on which information may be received, printed, or impressed—whether coherently or in confusion."[2] Like Rauschenberg's *White Painting* triptych of 1951 (fig. 1), in which the only points of respite from the blank expanse of the work are the slim, shadowy gaps between the abutting canvases, Hardy's "forms without features" experiment with the bareness of formal organization offered by one empty, white field being nothing more than "the limit of something else."

Like Rauschenberg too, Hardy wants to show us how ground can overtake figure, can emerge from its underneath position, can

FIG. 1. Robert Rauschenberg, *White Painting* [three panels], 1951, latex paint on canvas, 72 × 108 inches, San Francisco Museum of Modern Art.

reject the binarism of underneath and overtop, claiming our attention as an object in its own right.³ Ground might not only prepare the way for the mimetic image, it might signal to us that images do more than represent. Perhaps this is what Jean-Luc Nancy means when, considering the ontology of the image, its own way of imagining a relation between figure and ground, he writes that the image is "not a representation: it is an imprint of the intimacy of its passion (of its motion, its agitation, its tension, its passivity). It is . . . the stroke that marks the surface, the hollowing out and pressing up of this surface, of its substance (canvas, paper, copper, paste, clay, pigment, film, skin)." Following upon his shift from thinking of the image as a mimetic representation to thinking of the image as "an imprint" of movement, tension, hollowing, pressing, and so on, he offers a clarification of how the image finds its ontological support: "The imprint is at once the receptivity of an unformed support and the activity of a form: its force is the mixing and the resistance of the two."[4] Exceeding its function as mimetic representation, Hardy's blizzard scene, as literary image (and Nancy insists that literature produces images just as painting and photography do), performs the hollowing out and pressing up of the surface that Nancy describes. This scene opens to view the receptive but "unformed support" that grounds the image while simultaneously showing us what ground does, its work as "the activity of a form."

While Rauschenberg's white canvases hang on a gallery wall, still and flat, exposing and presenting the plane on which any picture must be built, Hardy's blizzard scene is just that—a scene, or series of images, drawn out of a narrative; a scene in which detail is scrubbed out but then slowly restored, features returning to populate form, as the narrator finally asks us to "turn our attention to the left-hand characteristics" of the vista, "which were flatness in respect to the river, verticality in respect of the wall behind it, and darkness as to both. These features made up the mass. If anything could be darker than the sky it was the wall.... The indistinct summit of the façade was notched and pronged by chimneys here and there, and upon its face were faintly signified the oblong shapes of windows." Outlines fill up with features again. Shades of darkness regain meaning. The narrator is finally able to return us, with some pained effort at clear vision, to the episode—the surreptitious meeting between two lovers, Fanny Robin and Frank Troy—that is the true subject of the chapter, as Frank himself emerges, a barely discernible *something*, from the obscurity: "A form moved by the brink of the river. By its outline upon the colourless background a close observer might have seen that it was small. This was all that was positively discoverable, though it seemed human" (86).

In this chapter, I follow the metaphor of groundwork through Hardy's fiction as a way of accessing the metaphysical problems that inform his ironic relationship to novelistic realism. As we'll see, "groundwork" is a word of which Hardy himself was fond. He uses the term across his fiction as a way of pointing to the seemingly inert field within which details—objects, events, features, steps, episodes—develop and move, as when in *The Return of the Native* (1878) he describes Thomasin Yeobright's face: "The groundwork of the face was hopefulness; but over it now lay like a foreign substance a film of anxiety and grief."[5] For Hardy, groundwork and what lies over it may be at odds, and this description of Thomasin seems to call out for us to strip away that dirtying "foreign substance" to reveal the pristine ground which glimmers through from underneath.

For groundwork contains and expresses an essential ontological truth. It's not the mere primer over which a painting takes shape; rather, it's the painting itself, or at least a rough sketch, temporarily obscured by an accumulation of grime. What Peter Casagrande once described as Hardy's "deteriorism"—his status as "a believer... in the absolute superiority of first things who was always tormented by the intellectual certainty that first things are beyond recovery"—might partially clarify the nature of Hardy's ambivalence about groundwork.[6] Is Hardy's groundwork a "first thing," the foundation upon which the world of the novel is built, which the novelist can expose only fitfully or indirectly? Or is it a last thing, the featureless sediment left behind when details deteriorate or decay, a corrosive force against which the narrator struggles to maintain the relationship between form and content, between outlines and the features that give them meaning?

I argue that in Hardy's fiction the question is left purposefully unresolved. Keeping alive the paradoxical interaction between these different kinds of metaphysical problems is precisely Hardy's intention as he asks us to reckon with the groundwork as a neglected, even forgotten, but nevertheless indispensable form: the form without features, divisible anywhere and everywhere; the pristinely open space whose still emptiness is itself a kind of chaos, an undecided and undecidable blizzard. Hardy famously declared that "'realism' is not Art," because the goal of art should be "a disproportioning—(i.e., distorting, throwing out of proportion)—of realities, to show more clearly the features that matter in those realities, which, if merely copied or reported inventorially, might possibly be observed, but would more probably be overlooked."[7] The groundwork is, paradoxically, just such a feature that matters: the featureless feature; the blank field which is overlooked but essential to all the things and locations that organize themselves within the open possibilities of its blankness; at the same time, it is the form as the last feature standing when everything is stripped away, the void that might reassert itself whether we like it or not, leaving us bereft and disoriented.

Hardy's conviction that the role of the novel is to disproportion and distort reality rather than to copy it is both a literary argument about the goals and protocols of realism, and a metametaphysical argument about which features of reality are most important to understanding reality's nature, about how we delimit the scope of metaphysics in the first place, and about how the novel makes available a unique way of seeing reality askance, bringing into view those features and those featureless forms that matter. Noticing how Hardy opens the groundwork to view might help us understand his vexation at a realism that would only copy or inventory or observe. He wonders what happens when that inventory of realist details becomes obscured to the point of blankness, the fictional world deprived of all but its barest outlines.

If Hardy's realism is not primarily a realism of reference or denotation (a mimetic realism) but is rather a realism of disproportioning and distortion (a metametaphysical realism), then it necessarily complicates our theories about how the realist novel refers and denotes. Even if Hardy wants to do something in excess of denotation, in other words, it's undeniable that his fiction does point to things, as all fiction does. The difference lies in the way he points, and in the difficulties that arise when the object of his pointing is the groundwork of the novel rather than its objects, characters, and details. Hardy's fiction asks us to attend to the obdurate but abstract presence of the blank groundwork rather than to that of concrete objects, to dark matter rather than to material things.

Methodologically speaking, to point our attention to the groundwork is an antihistoricist move (or, less polemically, an ahistorical one), whether on my part as critic or on Hardy's part as novelist, because it temporarily removes from consideration the grounds of historicist reading practices—material detail, the textures of ordinary life, the institutional mechanisms of ideology—in favor of a ground so featureless it gives us vertigo, or maybe thrills us by setting us loose, releasing us from the constraints of the physical into the speculative possibilities of the metaphysical. A great deal may be lost in turning our attention away from Hardy's interest in land, labor, and property (an interest which certainly does undergird many of the scenes I read in this chapter), but I hope that the turn away from the material and the historical may also make visible a set of questions about groundwork that are obscured when we take its "ground" and its "work" literally rather than metaphorically.

Hardy's fiction might, I argue, investigate metaphysical questions about fictional being that aren't available to a realism imagined as purely representational or denotative, or to a historicism interested in groundwork as a concept primarily of labor, economic value, and enclosure, or to a political formalism that might read Hardy's metaphors as analogous to or continuous with the social problems his novel engages. But Hardy has already shown in his blizzard scene that the rejection of mimesis, the return to the drawing board in order to find the ground of a fictional existence, while liberating, can also be terrifying. Or, as Sara Ahmed puts it, to upset the relationship between the ground and the body it supports—to "throw the body from its ground"—is to lose one's bearings: "Disorientation as a bodily feeling . . . can shatter one's sense of confidence in the ground or one's belief that the ground on which we reside can support the actions that make a life feel livable." But we might need such an experience of ungrounding, Ahmed insists, in order to start anew, to reorganize, to take up a queer orientation, "the possibility of changing directions and of finding other paths, perhaps those that do not clear a common ground, where we can respond with joy to what goes astray."[8] To point to the groundwork might be a way of expressing a desire for just such an openness of possibility, something like Roland Barthes's desire for "the neutral" as the "moment when within the original nondifferentiation something begins to be sketched, tone on tone, the first differences."[9] We might understand the novelistic denotation of a colorless field of mere "existence" or "being," in other words, as an evasion of reality and its pressures, the ruse of a writer fleeing to metaphysics in order to mystify the solidity of "the real."

But, on the contrary, I argue that Hardy points our attention to the groundwork in order to find a surer footing for realism, a deeper sense of how fictional reality feels, and a wider and solider foundation for the methods and metaphors by which we come to know and to formalize our sense of fictional being. As I'll argue later on, Hardy's groundwork attempts to conjure a different kind of "totality" from the one dreamed up by György Lukács as the novel's lost object, a smooth field somewhere underneath it all, usually hidden or just ignored, but which we can make visible with some effort, which is there even when our focus is elsewhere. As whiteness, blackness, and brownness emerge as constituting the basic color palette of Hardy's groundwork, however, we must also insist that his lingering in ontological abstractions—"being" and "totality"—with some freedom of movement and some authority is not only a neutral aesthetic experiment but also an assertion of power, and a function of the privilege that Fred Moten points to in his reading of the metaphysics of race, which I return to in chapter 2. If, as Moten insists, "blackness is prior to ontology, . . . ontology's anti- and ante-foundation, ontology's underground, the irreparable disturbance of ontology's time and space," then we must understand Hardy's movements in and around the blankness of the groundwork—a blankness that is sometimes white, but as we'll see is sometimes a brown face without features, sometimes an expanse of bestial, wounded black skin—as fueled by a set of racialized metaphors.[10] This is an aspect of Hardy's writing that has recently been taken up by S. Pearl Brilmyer, who points out how Hardy prioritizes the "racial logics" of "surface" over "outline": "in Hardy," she argues, "surfaces are not neutral canvases but rather the site where time and space collide to produce historical and social meaning."[11]

A long tradition within Hardy criticism has attempted to come to terms with Hardy's unique, ornery, or simply indeterminate relationship to the aims of realism and its pursuit of the ordinary world, but few have attended to the metaphysical paradoxes that prompted Hardy's sense that inventorying details, features, and things doesn't give us a deep or complex enough picture of reality, the kind of paradoxes that emerge in Moten's connection of the ontology of blackness to the social reality of black life. A succession of critics—Mary Jacobus, Elaine Scarry, J. Hillis Miller, Linda Shires, Michael Irwin, Megan Ward, and Audrey Jaffe foremost among them—have detailed Hardy's immanent critique of the pastoral mode and its reverence for nature and the landscape as stable grounds both for the literary imagination and for human work and inhabitation.[12] Others such as J. B. Bullen, Sheila Berger, Elaine Auyoung, and Jaffe again, have pointed to Hardy's self-consciousness about the artifice and the cognitive demands of realist mimesis and its analogues in visual perception, art, and drawing.[13] Recently, Anna Kornbluh has argued for the geometric abstraction underlying Hardy's realism by tracing *Jude the Obscure*'s meticulous attention to linear and typographic forms as analogues for the real and rigid force of social norms; and William A. Cohen, Elisha Cohn, Anna Henchman, Alicia Christoff, and Brilmyer have emphasized in different ways Hardy's abiding interest in the extreme instability of embodiment, psychological interiority, sensation, and racialization as ways of being in the world.[14]

I share with all of these critics a sense of Hardy's antifoundationalism: his deep skepticism, that is, about any thing, category, concept, or value that might seem uncomplicatedly to ground our understanding of reality, let alone fictional existence. As I've already suggested, however, I want to train our attention on the kinds of metaphysical perplexity, rather than only the epistemic uncertainty or political ideology, occasioned by this skepticism of foundations. What if fictional reality itself is uncertain and unstable, not only in our perception of it, but in its very being? What if the ground of that fictional world is not comparable to the ground of our own actual world? Where do those metaphors, including the metaphor of groundwork, find their limits as a way of imagining an ontological ground for the novel? The groundwork represents an important formal paradox for Hardy as he tries to reconstruct such metaphysical vertigo in the structuring of his fictional worlds: How do we reckon with the ground that also ungrounds, the blank field that presupposes no particular kind of organization, the underlying form that is simply a blank? But he also thematizes this formal problem frequently, as a pragmatic problem for characters within his novels. How does one find one's way in a world in which intervals and locations might be unreal, in which movement might be only wishful thinking? What if that blank groundwork, which threatens to unmoor me from the comforting solidity of the ordinary world like a fugue state or a delusion, is in fact just as real as anything?

The relationship of a stable "groundwork" to a contingent "finish" appears here and there as a kind of folk wisdom in Hardy's world. In *Under the Greenwood Tree* (1872), Reuben Dewy advises his son Dick that potential lovers "be all alike in the groundwork; 'tis only in the flourishes there's a difference."[15] In *Far from the Madding Crowd*, the destitute Fanny Robin's face is described as "young in the groundwork, old in the finish; the general contours were flexuous and childlike, but the finer lineaments had begun to be sharp and thin" (258). A minor character in *The Return of the Native* insults the appearance of Diggory Venn, the reddleman whose skin has been dyed red by the plying of his trade, only to excuse himself by insisting that "ye bain't bad-looking in the groundwork, though the finish is queer" (34). Of Mrs. Yeobright in the same novel, we're told that "The philosophy of her nature ... was almost written in her movements. They had a majestic foundation, though they were far from being majestic; and they had a groundwork of assurance, but they were not assured" (186).

In Hardy's fiction, characters and narrators share a sense that the groundwork is more essential and more valuable than the contingent, deceptive finish. A groundwork grounds, yet it's liable to disappear from view, unattended, and so it needs to be uncovered and reasserted in order to make its function clear. Early in *Jude the Obscure* (1895), for example, as a young Jude arrives at the farmer Mr. Troutham's field, where he's been tasked with scaring away birds, the narrator describes a plot of land on which "fresh harrow-lines seemed to stretch like the channelings in a piece of new corduroy, lending a meanly utilitarian air to the expanse, taking away its gradations, and depriving it of all history beyond that of the few recent months." Despite the smoothing over of the marks of history by the working of the ground, the land remains saturated by a memory that has after all only been covered over and made invisible, as if to begin anew: "To every clod and stone," the narrator clarifies, "there really attached associations enough and to spare—echoes of songs from ancient harvest-days, of spoken words, and of sturdy deeds. . . . But this neither Jude nor the rooks around him considered. For them it was a lonely place, possessing in the one view only the quality of a work-ground, and in the other that of a granary good to feed in."[16] Here, the work-ground is literally the space of agricultural labor, but it is also a plot of land stripped of its redolent narrative detail—its markings—and made new and unused as a fresh bolt of fabric, or perhaps a blank page.[17] This clearing happens not once but repeatedly, as part of the cycle of agricultural work, and yet this smoothing and working and resmoothing of the landscape never actually restores it to an original emptiness, or to what Megan Ward calls the "immaterial real," something like reality as such, for which the mythic image of an untouched, uncultivated nature is supposed to stand.[18] Although Jude sees a utilitarian ugliness in the freshly plowed land, a mere work-ground in which to sow, the narrator allows us to see how human intervention can never be thorough enough to return us to a moment before human intervention, before harvests, songs, and deeds have attached to the bare land and made it part of a narrative. Having been worked over, it now seems to offer to Jude no purpose other than to be worked and worn again, to be marked with features and figures, to be shaped.

It seems, then, that uncovering the groundwork unsettles as much as it enlightens, whether we're talking about faces or about the landscapes that Hardy so often compares to faces.[19] J. Hillis Miller, for example, has shown how Hardy connects the landscape to the face frequently through catachresis. I diverge, however, from Miller's deconstructive idea—which follows a Heideggerian phenomenology of the ground of the artwork— that we can never find an ultimate "ground" subtending Hardy's landscapes, which leads Miller to consider "the landscape as such" or "the topography of topography" as the central problems for Hardy's development of a mappable, habitable world. Instead, I argue, we need to change our sense of what "ground" we seek: not a set of "determining causes," in Miller's terms, but rather a field that is by definition without precise positionality, that doesn't "cause" the world that takes shape within it but makes space for it. Indeed, while Miller insists that "landscape in a novel is not just an indifferent background within which the action takes place," and "space not . . . something pre-existent, neutrally lying out there," I hope that it will already be clear that my argument runs precisely counter to these assumptions, as I aim to show how an "indifferent" and "neutral" field might be precisely that which Hardy understands as the ground of the novel; or that landscape isn't primarily about what Miller calls a "figurative mapping" but often figures something entirely other than an "actual" landscape, becoming metametaphysical in its meaning precisely when it is made most blank.[20]

We can look to one particularly striking example of Hardy's comparison of landscape to a pair of strangely blank faces to see how this metaphor comes to stand for something like Ward's "immaterial real" rather than for the problem of topography that interests Miller. In *Tess of the d'Urbervilles*, as Tess and her friend Marian work in a turnip field, we're told that, the livestock having eaten the leaves of the buried turnip bulbs,

> the whole field was in colour a desolate drab; it was a complexion without features, as if a face from chin to brow should be only an expanse of skin. The sky wore, in another colour, the same likeness; a white vacuity of countenance with the lineaments gone. So these two upper and nether visages confronted each other, all day long the white face looking down on the brown face, and the brown face looking up at the white face, without anything standing between them but the two girls crawling over the surface of the former like flies.[21]

Hardy echoes his metaphor of seventeen years earlier, the "forms without features" of the moor besieged by snow having now become the "complexion without features" that characterizes the turnip field stripped of its green shoots. To expose the groundwork is often to get at the truth, but Hardy insists that it's just as often to disorient—a grotesque flattening of detail and texture by which the expressive face becomes only a horrifyingly mute expanse of skin, across which skitter two flies. The syntax of the final sentence of this passage confuses even the location of Tess and Marian, who are said to crawl over the surface of "the former" of the two featureless expanses—but the chiasmus with which the two faces' mutual gaze is described makes it somewhat ambiguous which is the former and which is the latter. Do they crawl across the brown field as we assume they must? Or does nothing ground them any longer as the scene fades to near colorlessness, so that they might crawl just as easily across that blank white ground, the sky? As we'll see later on, when we look at *The Return of the Native* and Mrs. Yeobright's near-death experience in that novel, such fantasies of escape from the solid brown ground, the earth itself, are often central to those moments in which landscape fades away and groundwork appears.

The groundwork, then, is always a metaphor, or an approximation, in Hardy: the snow-filled scene retains some after-image of the more detailed scene that's just been described for us, that we know remains hidden behind the whiteout; the image of the featureless face can only be effective because of our sense of its unnaturalness, our idea of the features that should be there to restore to that "vacuity of countenance" its missing pieces, its natural above-or-below position in the scene. Indeed, Hardy often associates the landscape's loss of its features, its reduction to mere form, as a living process of decay, or desire, or breath, by which the obliteration of detail is bound to be repeated, so that the process is never quite complete. Take, for example, the description of Egdon Heath that fills the opening chapter of *The Return of the Native*, and which is strikingly echoed in the turnip field of *Tess*. The heath, like the turnip field, is imagined in the chapter's title as a face, "A Face on which Time makes but Little Impression," since it appears even darker than the night sky above it, as if out of joint with the rotation of the earth: "The face of the heath by its mere complexion added half an hour to evening; it could in like manner retard the dawn, sadden noon, anticipate the frowning of storms scarcely generated, and intensify the opacity of a moonless midnight to a cause of shaking and dread" (9). Blacker than the blackest night sky, this landscape again threatens a topsy-turvy reversal of sky and land; it has its own rhythms, and according to those rhythms its own ways of hiding and revealing its details and textures that don't rely upon the cycle of day and night.[22]

The moments in which the landscape becomes so dark as to be featureless, we're told, in fact reveal rather than conceal the truest image of the heath:

Nobody could be said to understand the heath who had not been there at such a time. It could best be felt when it could not clearly be seen, its complete effect and explanation lying in this and the succeeding hours before the next dawn; then, and only then, did it tell its true tale. The spot was, indeed, a near relation of night, and when night showed itself an apparent tendency to gravitate together could be perceived in its shades and the scene. The somber stretch of rounds and hollows seemed to rise and meet the evening gloom in pure sympathy, the heath exhaling darkness as rapidly as the heavens precipitated it. And so the obscurity in the air and the obscurity in the land closed together in a black fraternization towards which each advanced halfway. (9)

Total blackness offers the "complete effect and explanation" of the heath, and yet the narrator deprives us of the specific effects he means, the specific content of the heath's explanation, working by the kind of indirection that tends to attach to these moments in Hardy where the groundwork shows through. The heath, moreover, "exhales" its darkness. Darkness does not cover the heath like an opaque cloak; rather, the heath in all its vivid and precise detail is itself a kind of cover for the black groundwork that lies underneath and is periodically exhaled, like a black fog that rises up to meet the sympathetic blackness of the night sky. The dissolution of detail is figured here as a kind of erotic longing in which dividing lines and contrasts fall away in favor of sheer undifferentiation.[23]

In the third chapter of *The Return of the Native*, we watch as the disorienting black featurelessness of the heath comes back to life with the lighting of various bonfires to commemorate Guy Fawkes night. As we might expect, the popping up of these lights reorients us as well as the characters who populate this landscape, but it also retains the organizing field of the groundwork, which we can no longer push entirely into the back of our minds. Having been "nearly obliterated by shade" (19), in a turn of phrase that recalls the "obliteration by snow" with which we began, the scene regains its features slowly and uncertainly, as if searching for the right kind of metaphor that will embed those bright fires in the black ground out of which they emerge:

> None of [the heath's] features could be seen now, but the whole made itself felt as a vague stretch of remoteness.
>
> While the men and lads were building the pile a change took place in the mass of shade which denoted the distant landscape. Red suns and tufts of fire one by one began to arise, flecking the whole country round. They were the bonfires of other parishes and hamlets that were engaged in the same sort of commemoration. Some were distant, and stood in a dense atmosphere, so that bundles of pale straw-like beams radiated around them in the shape of a fan. Some were large and near, glowing scarlet-red from the shade, like wounds in a black hide. Some were Mænades, with winy faces and blown hair. These tinctured the silent bosom of the clouds above them and lit up their ephemeral caves, which seemed thenceforth to become scalding cauldrons. Perhaps as many as thirty bonfires could be counted within the whole bounds of the district; and as the hour may be told on a clockface when the figures themselves are invisible, so did the men recognize the locality of each fire by its angle and direction, though nothing of the scenery could be viewed. (19)

The blackness serves as a blank slate, allowing the fires that burst onto the scene to appear as varied images—fans, wounds, Mænades, cauldrons—each presupposing a different kind of relationship of feature to groundwork. It's a particularly complex example of what Elaine Scarry has called "radiant ignition," a technique by which the appearance of moving lights seeming to lift off from a dark ground aids us in our cognitive visualization of the world being described to us—although in this case the lights that spring up remain embedded in their organizing field rather than taking flight.[24] The fan or the Mænad is an image drawn upon the heath; the wound, on the other hand, punctures through the dark to reveal it as animal and fleshy; the cauldron, finally, is formed out of the reflection of light from ground and sky, radiating between the two featureless "faces" of the scene. Finally, the fires lighting the heath are compared to the hands of a clock without "figures," which point to relative positions on a blank field rather than to precisely marked numerical positions; although the field is blank, its circular form allows us to orient ourselves within its horizon, just as the edges of Rauschenberg's white canvases offer us some relief, some promise that blankness won't overwhelm the world and that we can retain form even as we tip perilously close to formlessness.

In *Far from the Madding Crowd*, Hardy dedicates a full chapter to the excruciating journey of Fanny Robin, destitute, pregnant, and physically hobbled, her face, as we've already heard, "young in the groundwork, old in the finish," as she travels by foot to Casterbridge to seek refuge in a workhouse after being abandoned by her erstwhile lover, her forward movement eventually having "dwindled to the merest totter." She cries out in despair, "If I could only get there!" In his painstaking description of the journey from *here* to *there*, Hardy also narrates the breakdown of Fanny's mechanisms of orientation as she moves ahead into a thoroughly blank landscape, "the depths of a moonless and starless night" (258). In turning to a reading of this chapter, I also turn to a somewhat different problem posed by what we might call the smoothness of the novel's groundwork. Fanny tries to get from here to there by putting one foot in front of the other, but how can she measure the reach of a step upon a smooth, continuous ground with no points of orientation? Hardy draws unmistakably upon Zeno's ancient paradoxes of motion in order to wonder about our capacities and incapacities when it comes to dividing the smooth groundwork into countable steps. He makes what has been a formal problem for the novelist's descriptive project into a detailed pragmatic problem for a character who tries to find her way across unreal ground.

Fanny first counts the chimes of a clock in order to know how long she has been walking, to orient herself in time even if she can't orient herself in space, and discerns only one chime. But she's uncertain: the clock sounds in a "small, attenuated tone," as if its chimes might have thinned out to the point of blurring together, no longer separable, so that what seems like a single chime might in reality be many chimes blurred together in Fanny's perception (258). Earlier in the novel, Bathsheba Everdene registers the visual version of this same problem when she notes the many gleams of light that appear in the sky after a rainstorm, which overlap in perception, making for the kind of dizzying disorientation that comes from losing one's ability to point and to count: "The sky was now filled with an incessant light, frequent repetition melting into complete continuity as an unbroken sound results from successive strokes on a gong" (247). When a passing light from a carriage reveals to Fanny Robin a milestone nearby, however, she finally feels she has come upon a real, countable interval in space—the distinct line between one mile and the next. She learns that she has two miles remaining in her journey to Casterbridge, and this knowledge buoys her spirits.

But, alas, she continues to lose her way (and her hope) between these milestones. Echoing and resharpening the dissolving chimes of the clock, the bark of a fox sounds, "its three hollow notes being rendered at intervals of a minute with the precision of a funeral bell." As if energized by the distinctness of the fox's barks, Fanny remembers that she must only walk "a little over a mile, and there I am!" The hopeful exclamation—"there I am!"—collapses *here* and *there*, fantasizing the present-tenseness of the destination. In order to make this fantasy more concrete, and orientation more precise, Fanny tries to calculate the number of steps that it will take to reach her destination: "Five or six steps to a yard—six perhaps. I have to go seventeen hundred yards. A hundred times six, six hundred. Seventeen times that. O pity me, Lord!" Since this kind of counting can lead only to terror (or math anxiety), she fools herself through a different kind of counting, pretending that each segment of five posts of the fence that she follows will get her to her destination: "I'll believe that the end lies five posts forward, and no further, and so get strength to pass them." The novel then enters into a chanting repetition, a call-and-response between narrator and character: "She passed five more. 'It lies only five further.' She passed five more. 'But it is five further.' She passed them" (260). The indifference of Hardy's narrator is palpable in the alternation between direct discourse and spare narrative commentary. For a moment the narrator withholds judgment, allowing Fanny to pursue her experiment, to communicate her desperate belief, without muddying the waters through the use of free indirect style or other techniques of psychological interiority.

Fanny realizes with a sinking feeling that even after four five-post journeys, she has almost half a mile left to traverse, and the narrator's tone shifts as her experiment finally fails. He describes her sinking feeling, the come-down from the fantasy of the divisible to the horror of "the lump," suddenly naming the willful delusion that has been sustaining her through the scene we've just read, but also hinting that Fanny's "artifice" might nevertheless point the way to a deeper, more disorienting truth:

> Self-beguilement with what she had known all the time to be false had given her strength to come over half a mile that she would

have been powerless to face in the lump. The artifice showed that the woman, by some mysterious intuition, had grasped the paradoxical truth that obtuseness may operate more vigorously than prescience, and the short sighted effect more than the far seeing: that limitation, and not comprehensiveness, is needed for striking a blow.

The half-mile stood now before the sick and weary woman like a stolid Juggernaut. (261)

At the heart of this scene, there is a paradox. Only by hanging on to the obtuse fantasy of counting steps, counting posts, counting chimes, can Fanny overcome the stolid impossibility of getting there that ends up facing her like a juggernaut, blocking out the view of Casterbridge that has beckoned to her in the distance. We see that the narrator's refusal of intervention as she passes post after post might be motivated by a desire not to get in the way of a psychological strategy that really is working, that allows Fanny to move. Fanny has managed thus far to avoid the "far seeing" insight that there is always a halfway point between here and there, and always a halfway point between here and *there*, and so on, ad infinitum. Counting is comforting, but it is also in some sense unreal, a fiction about movement across space that makes it impossible to arrive at one's destination, since there will always be one more half-interval left in the journey.

Fanny's journey performs a version of one of Zeno's ancient paradoxes of motion, passed down to us secondhand by an account in book 6 of Aristotle's *Physics*. The relevant paradox insists that to get from here to there is always impossible so long as we imagine space to be divided into countable steps by which we move along a line from point A to point B, since one can continue to divide each step forward into halfway points within halfway points, infinitely. As Aristotle describes Zeno's argument, in order to move, one would need to do the impossible, "to pass over or severally to come in contact with infinite things [i.e., infinite points in space] in a finite time" (*Phys.* 233a22–23). Aristotle's solution to Zeno's paradox is to insist that "while a thing in a finite time cannot come in contact with things quantitatively infinite," or the actually infinite series of points that Zeno imagines, "it can come into contact with things infinite in respect of divisibility," or simply a continuous line that could *potentially* be divided at any point (*Phys.* 233a25–28). And of course, that is the way we often want to imagine movement, walking, getting there: we take one step, then the next, we put one foot in front of the other, over and over again, "and there I am," since there is no other possible result of moving step by step, or even feebly tottering. We feel ourselves pass through the smooth continuity of space, not herky-jerky through an infinite series of adjacent but separate points.

In his commentary on Aristotle, Simplicius describes one famous response to Zeno's paradoxes of motion when he recounts that "Diogenes the Cynic, having heard these puzzles once, said nothing in reply to them, but stood up and walked."[25] There is a kind of cynical confidence about the reality of one's own experience that seems able to sidestep Zeno's argument altogether rather than addressing it methodically as Aristotle does. But the effects of Zeno's paradox and its Aristotelian solution retain their force in Hardy's world, suggesting the terror of a world smoothed into an undivided continuum, with no discernible points available for counting. As Anne Carson puts it, describing the painful irresistibility of Zeno's paradoxes, "You love Zeno and you hate him. You know there is a ruse operating in his paradoxes, yet you keep going back over them . . . because you like trying to understand what kind of a thing a paradox is. You like being situated at that blind but lively point where your reason is viewing itself."[26] We can easily reimagine Carson's metaphor as a novelistic one: the lively point where the omniscient narrator views the tottering woman, wanting to see if the paradox will play out, awaiting and fearing the moment when the illusion might dissipate.

Jean-Luc Nancy, on the other hand, sees Zeno's paradox of motion as a crucial analogy for the way in which landscape forms itself in art not as a mimetic representation of an actual place but rather as "the presentation of a given absence of presence," a fictional existence:

> A landscape is always the suspension of a passage, and this passage occurs as a separation, an emptying out of the scene or of being: not even a passage from one point to another or from one moment to another, but the step of the opening itself. This *step* is the immobilization in which forward movement is grasped as a basis or a "footing," a span of the hand, the marking out of a measure according to which a world can be laid out.[27]

Grasping at milestones, hanging on to posts, counting from one to five, all provide for Fanny ways of anchoring and orienting herself, finding what Nancy calls "basis" or "footing," in an unreal scene that threatens to dissolve into blackness, to lose its orienting features and become only smooth groundwork forever and ever; and yet it's also such counting that leads her irrevocably to paradox, to a horrifying realization that maybe it's all been only a comfort, not a reality.

Or, as Carson says, maybe that "blind but lively point" at which the paradox takes hold is not only terrifying but also a desirable moment of surrender to stillness and incapacity, the inaccessibility of forward motion—the point at which Fanny decides to give up and allow a dog, who appears to her out of the blank shadows as "a portion of shade" that "seemed to detach itself, and move into isolation," a feature appearing out of the featurelessness of the black night, to carry her the rest of the way to Casterbridge (261). Fanny reaches that point of surrender as she realizes that the last half-mile is not only a juggernaut but also "an impassive King of her world" (261). In that phrase, we also hear "impasse": in this case, the impasse by which one's movement forward is arrested, made suddenly impossible and uncountable, the subject of a profound aporia—so long as we insist that space is made of countable units that divide the flat and continuous groundwork into parts.[28]

It's worth noting by way of comparison that the novel's protagonist, the shepherd Gabriel Oak, is first introduced to us in the novel's second chapter as a master of stasis, a person whose survival to the end of this corpse-strewn novel we might in hindsight chalk up to his ability simply to remain still, to become the pivot around which the entire world of the novel moves. "Oak's motions," we're told, "though they had a quiet energy, were slow," and "his special power, morally, physically, and mentally, was static, owing little or nothing to momentum as a rule" (16). The narrator has led us to Gabriel's introduction with a meditation upon what it feels like to look up at the stars and feel oneself carried through the universe by the celestial movement of the earth:

> To persons standing alone on a hill during a clear midnight such as this, the roll of the world eastward is almost a palpable movement. The sensation may be caused by the panoramic glide of the stars past earthly objects, which is perceptible in a few minutes of stillness; ... but whatever be its origin the impression of riding along is vivid and abiding. The poetry of motion is a phrase much in use, and to enjoy the epic form of that gratification it is necessary to stand on a hill at a small hour of the night, and ... long and quietly watch your stately progress through the stars. After such a nocturnal reconnoitre it is hard to get back to earth, and to believe that the consciousness of such majestic speeding is derived from a tiny human frame. (15)

Whereas Fanny Robin finally succumbs to the impossibility of forward momentum, allowing a dog to drag her onward, in this earlier passage the narrator describes a different kind of assisted movement. The hypothetical person alone on the hilltop, whom Gabriel Oak swiftly enters into the novel to instantiate, feels himself carried along but doesn't move himself. The ground under his feet remains in place, unmysterious, while some wider or deeper or more distant ground—the cosmos—becomes the dizzying and majestic new field in which motion becomes possible and indeed effortless.

(After all, as Lukács puts it in the opening sentence of *The Theory of the Novel*, describing the lost golden age of the epic, "Happy are those ages when the starry sky is the map of all possible paths.")[29]

In order to access this weird combination of movement and stillness, one must practice a particular kind of detachment, observing as if from above one's own "stately progress through the stars" while at the same time experiencing phenomenologically "the panoramic glide of the stars past earthly objects." It is only by setting one ground against another, becoming momentarily unmoored from the specificity and countability of stars and of earthly objects like milestones, and attaching instead to the clearness of midnight, that this fictional observer and this fictional narrator together make the ontological problem of the groundwork visible and comprehensible, if only for a moment.[30] Of course, a different problem of ontological disorientation than Fanny's then emerges: it's "hard," in the end, "to get back to earth" after such a sojourn between grounds.

Fanny finally does arrive at the door of the workhouse in Casterbridge, but this arrival is only described in hindsight by minor characters, and it is followed immediately by her death. It's as if the conditions under which her journey has been represented make the direct narration of her arrival impossible. For Fanny, and for Hardy as a novelist interested in building a fictional world upon a dark, blank groundwork, the act of counting intervals necessarily leads to this kind of impasse or arresting paradox: the paradox of infinite steps and the problem of impassibility that Zeno makes so irresistible. Hardy conjures, if only obliquely, the field of existence that lies in the interstices between the smallest intervals, the infinitesimal point at which stepping turns to gliding—and in doing so, he makes this field of pure being that we see around the edges of the countable somehow ordinary, even tragically ordinary, an affair of hobbling steps and milestones and the sharp barking of a fox.

In *The Return of the Native,* Hardy describes another exhausting journey that, like Fanny Robin's, ends in death: Mrs. Yeobright's journey across Egdon Heath in intense heat to visit her future daughter-in-law Eustacia Vye in hopes of reconciling their differences. As opposed to Fanny Robin in *Far from the Madding Crowd,* who becomes disoriented in the dark of a moonless night, Mrs. Yeobright finds that a landscape that is normally colorful, marked with clear paths, has been scorched and blighted by the sun, which "had branded the whole heath with its mark, even the purple heath-flowers having put on a brownness under the dry blazes of the few preceding days. Every valley was filled with air like that of a kiln, and the clean quartz-sand of the winter watercourses, which formed summer paths, had undergone a species of incineration since the sun had set in" (266). Recalling Tess and Marian, two flies on a brown, featureless expanse, or the novel's opening description of the heath that "embrowned itself moment by moment" as night falls (9), Mrs. Yeobright's journey is one of those scenes we've been following in Hardy in which the landscape seems suddenly to have lost its features and thereby to have detached itself from the "reality" it is supposed to represent, leaving us bereft of our own points of reference just as Mrs. Yeobright is of hers.

On this journey, however, it's the world of "infinitesimal matter" that offers Mrs. Yeobright an emblem of forward-looking hope analogous to Fanny Robin's fence posts and milestones, allowing her the conviction not only that she will reach her destination but that, when she arrives there, all will work out for the best:

> Occasionally she came to a spot where independent worlds of ephemerons were passing their time in mad carousal, some in the air, some on the hot ground and vegetation, some in the tepid and stringy water of a nearly-dried pool. All the shallower ponds had decreased to a vaporous mud, amid which the maggoty shapes of innumerable obscene creatures could be indistinctly seen, heaving and wallowing with enjoyment. Being a woman not disinclined to philosophize, she sometimes sat down under her umbrella to rest and to watch their happiness, for a certain hopefulness as to the result of her visit gave ease to her mind, and, between her important thoughts, left it free to dwell on any infinitesimal matter which caught her eyes. (266–67)

This tiny, "innumerable," "indistinctly seen" riot of shapes opens up for Mrs. Yeobright those interstitial places "between her important thoughts," and yet these tiny playful beings are not only a metaphor for the free play of the optimistic mind—they really exist, although sequestered, it seems, in "independent worlds," in an alternate dimension of tininess that often passes beneath our ordinary perception, a vaporous world under or alongside our own in which counting is necessarily futile or obsolete, or in which the illusion of counting has never been taken too seriously in the first place.

This scene also recalls an earlier description of the white noise of the heath momentarily tuned into by Eustacia Vye. Produced by "infinitesimal vegetable causes," and difficult to hear underneath (or perhaps above) the more audible notes—"treble, tenor, and bass"—produced by the wind's careening, rustling, ricocheting movements, this sound barely rises above silence to touch Eustacia's ear. "Below these in force, above them in pitch," the narrator tells us, this "peculiar local sound" is "the linguistic peculiarity of the heath.... It was a worn whisper, dry and papery, and it brushed so distinctly across the ear that, by the accustomed, the material minutiæ in which it originated could be realized as by touch.... So low was an individual sound from these that a combination of hundreds only just emerged from silence" (55). This dry paper of a sound brings us back to the image of the blank page, the empty canvas—and its tactile quality, as if brushing across the ear, as if touchable by those "accustomed" to the "material minutiæ" that lie not somewhere, but everywhere, beneath the visible matter of the heath itself, enacts the fantasy of touching the groundwork, finding a texture, a worn whisper, a primed canvas, a dull white noise, rather than only a forbidding silence.

This perhaps seems a different kind of groundwork than the one I started out with—the teeming realms of microscopic life rather than the blank canvas primed in white or black. And yet Mrs. Yeobright's sinking into the interstitial places of her thoughts and of the muddy earth, and Eustacia's experience of white noise, two moments in which a different kind of life rises to the surface, recall Egdon Heath exhaling its darkness into the sky, or the turnip bulbs growing just underneath the brown surface of the earth, or the living history mixed up and flattened out in the freshly plowed lines of Mr. Troutham's field. As in Zeno's paradox, Mrs. Yeobright seems to sink into a world that could be divided anywhere, at the most infinitesimal scales—but unlike Fanny's vertiginous response, her feeling of being unable to get from here to there, or Eustacia's unpleasant "tenseness" as she listens to that foreign noise emerging from underneath her own world (55), Mrs. Yeobright feels the paradox of scale as an unalloyed pleasure.

Once she looks up from that fetid puddle, however, Mrs. Yeobright once again loses her way. She "had never before been to her son's house," the narrator tells us, "and its exact position was unknown to her" (267). Finally, she returns to an "open level" to regain her bearings, and is told by an itinerant laborer that she should follow a nearby furze-cutter, whose destination is the same as hers. Somehow, Mrs. Yeobright fails to put two and two together: the furze-cutter is her son, Clym, who is also heading to his home. Without yet knowing whom she follows, she observes how Clym seems barely independent from the ground across which he moves, pieces of which he consumes as he goes along collecting furze to be used for fire-making: "He appeared of a russet hue, not more distinguishable from the scene around him than the green caterpillar from the leaf it feeds on. . . . He appeared as a mere parasite of the heath, fretting its surface in his daily labour as a moth frets a garment, entirely engrossed with its products, having no knowledge of anything in the world but fern, furze, heath, lichens, and moss" (267). Like Jude, who sees the landscape as a work-ground, a fresh bolt of corduroy, Mrs. Yeobright finds her way across the heath by understanding it, through Clym's eyes, as a work-ground for his insect-like labors, which allow Clym to be at home on the ground, to make of its rawness a resource.

When she finally recognizes Clym, Mrs. Yeobright tunes into his individuality with much less sympathy than characterizes her attunement to the "ephemerons" of that muddy puddle: "She was scarcely able to familiarize herself with this strange reality" (268). As with the hypothetical solitary observer of *Far from the Madding Crowd*, staying still while the earth itself hurtles him through space, or Gabriel Oak's gracefulness, which arises out of his refusal of momentum in favor of stasis, Clym's position on the ground, his slow and methodical and workmanlike grace, is presented to us as an ideal mode of orientation, an assuredness that the fictional landscape really is what J. Hillis Miller would call a "landscape as such," which can support one's movements, one's centrality, one's labor, if only by allowing us to nestle into it, to fade into its background, to consume it and to be likewise consumed by it. But precisely when Clym distinguishes himself from the landscape, ceases to be an insect and reveals himself as Mrs. Yeobright's son, she loses her bearings, made aware of the "strange reality" she's stumbled into, in which the relation between figure and ground has become unintelligible to her.

Mrs. Yeobright finally arrives at Clym's home, but a tragic misunderstanding leads her to believe that Eustacia, his wife, has closed the door against her, refusing the reconciliation she has come all this way to broker. In her desire to get away as quickly as she can, she isn't able to rest or to drink, having been made nauseated by the warm water offered her by Johnny Nunsuch, the small boy who finds her hiding out near Clym's home. And so she begins her journey home. We're told that her "exertions, physical and emotional, had well-nigh prostrated her; but she continued to creep along in short stages with long breaks between," reminiscent of Fanny Robin breaking her own journey down into manageable segments (278). But the heat threatens to burn her into the brownness of the landscape along with those singed heath-violets and those kiln-dried summer paths: "The sun . . . stood directly in her face, like some merciless incendiary, brand in hand, waiting to consume her. With the departure of the boy all visible animation disappeared from the landscape, though the intermittent husky notes of the male grasshoppers . . . were enough to show that amid the prostration of the larger animal species an unseen insect world was busy in all the fulness of life" (278). The world of ephemerons keeps on rioting unseen, now only heard, as if living on a different, more hospitable ground inaccessible to the woman being swallowed up into blankness and inanimacy by the ruthless sun.

As Mrs. Yeobright finally succumbs to heatstroke, seated on the only patch of green she can find, she watches a colony of ants at work—yet another tiny insect world just below the level of her own experience that emerges into view to occupy her thoughts. She then watches a heron take to the sky, facing the sun itself, "and as he flew the edges and lining of his wings, his thighs, and his breast were so caught by the bright sunbeams that he appeared as if formed of burnished silver. Up in the zenith where he was seemed a free and happy place, away from all contact with the earthly ball to which she was pinioned; and she wished that she could arise uncrushed from its surface and fly as he flew then" (278). It will be several chapters before Mrs. Yeobright dies—the cause is not the heat, in the end, but a snakebite—but in this near-death experience, she luxuriates for a moment in a fantasy of what I've been calling the groundwork, the idea that one could trade the constraints of this ground for the freedom of that one. She imagines that she can give up the limitations of existence in exchange for what Leo Bersani calls the "utopic notion" of "an expansive diminishing of being" made comprehensible by virtuality and fictionality, a desire to be at once less than, and more than, one is.[31] Perhaps, she thinks, flying at the sun, inviting its leveling fire, could be a kind of liberation?

The groundwork of Hardy's fiction might be understood more broadly, then, as a problem of form and its operation at different scales and brightnesses and textures; in other words, a problem of our different kinds of attunement to the formal underpinnings (or the living, rioting underpinnings) of the spatial reality of the novel.[32] These two things—form and life, white canvas and infinitesimal biological matter—may not for Hardy be so different. Both are fields that invisibly permeate our own and that threaten an existential disorientation when they are exhaled from under the surface or when the novelist tunes in to their white noise. The important thing is that such disorientation can be awful, as in Fanny Robin's suffering, or deeply pleasurable, as in the luxurious blackness of Egdon Heath or Mrs. Yeobright's bursts of optimism.

Recounting the main events of his life in 1886, Hardy inserts a brief, cryptic journal entry from that year about his reading of Hegel, which might help us to a clearer sense of his commitment to groundwork, which seems to hover between solidity and abstraction, the bare canvas and the empty space, the actual and the virtual, as an aspect of novelistic form:

> May. Reading in the British Museum. Have been thinking over the dictum of Hegel—that the real is the rational and the rational the real—that real pain is compatible with a formal pleasure—that the idea is all, etc. But it doesn't help much. These venerable philosophers seem to start wrong; they cannot get away from a prepossession that the world must somehow have been made a comfortable place for man.[33]

We may balk for a moment at the characterization of Hegel, he of the master and the slave, as one who presumes a comfortable world. But indeed, the dictum that Hardy alludes to, set down in the preface to Hegel's *Philosophy of Right*, makes precisely this argument about how reason can remain comfortable even when faced with the defects of the real—about how, as Hardy puts it, a "real pain" might be assuaged by a "formal pleasure."

Hegel's bold aphorism arises out of a more detailed example, a question prompted by a reading of Plato's *Republic*, about how the ontology of the ideal and the ontology of the actual might be less incompatible than we think. Hegel argues that while Plato may seem in that work to sketch "an empty ideal," a world of political concepts unmoored from the concrete reality that surrounded him, this ideal was in fact there, something that really existed in Plato's world, if only in an incipient form: "There was breaking into that life in his own time," Hegel insists, "a deeper principle which could appear in it directly only as a longing still unsatisfied.... His genius is proved by the fact that the principle on which the distinctive character of his Idea of the state turns is precisely the pivot on which the impending world revolution turned at that time."[34] Hegel's chiasmus—the real is the rational and the rational the real—insists upon a meeting point, a rapprochement, a pivot, between the ideal world and the actual world, or something like what Raymond Williams would later call "structures of feeling," a phrase he uses to describe "a kind of feeling and thinking which is indeed social and material, but each in an embryonic phase before it can become fully articulate."[35] The "empty" ideal gives rational form to the emergent feeling of an unsatisfied desire; an abstract principle can also function as a solidly rooted pivot; and it's therefore surprisingly difficult to separate the idea from the reality.

So much for Hegel's dictum. Why, then, does Hardy, mulling it over in the British Museum's reading room, find it so unhelpful, and even so untrue? The short answer is that for Hardy, the world is real all the way down—an uncomfortable world, he thinks, or at least a world that in its stolid realness is deeply indifferent to the comfort of rational subjectivity and its formalizing, idealizing work. A real pain is a real pain. Hegel paints us a reality in which reason feels at home; Hardy's reality is, as Freud would say three decades after Hardy's journal entry, *unheimlich*. This problem of what I'm calling the uncomfortable world, inescapably and oppressively real, indifferent to the rationalizing aims of the individual, animates Hardy's work as a novelist, and especially his vexed attitude toward the tradition of the realist novel. Hardy maintains that the reality of the novel's world doesn't provide us a respite from the discomfort of the actual. We could take comfort, in other words, in a fictional reality imagined as groundless, that allows us to fix the problems of the actual world by starting all over again in a world not bound by the ontological preconditions that shape our own. Hardy refuses that comfort, even in fiction, by imagining the ground of the novel as insistently real, alive, breathing, roaring, occasionally even viewable.

For Lukács, writing around the time that Hardy would have been at work on his autobiography, the novel is also the genre of the uncomfortable world, what he famously describes as "the epic of an age in which the extensive totality of life is no longer directly given, in which the immanence of meaning in life has become a problem, yet which still thinks in terms of totality" (56). Hardy might phrase this in a different way: for him, "the immanence of meaning in life" might lie elsewhere than in the totality that Lukács idealizes. It may lie in the groundwork of the novel, figured by Hardy as hovering between the immaterial and the material, the fictional and the concrete, or perhaps refusing the binary logic that would presume these as the two registers of ontology that need to be reconciled or brought into contact. Hardy prefers to think of the groundwork as something solid, something real, something uncomfortably opaque, a source of painful disorientation that doesn't promise release, even when we fantasize about rising uncrushed from its surface like Mrs. Yeobright's heroic heron.

For Lukács, the novel is best at representing the "world of distances," "sprawling and chaotic" (59), and thus stands opposed to the ancient epic that precedes it historically, in which "here" and "there" stand for a meaningless (or at least unimportant) differentiation, and his treatment of the spatial fields and scales of the novel can be helpful in understanding Hardy's ambivalent relationship to his novelistic groundwork. As Lukács puts it, in the world of epic, "there exist no qualitative differences which are insurmountable, which cannot be bridged except by a leap"; rather, "the ascent to the highest point, as also the descent to the point of utter meaninglessness, is made along the paths of adequation, that is to say, at worst, by means of a long, graduated succession of steps with many transitions from one to the next" (32). In the epic, there is no need to count steps because stepping is so easy. Every difference is surmountable, with no impossible leaps required. Even "at worst," the distances of the epic can be traversed by steps that are "graduated," transitioning smoothly from point to point: in some sense, in the ancient epic world idealized by Lukács, it's all *here*, never *there*. Lukács describes not only a form without features, but a space without distances, relations without differences—something like that infinitesimal singularity that precedes the Big Bang, in which nothing has yet separated from anything else. And yet there it all is. This is how Lukács arrives, finally, at that strange phrase, "the paths of adequation," paths that lead from here to here, from myself to myself, that "connect" equivalences rather than bridging gaps or negotiating differences; or perhaps the sturdy paths of unbroken connectedness that allow literature to remain adequate to its task, adequate to the totality in which gaps no longer exist between the world of fiction and its groundwork.

All of this is to say that in Lukács's utopian concept of the ancient world and the epic narrative that reflects its prelapsarian reality, counting steps is unimaginable, because counting the steps presupposes a way of dividing the world and measuring its distances in discrete units. Lukács instead imagines a world in which all movements, whether upward or downward, proceed by a barely graduated continuity—floating rather than stepping, gliding rather than counting. The image of the "step" persists even in Lukács's account, however, each one connected by "many transitions." Lukács clearly shares with Hardy an interest in Zeno's paradox and an intuitive sense of its importance to how we understand the ground of fictional being. After all, isn't the object of Zeno's critique, the idea that we proceed across distances "step by step," always only a fiction? In other words, we know that motion must be much more continuous than this, but we find it difficult to represent what such absolute continuity, without intervals and without steps, looks and feels like. The fiction of step-by-step movement might then also be the basis of fictional realism, which must begin from a countable interval to build a world upon the groundwork.

Strangely, given the ancient pedigree of Zeno's paradox, Lukács insists that the ancient epic represents a world in which this paradox is irrelevant, a world in which each step from here to there is continuous rather than divisible. And yet we must remember how Lukács balks: these steps are connected by *many* transitions but not by the *infinite* points upon which Zeno would insist. Even here, the groundwork remains a very near approximation. In this chapter, my claim has been that Hardy's fiction often reaches for a different kind of immanence than the one Lukács is after, what he called the "immanence of meaning in life" and designated as the central problem of the novel, its missing but longed-for end (56). In Hardy's novels, we find such immanence of meaning not in Lukács's concept of the lost "extensive totality" in which all is *here*, nothing ever *there* (56). Rather, for Hardy, the "far sight" that helps us to see past the place where counting ends is a gaze deep into a muddy puddle, the perception enabled by the close rather than the comprehensive gaze. Hardy wrote that "the Art of novel-writing" is predicated on "an observative responsiveness to everything within the cycle of the suns that has to do with actual life," or on what he elsewhere describes as his interest in "the substance of life only," to the exclusion of the "manners" that he imagines interest most other novelists.[36] And yet the "everything" (at least the everything of substance) to which the novelist must respond is surprisingly focused and flattened out for Hardy, used here as a way to describe the novelist's "blindness to material particulars" in favor of "a sensitiveness to the intrinsic," or to the smooth, blank field, as I've argued, in which those particulars take shape.[37] Counting steps in Hardy's novels is a rudimentary kind of denotation, to return to Freedgood and Schmitt's central term—relativistic, rooted in the individual body as it marks its position in space, the length of its own legs, the strength of its forward momentum—a denotation not of things but of points in space and time. If denotation can also mean a kind of orientation of the fictional body in fictional space, then it can in fact point us beyond the numerable and toward some more indistinct, more attenuated field that is nevertheless achingly, forbiddingly real.

TWO

Underground

"The full African moon poured down its light from the blue sky into the wide, lonely plain."[1] In this first sentence of Olive Schreiner's *The Story of an African Farm* (1883), the narrator begins to survey a silent and almost depopulated landscape, echoing those scenes that we've been tracing in Hardy that strip landscapes of texture, emptying them out, as if to reveal some more unaccountable groundwork for the world of a fiction beneath or beside the place described by that geopolitical adjective, African, attached in this case not to the land but to the moon. As with Hardy's fictional Wessex, which enacts a minor refusal of referentiality, both referring and not referring to the actual English landscape of Dorset, Schreiner in this opening scene moves "Africa" elsewhere, a source of reflected light, and transforms the South African plain itself into a dreamscape, a mirror-ball surface illuminated by the "weird, almost oppressive beauty" of moonlight. "In one spot only," we're told, "was the solemn monotony of the plain broken. Near the centre a small, solitary 'kopje' rose. Alone it lay there, a heap of round iron-stones piled one upon another, as over some giant's grave" (1). The kopje, or small hill, figured as a giant's grave, points our attention to the invisible underground that has already been implied by the karoo bushes that root in the earth, by the "tufts of grass" and "small, succulent plants" that have "sprung up among the stones" of the kopje itself, and finally by the "clump of prickly pears" that grows from the top of that giant's grave, their leaves reflecting the moonlight "as from mirrors," as if warding off the light of the African moon, which might otherwise threaten to penetrate the tomblike depth beneath.

The fact that "kopje," the word used to denote a small hill in the Afrikaans language, also means "head," makes the figure even more complex. The underground of the novel; the giant's grave; interiority. We don't seem, however, to be dealing with the psychological interiority of a character in this opening scene, delivered from the point of view of the omniscient narrator; we might imagine, instead, that the interiority glanced at, lying just beneath the world of the novel, is our own, the head within which this world's ground is being laid, or into the depths of which the novel roots.[2]

In Hardy, we've seen how novelistic grounds can double, one moving against the other, upper and lower, earth and cosmos, breathing heath and dissolving sky. But once the ground ceases to seem monolithic, monotonous, unbroken, a further, irresistible question arises: What grounds the ground?[3] If Hardy makes visible the bare canvas that underlies the artwork, what about the wooden struts that hold the canvas taut? We can easily fall into the problem of infinite regress (a problem that haunted Aristotle as he searched for the ultimate substance or form that grounds all being), perhaps especially when the grounds in question are fictional. Something, some further ground, must always lie beyond the reach of the novel, unaccountable, underneath, a dark continent. I use the Freudian metaphor advisedly: as I've already implied, and as we'll see more clearly in what follows, the underground of the novel is not only a figure for an ontological problem; it's also in this case a racialized and geopolitical figure, and this is a problem Schreiner approaches at best tentatively. Hardy's images of the groundwork as a grotesquely featureless brown face, or as wounded black skin, have already suggested to us the problems that arise when whiteness, brownness, and blackness serve as ways of imagining different and sometimes competing modes of blankness or emptiness. Schreiner registers the blackness underground as a figure for a ground even more primordial, both generative and unstable.

As the opening scene of *The Story of an African Farm* proceeds, the narrator turns our attention to the farm at the foot of the kopje, and to a young boy named Waldo, son of the farm's German overseer, who lays in his bed in a "complete darkness" under which "nothing was visible, not even the outline of one worm-eaten rafter," contemplating time, existence, and death. He listens to the "tick—tick—tick!" of his father's watch and realizes that "it never waited; it went on inexorably; and every time it ticked *a man died!* ... How many times had it ticked since he came to lie down? A thousand times, a million times, perhaps.... 'Dying, dying, dying!' said the watch; 'dying, dying, dying! ... Where were they going to, all those people?" (3). As if terrorized by the two-dimensionality of the scene that has preceded his introduction (the impenetrability of that reflective earth), he envisions with horror a flat world and its precipitous edge, over which the dying tumble:

> He saw before him a long stream of people, a great dark multitude, that moved in one direction; then they came to the dark edge of the world, and went over. ... He thought of how that stream had rolled on through all the long ages of the past—how the old Greeks and Romans had gone over; the countless millions of China and India, they were going over now. Since he had come to bed, how many had gone?
>
> And the watch said, "Eternity, eternity, eternity!" (3–4)

Wrestling with metaphysical profundities—existence, temporality, God, eternity—Waldo both universalizes and racializes the question of death. The precipice awaits us all as it awaited those old empires of Greece and Rome, but we hear something more specific in his image of the "dark multitude" whose constrained movement pushes them over the edge, into the oblivion that lies beyond the reach of Waldo's ontological theory, a specificity made more acute by the turn from Greece and Rome in the historical past tense to China and India in the continuous present tense.[4] In Waldo's mind, death is not quite universal: it moves, historically and geographically, its pull toward the edge intensified by the gravitational force of empire. This is not the actual world but a flattened fictional universe the edges of which are uncertain, flickering first here and then there and perhaps ultimately in all directions, a threatening circumference. As moonlight turns to sunlight, the underground, its more fertile verticality, continues to beckon to Waldo: "Midday had come now, and the sun's rays were poured down vertically; the earth throbbed before the eye" (6).[5]

In Waldo's image of the doomed multitude plunging over the edge of a flat world, we find an echo of a strikingly similar image in Dickens's *Bleak House* (1853), which makes even clearer that Waldo's intense terror might stand for a persistent formal anxiety about the precipices of fictional worlds. As the second chapter of *Bleak House* opens with Dickens's omniscient narrator whisking us "as the crow flies" from the muddy, foggy world of London to the bucolic world of the landed aristocracy, we are reminded that the latter "is not a large world. Relatively even to this world of ours, which has its limits too (as your Highness shall find when you have made your tour of it and have come to the brink of the void beyond), it is a very little speck."[6] From a scared boy wondering about the edge of existence, we turn to a confident narrator declaring that "this world of ours," the "this" seeming somehow to comprehend both his fictional world and my real one, has its limits—its brink—and a void beyond. We see how the limits of the novel's world can be seen from within or from above, from the perspective of Waldo's dread or from the perspective of the omniscient narrator's detached knowingness. These limits might separate my world from Waldo's, reality from fiction—or our worlds might have a different kind of relationship that takes shape under the sign of the first-person plural.

What neither vision quite allows for is a third novelistic dimension of movement—instead of moving across the surface of the world (theirs or mine or ours) which leads in all directions to oblivion, we might look up into the infinite reaches of sky, and we might then wonder, conversely, about what lies hidden underground. Could we find there the soil in which existence roots? In this chapter, I take *The Story of an African Farm* and its narrator's characterization of "existence" as "a something which has its roots far down below in the dark" (a phrase to which we'll return later) as a central, guiding example, in order to descend to the underground of the novel, which takes shape when we refuse the two-dimensional grounds laid out both in Waldo's vision and that of Dickens's narrator, in which there is no underneath, only "beyond." Rather than imagining that which exceeds the limits of the novelistic world as a void, Schreiner figures it as an underground: a hollow, a giant's grave, a depth of fertile earth. The underground to which Schreiner's narrator gestures, the dark and inaccessible source of existence, is an aspect of novelistic form that is visible (for the most part) only indirectly, the earth out of which a fictional existence grows and spreads its branches. If ontology is often understood as a philosophical pursuit of ultimate grounds, then the underground in Schreiner's work figures a deeper ground beneath, and with it the possibility that grounds might give way or erupt.

When it breaks away from realism and the bildungsroman toward the novel of ideas in its pursuit of metaphysical problems, *The Story of an African Farm* enters into conversation with a philosophical tradition that Schreiner would have accessed through her devoted reading of Plato, Aristotle, John Stuart Mill, Herbert Spencer, Walter Pater, and others; and while I consider some of these thinkers in relation to Schreiner's fiction, with a special focus on Spencer, I mostly resist the mode of straightforward contextualism that would leave aside the racialization of the metaphysical gnosis that so fascinates Schreiner.[7] Fred Moten's work on the ontological significance of blackness, for example, clarifies what's at stake in Schreiner's interest in the underground as a metaphor for the foundation of being. For Moten, blackness is not only a fact of social and political life. It's also an ontological ground; or more accurately, blackness precedes or opposes or underlies ontology, waiting to erupt from beneath its seemingly stable ground. He pursues the idea of a metaphysical blackness, which risks seeming depoliticized, without standing, or as he puts it, without standpoint,

> not just the absence but the refusal of standpoint.... What would it be, deeper still, what is it, to think from no standpoint; to think outside the desire for a standpoint? What emerges in the desire that constitutes a certain proximity to that thought is not (just) that blackness is ontologically prior to the logistic and regulative power that is supposed to have brought it into existence but that blackness is prior to ontology..., ontology's anti- and antefoundation, ontology's underground, the irreparable disturbance of ontology's time and space.[8]

Both the prerequisite (antefoundation) and impossibilization (antifoundation) of ontology, blackness in Moten's thought represents a position outside of ontology's very structures of thought, beyond the standpoint required to orient oneself in relation to being or to ground oneself upon being as ontology thinks it.

We often think of the "logistic and regulative" apparatus surrounding blackness as its own kind of fiction, the kind that we call ideology. Calvin Warren, for example, takes up the "invention" of black nonbeing (which he represents typographically as a strikethrough) as central to the history of metaphysics and argues that "the Negro is the incarnation of nothing that a metaphysical world tries tirelessly to eradicate. Black ~~being~~ is invented precisely for this function ontologically; this is the ontological labor that the Negro must perform in an antiblack world."[9] Moten says, however, that we might desire to think otherwise: we might refuse the standpoint assigned by that fiction and instead get close to another kind of thought. But how Moten hesitates and hedges in narrating the parabolic approach to "a certain proximity to that thought," seemingly impossible to arrive at once and for all, that blackness precedes ontology! Before or underneath ontology, beyond standpoint, is a place we can't in fact go to. As Nahum Chandler puts it, echoing Moten's underground metaphors, to think such an ontological position is to make an assumption about what lies beneath in a place we can no longer access except through a cavalcade of figuration, to suppose that "there must have been an explosion, an irruption somewhere, from the beginning of time, as time, and thus yet beyond time, neither time nor not time, indeed displacing time, before beginning, cavernous and massive, fractual, infinitely so; an earthquake or a volcano; a black hole in the whiteness of being, in the being of 'whiteness.'"[10]

Moten's image of blackness as the "irreparable disturbance" of ontology is only intensified when he goes on to insist that "I bear the hope that blackness bears or is the potential to end the world," shifting our attention from Chandler's image of Big Bang genesis to this image of apocalypse. Moten trains our attention on the underground of ontology that might erupt or might refuse that which takes root in it, the underground that Schreiner also positions as an "antefoundation" of ontology, but that in her version must remain in darkness. We'll see this darkness figured in her fiction as the darkness of night, an invisible rooting place, and an undisturbed grave. *The Story of an African Farm* is a novel "about" South Africa in which Black African characters remain hopelessly minor, named only by pejoratives, and so it's especially important to think about the narrative unavailability of the racialized zone "far down below in the dark" where this fiction lays its roots.

In the final section of this chapter, I will turn to Colson Whitehead's *The Underground Railroad* (2016) as a counterexample that both contextualizes and problematizes Schreiner's underground metaphors from the perspective of the Black novel. Like *The Story of an African Farm*, *The Underground Railroad* breaks from realism (in this case toward speculative fiction) to reckon with the underground that supports the novel's world. But Whitehead's novel takes what was a metaphor in reality (the historical Underground Railroad that was neither underground nor a railroad) and bases his novel upon the literalization of that metaphor, imagining a nineteenth-century United States undergirded by the tunnels of a railroad engineered and built by Black people. While Whitehead's conceit opens the underground to view, narrating it as a setting rather than an exoticized, oblique Blackness, that underground is also the point at which the novel becomes most purely fictional, refusing the tradition of realist historical fiction, which would look to the historical record as the ground of the novel's cohesiveness. I argue that Whitehead's experiments with genre and metaphor help to problematize and destabilize the Black underground of the novel. Where Schreiner sees the underground as a symbol of dark fecundity and rootedness, a set of images that naturalizes and authorizes colonial occupation and white settlement, Whitehead reveals the underground of the novel as a principle of contingency, instability, and constant fugitive movement.

As Waldo continues to wrestle with the question of metaphysical foundations in the opening chapter of *The Story of an African Farm*, he longs for a clear view that he imagines can come only from elsewhere, from beyond, or above, or indeed from beneath his limited human point of view: perhaps from a place beyond standpoint. When he laments to his friends—Lyndall and Em, both orphans, the niece and stepdaughter of the farm's Boer owner, Tant' Sannie—that even books can never tell you what you really want to know, he turns to the landscape itself, wishing that the ground would offer up to him its secrets: "If *they* could talk, if *they* could tell us ... then we would know something. This 'kopje,' if it could tell us how it came here! ... When I was little ... I always looked at it and wondered, and I thought a great giant was buried under it" (15). Waldo reveals that the metaphor comparing the kopje to a giant's grave belongs to him as much as to the novel's narrator, but also that he finds this metaphor immature and unsatisfying. He has used the mythic image as a mere placeholder, designating the impossible knowledge of what lies beneath the visible world. Having tried to fill in the gaps in that knowledge by consulting "the 'Physical Geography'" (15), he finds that he's still left seeking something more, wishing that the substance of the world could speak its truth to him more immediately.

Later on, Waldo turns from land to sky (perhaps prompted by Em, who says matter-of-factly that it's God who has arranged things as they are), and he visualizes the puniness of his own existence from the point of view of the stars above. Those distant points of light can make sense, or so Waldo believes, of the mystified relationship between visible surface and invisible depth. They possess the knowledge he longs for, having seen what passes from below to above and back again: "'We,' said the stars, 'have seen the earth when it was young. We have seen small things creep out upon its surface—small things that prayed and loved and cried very loudly, and then crept under it again. But we,' said the stars, 'are as old as the Unknown'" (87). Imagining the voice of the stars, who speak with an omniscience that seems to exceed that of any fictional narrator, Waldo is nevertheless led back to the ground, and to the underground, trying to comprehend how the world around him has been shaped partly by things that once made themselves visible but have long ago crept back beneath the surface.

When Waldo finally grows exhausted and intoxicated by deep thinking—the desire to see underneath the surface of things or to look to the dark place beyond—he finds relief in working with his hands on an invention, a new sheepshearing machine. "After struggling to see the unseeable," the narrator tells us, "growing drunk with the endeavour to span the infinite, and writhing before the inscrutable mystery, it is a renovating relief to turn to some simple, feelable, weighable substance; to something which has a smell and colour, which may be handled and turned over this way and that" (72). It's this pleasurable kind of oscillation between the unseeable and the feelable, the infinite and the weighable, between the drunkenness of intense thought and the sobriety of solid ground that characterizes the work of metaphysics, a discipline of philosophy that asks of us a unique kind of asceticism, a mortification of the concrete self who must transcend the limitations of mere human existence in order to access an impossible kind of knowledge.

As the British idealist philosopher F. H. Bradley puts it in the introduction to *Appearance and Reality* (1893), "To say the reality is such that our knowledge cannot reach it, is a claim to know reality; to urge that our knowledge is of a kind which must fail to transcend appearance, itself implies that transcendence. . . . Is it possible to abstain from thought about the universe?" Bradley insists that even if we reject metaphysical knowledge as impossible because it exceeds the epistemic limits set by our limited human experience, we make a claim to know something about reality itself, if only in negative. We know enough about it to say we cannot know it; so that even when we claim that transcendence is impossible, we assert a kind of intimacy with its foreclosed movements. As he begins to theorize the ontological nature of space, for example, Bradley's writing revels in the ineffable "beyond" or "between" required by metaphysical thought, the same kind of "beyond" which we have already seen activated to different ends by Moten: "Space, to be space, must have space outside itself. It forever disappears into a whole, which proves never to be more than one side of a relation to something beyond. And thus space has neither any solid parts, nor, when taken as one, is it any more than the relation of itself to a new self.... Space is a relation between terms, which can never be found."[11] Bradley's description of space as always disappearing "into a whole," with its homonymic punning on "hole," suggests how the metaphor of the underground hollow (this specific metaphor, but perhaps also metaphor more broadly) helps us to mark out the zone of the unknowable, the unreachable "beyond" that must always structure our metaphysical theories. (It's a phrase that I'll return to in my reading of *The Underground Railroad*, a novel structured by repeated descents underground and journeys through dark tunnels, in search of a permanent settlement that seems always beyond the novel's grasp.) I can know something about the reality I occupy, and Schreiner's narrator can know a great deal about the fictional existence that she surveys; but as Bradley points out, as Waldo realizes with terror, and as Dickens's narrator wants to explain, even space itself, which feels to us so limitless, can only be understood properly as a "relation" to a space beyond its limits, a relation that in the end "can never be found." We might decide at some point simply to live with the infinite regress implied here, and we might use metaphor to make the unknowable beyond feel more solid, a ground to root in rather than a void of unbeing.

We can see in Moten and in Bradley, in other words, the kind of impulse that drives Waldo to his various metaphoric vehicles for the tenor of this "something beyond": a giant buried underground, a dark edge, a throbbing earth from which something seems ready to sprout under the energy of the sun. To stay poised at the edge where the actual and the concrete abut the metaphysical and the unreal might be to find what Sara Ahmed has called "a way of inhabiting the world at the point in which things fleet."[12] Ahmed's phrase denotes in phenomenological terms a queer orientation that pivots upon the point at which the things around us seem to become ungrounded or unstable, and to move swiftly and unpredictably. But we might also return to the more archaic use of that intransitive verb, "to fleet": the point at which things vanish as they give way to the transcendent, immaterial forms of metaphysics.

Or, as Herbert Spencer argues in *First Principles* (1860), a book that Schreiner described as having "showed me the unity of existence" at the age of sixteen, we cannot avoid reckoning with the realm of "nescience" that necessarily lies on the other side of our expanding and yet relatively feeble human knowledge.[13]

> At the uttermost reach of discovery there arises, and must ever arise, the question—What lies beyond? As it is impossible to think of a limit to space so as to exclude the idea of space lying outside that limit; so we cannot conceive of any explanation profound enough to exclude the question—What is the explanation of the explanation? Regarding Science as a gradually increasing sphere, we may say that every addition to its surface does but bring it into a wider contact with surrounding nescience.[14]

Spencer, like Bradley after him, felt certain that even as our ontological theories become more and more comprehensive, seeking more and more fundamental truths about the nature of being, "the reality existing behind all appearances is, and must ever be, unknown."[15]

When we try to determine the source of a mysterious sound in the bushes, Spencer explains, we might find upon investigation that it was caused by an injured pheasant. But if we're looking for the deeper cause or essential nature of that noise we heard, the discovery of the pheasant isn't enough. It leads to the pursuit of more and more general kinds of knowledge, about the anatomy of the pheasant's organs of vocalization, about sound waves, and electricity, and so on. How general can such knowledge become before it exceeds our capacity for understanding? "Of necessity, therefore," Spencer concludes, "explanation must eventually bring us down to the inexplicable. The deepest truth we can get at, must be unaccountable. Comprehension must become something other than comprehension, before the ultimate fact can be comprehended."[16] There's a deconstructive logic to Spencer's argument here: our accounting can only reach its fulfillment when it accounts for the unaccountable; we find the apotheosis of our comprehension when it passes over into an acknowledgement of incomprehension. Knowledge is shaped from the outside by nescience.[17]

The scene of Waldo in the darkness, which sets up so many of these metaphysical ideas as crucial for our understanding of the novel, reworks a similar scene in Schreiner's earlier novel *Undine*, drafted in the 1870s but left unpublished until after Schreiner's death. In this case, it's the novel's title character Undine who lays awake at night as a child, thrown into existential crisis by darkness: "emptiness, and black space, above, around, below, and she was one alone. Oh, how the silence ached!" Like Waldo, Undine tries (and perhaps still fails) to find her bearings by turning to the solid ground: "She crept out of the bed trembling and lay down on the cold mud floor; that at least was hard and solid, and it seemed to calm her. She pressed her face onto it, and a few burning tears fell on it; then she lay as still as though she were asleep. How comforting it was, that solid earth, but it was deadly and cold, and she would like the touch of something warmer."[18] There is some comfort in the concreteness of the ground, simply as a support for the body. It's better at least than "emptiness and black space" in every direction. But it's also a lingering reminder for Undine of death. When Schreiner's fiction turns to the ground, the image of the grave is never far away.

Undine touches the warm body of one of the girls asleep in the next room; she reads from the Christian Bible; yet she still feels adrift. In the end, very much unlike Waldo, Undine takes comfort by simply inhabiting the night and finding the specific contours of its darkness, learning to see that what has seemed empty may in fact be full:

> She sat up and pressed her little burning cheek against the window pane. How calm and still the outside world was. . . . Through that subtle sympathy which binds together all things, and to stumps and rocks gives a speech which even we can understand, the night spoke to the little child the sweet words of comfort which she had looked for in vain in the brown Testament. She left off thinking and only sat and listened, and the sweet night wind blew in through the broken pane and touched her softly, till the weary eyelids closed and the little head found rest once more on the window seat.[19]

Pressing her face against the windowpane, Undine finds a firm support that is also a transparent opening onto the darkness of "the outside world," the dark space that she has experienced as terrifyingly limitless settling into what Bradley might call a "relation between terms." The terror, she realizes, came from trying to think her way to a conclusion. Listening rather than thinking, she learns to understand the language of darkness, its soft touch, its whispering and hardly audible wisdom of the "subtle sympathy which binds together all things." These scenes in Schreiner's novels of children afraid of the dark, each of which opens the novels from which it's drawn, help not only to show us the everydayness of metaphysical disorientation and its roots in childhood fears of solitude, abandonment, or death itself; but also to lay the ground of the novel, by positioning it from the outset in relation to the darkness, blackness, or emptiness that lies beyond—beyond the bed, beyond the window, beyond the reach of vision or thought, or underneath the supportive but cold and deadly ground.

We've already seen how Hardy's descriptions of the landscape of the Wessex heath at night, exhaling darkness, longing to merge with the black sky, act as figural approximations of the blank groundwork within or upon which the novel takes shape. Schreiner's nighttime scenes belong, perhaps, to the same family. The metaphoric association of the immersive darkness of night with the forbidding unknowability of being crops up in Emmanuel Levinas's idea of the *there is*, too. "We could say that the night is the very experience of the *there is*," Levinas writes. We *could* say that night is the experience of this murmur of being, just as Waldo and Undine conjure awful visions and soothing whispers from the darkness in which they find themselves suddenly suspended and adrift, except that Levinas goes on to qualify that "experience" seems an odd word "for a situation which involves the total exclusion of light.... When the forms of things are dissolved in the night, the darkness of the night, which is neither an object nor the quality of an object, invades like a presence."[20] It becomes increasingly difficult to talk about the experiencing subject, or even subjectivity itself, as this invading darkness of the *there is* pushes back against us, assuming its own ominous subjectivity. Levinas shares in Schreiner's racialization of these ontological metaphors: the mystery of being is compared not only to the darkness of night but also to an invasion of subjectivity by an unruly metaphysical "object" that seems to have reclaimed its sovereignty. Here is an example of what Stephen Arata has called the fantasy of "reverse colonization" that characterizes much late Victorian writing on empire, and the thread of that fantasy works its way forward into Levinas's moment as well.[21] Levinas's figure shimmers as the mirror image of Waldo's vision, in which dark multitudes are pushed out into the darkness of the void that lies beyond the reach of metaphysical theories.

In Schreiner's other posthumously published novel, *From Man to Man, or Perhaps Only—*, which she worked on for decades but left unpublished at her death in 1920, we see the underground, and particularly the image of the grave, return as a more concrete metaphor for the unreachable darkness of being. This scene is again an early scene, establishing the world of the novel by problematizing the underground and its relationship to metaphysical knowledge. The novel's protagonist, Rebekah, understands with a flash the death and burial of her younger sister, one of a pair of twins, and this epiphany about the grave is brought on by an epiphany about the reality of mathematical truths. Going over her math lessons, she repeats to herself several times "six times six is thirty-six," before trying to speak into existence an impossible alternative, "six times six is thirty-seven":

> In a moment, something had flashed on her! . . . In an instant she knew well, and with an absolute certainty, that if she went down to the great dam behind the willow trees beyond the new lands, she would find there a little mound of earth, and that the baby from the spare room would be under it. . . . She knew, also, something else; she knew at that moment—vaguely, but quite certainly—something of what birth and death mean, which she had not known before. She would never again look for a new little baby, or expect to find it anywhere; vaguely but quite certainly something of its genesis had flashed on her.[22]

The conditional works in this passage as a counterpoint to Rebekah's avowal of certainty. What does it mean for her to know with certainty what she *would* find *if* she were to dig up the child's grave? The narrator offers her own qualification when she says (twice within as many sentences) that Rebekah's knowledge of the meaning of birth and death and genesis are at this moment simultaneously vague and certain.

Even in the image of the grave conjured in Rebekah's mind, no digging actually takes place. She knows that if she goes to the plot of land behind the willow tree she will see a mound of earth; and she knows that underneath that mound of earth lies the baby's corpse. She does not or perhaps simply will not imagine the corpse unearthed and therefore confirmed, the underground that holds the meaning of birth and death opened at last to view. The concrete image of that mound of earth serves for Rebekah (just as the image of the giant's grave serves for Waldo) as a placeholder for a much more abstract knowledge about what it means to come into being and to pass out of it, about how shaky and tenuous "genesis" can be, and about the obscurity of the underground of existence. That underground where birth, death, and genesis live: it is vaguely but certainly *there*, but it must not be turned up into the light, or something of its constitutive mystery dissolves. Rebekah vows never again to look for, or to expect to find, a new little baby, now her symbol for genesis itself.

The scene of Rebekah's epiphany follows upon a brief prologue to the novel which shows her already carefully thinking about grounds and undergrounds and foundations. While her mother is in labor to deliver the twins, Rebekah lingers outdoors, and comes to "a spot just behind the kraal where the ground was flat and bare; the surface soil had just been washed off, and a circular floor of smooth and unbroken stone was exposed, like the smooth floor of a great round room."[23] Here the underground is not loamy or dark, not the site of death and decay; rather, clearing away the "surface soil" reveals a pristine ready-made foundation, "smooth and unbroken." We're told that Rebekah has been using this spot for just this purpose, as the foundation for a miniature stone house designed for mice. The underground functions here as part of a different and more hopeful genesis myth—a *mise en abyme* of the laying (or simply the discovery) of novelistic foundations. The death of Rebekah's sister arrives to shatter and reorient the ideal of smoothness and stability that this scene establishes, transforming the underground into a forbidding hollow rather than a steady site for construction.

Halfway through *The Story of an African Farm*, as we've been following Waldo's deepening religious crisis, we finally arrive at a chapter called "Times and Seasons," in which we step back from the specificity of Waldo's life and enter into the indefiniteness of the first-person plural, the religious and philosophical *Bildung* of a universal "we"; and in its piling up of metaphors of grounding, groundlessness, and the underground, we can see how Schreiner shifts away from the conventions of realist fiction and into the register of philosophy, or at least the novel of ideas, in order to imagine what grounds the novel.

In this section of the novel, theologies and metaphysical theories develop along with the phases of childhood and adolescence only to be found in every case inadequate, often because they lead to an antifoundationalism that throws the world into wretched disarray, in which nothing grounds anything, and God is dead: "The human-like driver and guide being gone, all existence, as we look out at it with our chilled, wondering eyes, is an aimless rise and swell of shifting waters. In all that weltering chaos we can see no spot so large as a man's hand on which we may plant our foot" (115). Without God as a guarantee of metaphysical order, we lose our bearings in the deluge. For Schreiner's narrator, only dry land, the constant and the consistent ground of the real, will do. "Was it possible," the narrator continues, "for us in an instant to see Nature as she is—the flowing vestment of an unchanging reality?" (114).

At the culmination of this philosophical journey, however, we begin (with the narrator, and at her prompting) to look at nature and to see its patterns and repetitions, which might, it seems, point the way to a Platonic ground, an ideal form or "unchanging reality" underlying it all, of which all of nature's specific shapes are imitations. Dissecting a gander, we observe the branching blood vessels emanating from a central trunk, and then think of the branching patterns that exist in so many things: trees, the metallic veins in rocks, the paths of a river branching around dams, "the antlers of the horned beetle," and so on. We ask, finally:

> How are these things related that such deep union should exist between them all? Is it chance? Or, are they not all the fine branches of one trunk, whose sap flows through us all? That would explain it. We nod over the gander's insides.
>
> This thing we call existence; is it not a something which has its roots far down below in the dark, and its branches stretching out into the immensity above, which we among the branches cannot see? Not a chance jumble; a living thing, a *One*. The thought gives us intense satisfaction, we cannot tell why.
>
> And so, it comes to pass in time, that the earth ceases for us to be a weltering chaos. We walk in the great hall of life, looking up and round reverentially. Nothing is despicable—all is meaningfull; nothing is small—all is part of a whole, whose beginning and ending we know not. The life that throbs in us is a pulsation from it; too mighty for our comprehension, not too small. (118)

In this passage, the narrator turns away from the Platonic ontology we've been led to expect. It's not that antlers, rivers, blood vessels are all mere copies of an ideal shape that exists somewhere out there, or at least if this is true it can only be part of the solution. Rather, the arboreal metaphor pictures each of these branching shapes as themselves branching off from a central trunk, which in turn roots in the earth, in the "far down below in the dark" of the underground. The third-person point of view and its privileges are deactivated here by the question of ontology: "we among the branches cannot see" existence—that is, we existing beings, whether real or fictional, cannot see our own existence as if from outside, beyond standpoint, disappearing into a whole. And we certainly cannot burrow into the underground where existence has its roots.

Like Undine, whose fear of endless empty darkness turns to comfort as she learns to tune into the particular frequency of nighttime, the narrator here describes a shift from fear of the forbidding blankness of "nothing" to fulfillment by the plenitude of "all." We've seen how sensitive Schreiner is to the awful sensation that our reality is surrounded by nothing, or by what Spencer called nescience—that is, the feeling that at any moment we might tip over the edge, or sink into the pit, falling forever into the void. And worse yet, what if that "nothing" beyond is also the home to the meaning we long for? Suddenly it seems as if we're destined to live forever in thrall to nothingness.[24]

But the soothing finale to "Times and Seasons" reverses this presumed relationship between the world we can know and the nothing that lies beyond our reach. It's tempting to read that sentence, "Nothing is despicable, all is meaning-full," as an ethical claim: we see now that it is wrong to despise any existing thing, and that every being is filled with meaning. This ethical claim is certainly part of the sentence's thrust.[25] But I think there's an ontological claim here too, about where we imagine the nature of being can be found. Now we are able to see "nothing" as simply beside the point, "despicable," "small." We inhabit instead the "all" that is our comfortable home, "meaning-full" and "part of a whole, whose beginning and ending we know not." As Bradley puts it, space always "disappears into a whole," and yet in Schreiner's narrative of philosophical development we see a thinker learning to be at ease with that disappearance, convinced that even if the "all" that houses me is only a part of a larger whole, the pursuit of beginnings and endings is a metaphysical red herring. All the meaning we need lives right here in our world.

Schreiner rejects the Quinean view—the ontology that would only list a chance jumble of existing things—in favor of Schaffer's "grounding questions." But the best that even omniscience can do in investigating the ontology of this fictional world is conjecture, metaphor, approximation. The narrator gives us an indirect and metaphorized glimpse of the space that lies beyond the "all" included in the novel, and figures that space beyond not as a measureless void but as immense sky and fertile soil. In the final third of the novel, Waldo's long-time friend Lyndall in fact scolds him for his metaphysical burrowing in terms that echo the wisdom of "Times and Seasons." She warns him against digging deeper and deeper for ultimate truths and urges him to be satisfied with a more sensuous or immediate ontological knowledge:

> It is enough for me . . . if I find out what is beautiful and what is ugly, what is real and what is not. Why it is there, and over the final cause of things in general, I don't trouble myself; there must be one, but what is it to me? . . . But you Germans are born with an aptitude for burrowing; you can't help yourselves. You must sniff after reasons, just as that dog must after a mole. He knows perfectly well he will never catch it, but he's under the imperative necessity of digging for it. (163)

Waldo responds by insisting upon the fantasy of so many metaphysicians: "But he *might* find it" (163). Lyndall, however, is a thoroughgoing Quinean. She seeks to know what is real and what is not; the rest is never-ending, restless, exhausting digging.

The Story of an African Farm is on the one hand deeply sympathetic with Waldo's longing, and on the other hand eager to point out along with Lyndall that unearthing and upturning cannot reveal the mole that dog sniffs after. Lyndall insists that Waldo can never catch that mole, but why? Certainly dogs do catch moles sometimes, with some luck and some hard work, and Waldo's optimistic rejoinder only seizes upon that clear fact. But Lyndall is maybe right to think the work is futile. Moles are more at home underground than dogs are. It's in their nature to recede further into their hollows, pulling away from the sniffing nose until it loses the scent. Moreover, in this extended metaphor, to catch the mole is to maim and kill and devour it, and only after having ruined its underground habitat by bringing it violently above ground. The object is caught but also killed, and here we remember Rebekah in the opening chapter of *From Man to Man*, knowing "vaguely but certainly" that the dead body of her sister lies under a mound of earth but refraining from unearthing the corpse, even in imagination.

In the novel's second digressive philosophical parable, which follows immediately upon the "Times and Seasons" chapter, Waldo meets a mysterious stranger by the roadside, who narrates an allegorical tale that makes much the same point as Lyndall does in warning Waldo against digging for what he can never find. The story tells of a hunter who catches a brief glimpse of a strange and beautiful white bird reflected in a lake. He becomes obsessed, and he tells his friends that "now I desire nothing more on earth than to hold her" (124). Wandering around, "heartsore and weeping," seeking the elusive bird, he encounters an old man who declares, "I am Wisdom, . . . but some men call me Knowledge." Wisdom tells the hunter that the bird he seeks is called "Truth" and that "he who has once seen her never rests again. Till death he desires her" (124–25). The tale continues, detailing the hunter's dogged labors to seek out Truth, eventually learning that in order to catch her, he will need to scale an impossibly high mountain: "The mountains of stern reality will rise before him: he must climb them: *beyond* them lies truth." (In the world of this novel and its several beyonds, if existence has its roots deep down below, then truth lies somewhere beyond the immensity of sky into which the branches of existence extend.) He discovers that the mountain itself is littered with the graves of those seekers who have gone before him; creatures look out from crevices and hollows, tempting him to give up his labor. There is a tension in this fable between the upward-pointing promise of truth and the more dangerous, alive pull of the underground: "in the lava-like earth chasms yawned" (130). In the end, the hunter dies alone on the mountain, finding solace in the idea that his work has only been a part of an ongoing collective effort: he has carved footholds into the mountain that will allow others to mount higher. As he dies, a feather flutters down from the sky, and he dies clutching it (133).

Waldo reacts to the stranger's story with surprise, as if the story is his own and the stranger has read his mind. "How did you know it?" he asks. It is not written, Waldo thinks to himself, on the piece of wood on which he has been carving intricate patterns, the object that initiated the conversation between the stranger and himself.

"Certainly," said the stranger, "the whole of the story is not written here, but it is suggested. And the attribute of all true art, the highest and the lowest, is this—that it says more than it says, and takes you away from itself. It is a little door that opens into an infinite hall where you may find what you please.... There is nothing so universally intelligible as truth. It has a thousand meanings, and suggests a thousand more." He turned over the wooden thing.

"Though a man should carve it into matter with the least possible manipulative skill, it will yet find interpreters.... Whosoever should portray truly the life and death of a little flower—its birth, sucking in of nourishment, reproduction of its kind, withering and vanishing—would have shaped a symbol of all existence." (133–34)

In the stranger's excursus on art, the metaphysical problem of the inaccessible "beyond" aligns with a novelistic problem. The novel, like all art, "takes you away from itself": even while conjuring and circumscribing a fictional universe, it also opens a "little door" into a more infinite kind of extension. The space of the novel, like any space, is as Bradley says "a relation between terms, which can never be found." Even a fiction that represents something as concrete and narrow as the germination, nourishment, and growth of a flower (or indeed the growth of a great tree out of the darkness below) can therefore stand as "a symbol for all existence," the particularity and limitedness of mimesis always necessarily opening out into a more infinite space beyond the edge of the novel, outer space and underground.

Although Schreiner held complex and in some ways progressive ideas about race, Paula Krebs points out that "Africans remain fantasy figures or metaphors in most of her writing."[26] Anne McClintock argues similarly that Schreiner's focus on "metaphysical abstraction . . . served to conceal and thereby ratify . . . the very real imbalances in social power around her," and that "Schreiner's early reluctance to look squarely at the politics of race is rendered most vividly in the figure of the hostile, ominous and unsympathetic 'Hottentot' (Khoikhoi) who stalks through many of her stories."[27] Krebs offers a passage from Schreiner's introduction to

Thoughts on South Africa (1923) to demonstrate the nature of her inconsistent thinking about race. Here, even as Schreiner admits and works through her own prejudice against the Boers, whom she sees as a racialized group, she frames it with an account of a racism against Indigenous Africans that she considers entirely unremarkable:

> One of my earliest memories is . . . making believe I was Queen Victoria and that all the world belonged to me. That being the case, I ordered all the black people in South Africa to be collected and put into the desert of the Sahara, and a wall built across Africa shutting it off; I then ordained that any black person returning south of that line should have his head cut off. I did not wish to make slaves of them, but I wished to put them where I need never see them, because I considered them ugly.[28]

As Krebs argues with reference to Carolyn Burdett's biography of Schreiner, this is a prescient fantasy of apartheid.[29] I want to suggest the fantasy also has its parallel in the ontological theorizing of Schreiner's novel, in which the underground is imagined as a racialized ontological foundation, the loamy underside of things turned up only by a rare and fleeting gnostic insight.

Throughout this chapter I have been hoping to challenge McClintock's understanding of metaphysical abstraction as necessarily an evasion of race and racism. But the basic point remains: although I have wanted to keep race in view even as I turn again and again to the largest and fuzziest abstractions, my reading of Schreiner, which often luxuriates in the beauty of her writing about being, runs the risk of confirming her romanticization of Blackness as a figure for a sublime and even eroticized kind of metaphysical knowledge. And these metaphors indeed "conceal and ratify," to return to McClintock's language, the problem of colonial occupation and white settlement in *The Story of an African*

Farm. If the underground is never to be dug up or burrowed into, it can instead be imagined indirectly, as a black fecundity, a place in which to root, and therefore as a solid and unquestioned foundation for colonization—all while Black characters are pushed to the edges of the novel's world.

In this final section, I want to think more carefully about Schreiner's racism and about the limitations of her figuration of ontology's black underground as invisible and unreachable. Schreiner's black underground is soft and earthy but also thoroughly unreal, metaphorized as soil through which the roots of existence itself can branch, and in which the grave of genesis can be dug. As Elaine Freedgood argues, there's something odd about fictions, especially imperial fictions such as this one, that place fictional characters in "real" landscapes—but real landscapes that are nonetheless as good as fictional to most of the novel's readers. Such a conceit is a potent example of metalepsis, Freedgood claims, borrowing the term from Gérard Genette and defining it as "a breakdown of the boundary between levels of narration." An interest in the permeability of narrative levels and frames makes perfect sense, she writes, when what we want is a clearer, bigger, maybe even global view, since the breakdown of narrative frames enacts a fantasy of free movement and identification across the boundary that separates the fictional from the actual: "Narratives frame us rigidly. . . . But narrative frames also frame us rigidly. Diegetic space is claustrophobic—ontologically and narratively. We want sometimes to be on the outside looking in, or on the outside looking out."[30]

Freedgood has continued to deepen this theorization of the novel as a literary form characterized by its circumscription of diegetic space and by its experimentation with the metaleptic figures that promise to disrupt that circumscription. "If [nineteenth-century] novels have a 'form,'" she argues, "it is ragged and broken in its diegetic dispersion of a coherent world," and it is this raggedness that allows us readers the arrogant and too often unexamined fantasy that we can inhabit "multiple ontologies."[31] Or, as Katherine McKittrick argues from within the theory of geography, we must challenge "the idea that space 'just is,'" which tends to occlude blackness, and attend to "the 'where' of black geographies and black subjectivity. . . . If space and place *appear* to be safely secure and unwavering, then what space and place make possible, outside and beyond tangible stabilities, and from the perspective of struggle, can potentially fade away." Even in her theorizing of black geographies, it's important that McKittrick draws frequently upon novelistic examples: "imaginative configurations" of space, "metaphoric places," the novels of Octavia Butler and Toni Morrison, all offer ways of imagining and problematizing what McKittrick calls "impossible black places."[32] Schreiner positions the underground as just this kind of impossible black place, or the antefoundation of ontology imagined by Moten but exposed to view only indirectly, hypothetically, in the language of fiction and figuration. An impossible place, a metaphoric place, an imaginative configuration, an antefoundation: we can understand these concepts as somehow proper to the novel, not "extradiegetic" or metaleptic in Freedgood's sense, even while they register a haunted awareness that something lies beyond or underneath the novel's cosmos. To use the terms employed by Étienne Souriau as he argues that virtual being exists, and exists as something other than a mere "possible," we can understand that "some reality conditions it, without thereby including or positing" that external reality in our analysis of virtual being.[33] This is an antimetaleptic gesture, or at least one that holds metaleptic disruption at bay.

Ivan Kreilkamp describes Schreiner's aesthetic mode as an "experimental realism," and I would suggest that this designation would apply equally well to Colson Whitehead's *The Underground*

Railroad: both Schreiner and Whitehead shuttle back and forth between realism and other modes in order to call our attention to the metaphysical underpinnings of fictional worlds, to bring into view that which realism cannot see but upon which it nevertheless rests.[34] Ramón Saldívar has used the term "speculative realism" to similar effect to describe Whitehead's work, and he even links this melding of aesthetic modes to an earlier moment in the history of the realist novel, Walter Scott's "generic mix of history and romance to invent the genre of the historical romance."[35] There's a *longue-durée* story to be told here about the development of experimental realisms across the history of the novel, and this concluding section makes a small contribution to that story. But what connects Schreiner to Whitehead for me, more than anything, is simply a shared metaphor of fictional being worked to such different ends in the hands of these two very different writers. They share an interest in the underground and its earth, how it represents in the novel a raw material for the structuring of a fictional universe. But where I've been indicating how Schreiner often makes the underground the object of an ineffable, mystical gnosis, Whitehead truly goes there in his novel, seeming to comprehend how the full representation of the novel's underground ontological infrastructure might recuperate the underground as a support.[36] In that sense Whitehead's novel runs counter to Moten's argument about blackness as ontology's irreparable underground disturbance. In *The Underground Railroad*, the underground is instead a network of Black being and a mechanism of the novel's structure.

The novel begins "down there in the dark," a phrase that seems to echo Schreiner's "far down below in the dark."[37] But Whitehead's description is not metaphysical metaphor: we are in the hold of the ship where Ajarry is imprisoned on her journey across the Atlantic. The novel begins in darkness, begins in the literal beneath of the ship's hold; but in this novel concerned so thoroughly with the meanings and possibilities of "beneath," the space of the ship's hold may signify more than a setting. It is that space that Christina Sharpe figures, for example, as "a factory producing blackness as abjection," producing the "non/status" and "non/being-ness" of blackness, and in that sense still standing metonymically for the problem of distinguishing being from nonbeing.[38]

The novel's protagonist, Ajarry's granddaughter Cora, is born into the plantation, raised on stories of her grandmother's fierce protection of her small garden plot, only "three yards square." For Ajarry, "to escape the boundary of the plantation was to escape the fundamental principles of your existence: impossible" (8), and so she extends her being vertically into the underground while the plantation expands its acreage: "Ajarry's plot remained in the middle of it all, immovable, like a stump that reached down too deep" (14). When the plot passes to Cora, she comes to share Ajarry's understanding of the small parcel of land as a resource but also as a metaphor for standpoint, history, narrative, in opposition to the eradication of Black life that is the goal of plantation slavery: "The dirt at her feet had a story, the oldest story Cora knew" (13). This section of the novel enacts in miniature the tension between "plot" and "plantation," between use-value and exchange-value, that Sylvia Wynter identifies as a fulcrum for the history of the novel and its ontological claims: like the "plot system" by which enslaved people were often granted "plots of land to grow food on which to feed themselves in order to maximize profits," Wynter argues, the novel becomes "in literature terms ... the focus of resistance to the market system and market values," a form of "folk culture" that promises a position outside of or "against the impossible reality in which we are enmeshed."[39] We might hear the echo of Bradley again, pursuing a space outside of space, but here imagined as a site of resistance to the "impossible" terms that organize our idea of reality. But for Ajarry, the plot is not quite the resistance to or even escape from "impossible reality" Wynter has in mind. "She knew that the white man's scientists peered beneath things to understand how they worked," we're told, and so "Ajarry made a science of her own black body and accumulated observations.... She minded her place" (6–7). Ajarry minds her place. She keeps to herself, a stump rooted too deep to move. She tends to her place, the tiny parcel of ground upon which she dares to lay a claim. She stays within what she imagines to be her own sphere of inquiry, congruous with the limits of her own body and experience, indifferent to the white man's metaphysical burrowing. She stays put, having been made unable to imagine otherwise. "To escape the boundary of the plantation was to escape the fundamental principles of your existence: impossible."

And while at the outset of the novel Cora follows her grandmother's influence, refusing an offer from her friend Caesar to escape the plantation, she eventually changes her mind and decides to follow the different influence of her mother Mabel, whom Cora believes has escaped years earlier, leaving her behind. Cora joins Caesar, and the novel proceeds to narrate her indirect journey along the Underground Railroad from Georgia toward the North, with stops in South Carolina, North Carolina, Tennessee, and Indiana. Even before the escape, we get a hint at Cora's drive toward the underground as a mechanism of movement "through" and "beyond" enslavement: "Cora's last day in the field she furiously hacked into the earth as if digging a tunnel. Through it and beyond it is your salvation" (54). Leaving the plantation, Cora and Caesar (and Lovey, who surprises the pair by absconding with them) must navigate a swampy territory, drawing upon Caesar's knowledge of the area and "how to find the islands of sure ground" that will get them through the muck to safety.

The scenes of Cora's descents into the stations of the railroad, and her journeys along its tracks, are transitional, linking one episode of the novel to the next. Whitehead sees the underground of his fiction as the guarantee of its episodic form, the network of tunnels that holds it all together through the mechanism of what Cora often calls "the slave's choice," a kind of minimal agency by which one moves "anywhere, anywhere but where you are escaping from" (311). When she first enters one of the stations of the railroad, Cora is awestruck at "the sheer industry that had made such a project possible. . . . The steel ran south and north presumably, springing from some inconceivable source and shooting toward a miraculous terminus" (68). The "inconceivable source" and "miraculous terminus" of this underground place demonstrate to us that we haven't entirely left Schreiner's mode behind, nor have we gotten away from Spencer's conviction that expanding our view can't cancel out the nescience that always lies beyond the edge of our vision: even as this novel moves underground, further reaches remain in darkness.

But at the very least, by imagining the railroad as a product of Black engineering and labor, the novel works to concretize even the unimaginable reaches of its tracks: "The tunnel pulled at her. How many hands had it required to make this place? And the tunnels beyond, wherever and how far they led? . . . The tunnel, the tracks, the desperate souls who found salvation in the coordination of its stations and timetables—this was a marvel to be proud of" (70). Rather than experiencing terror or vertigo as she thinks of the dark reaches of the tunnel, Cora experiences pride and wonder, the "pull" of the tracks that might carry her onward and onward.[40] And yet, "she wondered if those who had built this thing had received their proper reward" (70). The work that builds the Underground Railroad is opposed to enslavement, liberatory, but at the same time uncomfortably adjacent to enslavement, a forced and unremunerated labor made necessary by the institution of slavery from which the tunnel builders must engineer an escape.

In other words, descending to the underground of this novel, we find another figure of ontological support—a network of darkened tunnels that holds the novel together and insists upon its fictionality, its departure from historical fact—but also a figure of limbo, a tunnel between enslavement and freedom, a figure, perhaps, for what Moten calls "the underprivilege of being-sentenced to the gift of constant escape," or of what Stephen Best and Saidiya Hartman call the "loophole between hope and resignation," "the political interval in which all captives find themselves—the interval between the no longer and the not yet."[41]

The Underground Railroad in this novel is not so much a figure, though, as an ironic literalization of a metaphor so entrenched in American history that it has turned into a dead metaphor. It works in that sense as a metafictional device, Madhu Dubey argues. Dubey sees Whitehead as engaging in a practice of novelistic "racecraft" that works to understand race as a "fiction rather than a lie": "Fictions, unlike lies, are invested with truth claims, so the new strategy of race critique focuses on the presumed rationality of the fiction, on its distinctive conditions of credibility, rather than on its inadequacy to the real." In an argument that resonates with Freedgood's analysis of novelistic metalepsis, Dubey claims that many contemporary American novels, including *The Underground Railroad*, "try to reckon with the muddle of truth claims about race through a deliberate conflation of literal and figurative levels of meanings . . . sometimes lending heft to the category of race and at other times satirizing its ongoing reification."[42] Whitehead's turning of metaphor on its head ("What if it *weren't* a metaphor but literally a railroad?") enacts the mixture of the figurative and the literal that Dubey notes, and it also complicates the picture that I've been drawing in this book, by which novels make use of metaphor to figure the grounds of fictional being. In this case, metaphor is forcefully demetaphorized, but the effect is not to make the novel more realistic, it's rather to advertise the novel's fictionality, the points at which it withdraws from the real and into the self-sufficiency of its own fictional being. Perhaps Whitehead's goal is something like Zakiyyah Iman Jackson's goal of "rethinking ontology" in relation to Black being, problematizing "the nature of what exists and what we can claim to know about existence" through texts that offer "unruly yet generative conceptions of being—generative because they are unruly."[43] Dubey helps us to see how such a move might work metafictionally: satirizing the reification of realism, the novel refuses reference and mimesis every time it descends onto those tracks underground, helping us to think about how fictions (whether novelistic fictions or ideological fictions of racialization) ground themselves.

The novel's conclusion, I argue, works to clarify how the literalized but still fantastical and speculative Railroad both formalizes and problematizes the image of the underground as the foundation of the novel's fictional being. As Cora takes on the labor of the Railroad's construction in her final escape from the novel's villain, the slave catcher Ridgeway who pursues her from state to state, she comes to understand something new of the nature of the Railroad's construction and purpose.

Late in the novel, Cora is beginning to make a life on a farm in Indiana run by formerly enslaved Black people, a refuge growing increasingly unsettled as white settlers populate the area surrounding it and as infighting develops among the farm's residents over the politics and possibilities of Black freedom. A new friend, Royal, takes her to see the "ghost tunnel" nearby, an abandoned branch of the Underground Railroad that reminds us that in this novel, as in Schreiner's, the underground and the grave are inextricably linked, but here the underground is figured as a space beyond death, what I called earlier a limbo, haunted by ghosts, a "deathless tunnel" (100). Royal explains that he wanted to show her the ghost tunnel "because you've seen more of the railroad than most.... I wanted you to see this—how it fits together. Or doesn't." When Cora responds humbly, "I'm just a passenger," we feel her resistance to the kind of narrative centrality and authority Royal wants to ascribe to her, the omniscience that could see the plan of the railway whole. I can't help but think of the opening to George Eliot's "The Natural History of German Life," which, in its defense of extensive empirical knowledge of the world as the raw material of realist art, compares the understanding of two different men on hearing the word "railways." The first man, "not highly locomotive," conjures up concrete images from his own experience, "of a 'Bradshaw,' or of the station with which he is most familiar, or of an indefinite length of tram-road." The second man, who may have "the experience of a 'navvy,' an engineer, a traveler, a railway director and shareholder, and a landed proprietor in treaty with a railway company," responds differently to the word, seeing in his mind a more abstract image of "all the essential facts in the existence and relations of the *thing*." While the first man, Eliot argues, may "entertain very expanded views as to the multiplication of railways in the abstract, and their ultimate function in civilization, ... it is evident that if we want a railway to be made, or its affairs to be managed, this man of wide views and narrow observation will not serve our purpose."[44] While the second man's knowledge may seem abstract, Eliot claims, it is developed out of extensive experience on the ground, a wide and far-reaching but also hard-earned kind of knowledge.

Similarly, Royal insists that even in Cora's role as a passenger, she might approach a fuller knowledge of how the tunnels of the Railroad work, simply by continuing to travel the rails. She might even come to know that the Railroad is itself a kind of pervasive ground for the world of this novel, not only a set of mappable tunnels but also a mechanism of escape and fugitive movement that runs "everywhere" underneath them: "It goes everywhere," Royal says, "to places we know and those we don't. We got this tunnel right here, running beneath us, and no one knows where it leads. If we keep the railroad running, and none of us can figure it out, maybe you can." Cora again refuses the role Royal imagines for her: "She told him she didn't know why it was there, or what it meant. All she knew is that she didn't want to run anymore" (272). Cora's mastery of the Railroad would require her to keep using its tracks, to keep up the movement of forced escape that has been the engine of the novel's plot, and she would rather find a world in which tunnels aren't necessary, a life rooted upon solid ground instead of a life that might at any moment require a descent into the darkness and an unpredictable, contingent movement, anywhere and everywhere. We might say that Whitehead's literalization of the figure of the Underground Railroad allows him to dramatize this tension between ground and underground, stasis and movement, rootedness and fugitivity.

In the novel's climactic scenes, white terrorists attack the Indiana farm, and Cora is again captured by Ridgeway, who forces her to bring him to the ghost tunnel. To him, the unearthing of the Underground Railroad, its exposure as more than a metaphor, would be the greatest possible victory, like tapping into a vein of buried ore: "'Most people think it's a figure of speech,' he said. 'The underground. I always knew better. The secret beneath us, the entire time. We'll uncover them after tonight. Every line, every one.' . . . For the slave catcher the tunnel was all the gold in the world" (307). But Cora escapes, grappling with Ridgeway as she pulls him down the stone stairs that lead into the station. As he lays dying, she boards the spartan handcar that will lead her through a tunnel as yet only partially cleared, "into the tunnel that no one had made, that led nowhere" (309). As the car moves forward, powered by the pumping of her arms, Cora becomes a builder of the railroad, a digger of the tunnel, occupying the position that Royal had imagined for her, the directionless passenger who is also somehow developing an intimate knowledge of the darkness that undergirds this novel's world. Cora wonders about the nature of her movement through the railroad's tunnel as she continues to bore toward the "miraculous terminus" it has promised:

> Was she traveling through the tunnel or digging it? . . . Who are you after you finish something this magnificent—in constructing it you have also journeyed through it, to the other side. On one end there was who you were before you went underground, and on the other end a new person steps into the light. The up-top world must be so ordinary compared to the miracle beneath, the miracle you made with your sweat and blood. The secret triumph you keep in your heart. (309–10)

The miracle you made: the novel. Its underground is no longer a dark and invisible rooting place, but a network, a structure, or perhaps a garden plot, built by precisely those invisible fictional people who exceed the novel's narrative frame. Cora brings the labor of the underground to the center of the novel—not only its power to end the world but its power to form it.

But the conclusion of the novel is haunted by its penultimate chapter, which finally narrates the brief escape of Cora's mother, Mabel, from the Georgia plantation where the novel had begun. We discover that Mabel made it as far as the swampland adjoining the plantation, following a method similar to Caesar's: "There were islands in the swamp—follow them to the continent of freedom" (299). And in a sense, she does reach that destination, stopping on one of those swampy islands to live for a moment in liberty.[45] As she lays on her back, listening to the sounds of wildlife and watching the stars roll past, there are "no patrollers, no bosses, no cries of anguish to induct her into another's despair. No cabin walls shuttling her through the night seas like the hold of a slave ship. . . . On the bed of damp earth, her breathing slowed and that which separated herself from the swamp disappeared. She was free" (300).

This is, like the dark tunnels of the Underground Railroad, a limbo ground, barely past the edges of Mabel's prison, somewhere between, a ground not quite solid but not quite unsolid.

After only a "moment" of freedom, she feels herself pulled back to the plantation, realizing that she cannot abandon her daughter, that she must instead return and relate to Cora her experience of foreclosed emancipation: "the girl would understand there was something beyond the plantation, past all that she knew," that one might strike out into the darkness beyond and beneath the plantation, beyond and beneath being as it is framed by enslavement—and perhaps also by the hard limits of realist fiction—and emerge on the other side.

But then Mabel, like Hardy's Mrs. Yeobright before her, has her moment of illumination canceled out by a deadly snakebite. She tries to continue moving, disbelieving her impending death, but finally "she stumbled onto a bed of soft moss and it felt right. She said, Here, and the swamp swallowed her up" (301). The novel ends with Cora emerging from the Underground Railroad, embarking on yet another leg of her journey, and we remain unsure whether she will ever arrive at a solid ground on which to flourish. But we are meant, I think, to be optimistic about her chances after we have followed her through so many harrowing escapes. Her mother, on the other hand, is freed only by death, swallowed by a ground that will not heave her back up again into the light. Whitehead's novel makes the underground into a setting, and sometimes into a utopian possibility of movement beyond enslavement, but he is keen on reminding us of this other possibility, this descent without re-emergence, a woman looking for freedom and finding it for only a brief suspended instant before sinking into the gulping ground, to find no tunnel beneath.

THREE

The Ground Gained

It's a perilous job, "renewing acquaintance" with an old novel, perhaps especially perilous if you yourself wrote it: as you open the volume and begin rereading, you might say that "experience" ventures forth into that "admirable immensity" of a fictional world, beset by "fear... of losing its way." But thankfully you yourself, the reader, linger behind in your own world, experience your emissary. Experience is watchful for pitfalls and a master of the terrain; it even brings along its "explorer's note-book," that "endlessly receptive" log of "aspects and distances, . . . steps taken and obstacles mastered and fruits gathered and beauties enjoyed," and so manages not to lose its way, keeping clearly in view the limits that bound and organize this immense place.[1]

You remember when you first made this place, although *made* feels like the wrong word somehow. The surface upon, within, around which it took shape was there already, a raw material; you might think of that past self (the writer, not the reader, not the reviser) less as a godlike creator of a world *ex nihilo* than as "a young embroiderer of the canvas of life," passing the needle of your prose from one side of the fabric to the other and back again, "in terror, fairly, of the vast expanse of that surface" upon which you draw your "many-coloured flowers and figures" in thread, overwhelmed by "the boundless number of . . . distinct perforations for the needle," into any one of which you might plunge the needle next. Oh, the "immense counting of holes," the "careful selection among them"; it is, you have come to realize, "the very nature of the holes so to invite, to solicit, to persuade, to practice positively a thousand lures and deceits" (*AN* 5–6).

This is the allegory of rereading that opens Henry James's preface to the New York Edition of *Roderick Hudson*, and the first of the prefaces as later collected in *The Art of the Novel*. But "allegory" in the singular misleads. Jamesian allegory is always plural and fractured rather than cohesive and consistent. Already in these first pages we have the rapid movement from one organizing metaphor to the next: first, the novel as a mappable but hazardous terrain, once so familiar to the writer who shaped it and now somewhat strange to the reader who returns to it; but then second, the novel as an embroidered canvas, with the rereader remembering the difficulty of forming figures out of mere thread, his fear of piercing in the wrong place. In James's writing, metaphors, those little miracles of comparison, often pile up in this way, so that they themselves become second-order vehicles and tenors, metaphors compared to metaphors, and the ground that subtends them, the original object of puzzlement that metaphor is supposed to illuminate, receding further and further into the depths.

Taking these two initial metaphors together, we see James seeking in their juxtaposition an illustration of the novel's ontological guarantee, which is also the dimension of the novel that remains alien and unknowable to writer and reader alike, approachable only through the work of figuration. The novel's "vast expanse," the novel's illimitable and infinitely perforated canvas:

both seem not really to belong to the novel, as my possessives would suggest, but rather to preexist the novel, constituting what James describes vaguely as "the continuity of things" that he approaches as he begins his work of imagining a fiction. This continuity "is never, by the space of an instant or an inch, broken," so that James's "perpetual predicament" is that "to do anything at all, he has at once intensely to consult and intensely to ignore it" (*AN* 5). Perhaps metaphor is a way of resolving the predicament by doing both at once, intensely consulting the thing one wishes to illuminate while at the same time intensely ignoring it, indeed replacing it, swapping a forbiddingly unbroken continuity for images of work-grounds more receptive or at least more human: the surveyable landscape full of masterable obstacles; the canvas riddled everywhere with soliciting holes. The mood of trepidation that runs through these metaphors is further evidence that James imagines the ontological ground of the novel as a given, an *a priori* foundation for the work of novel-making, rather than as an object of his creation. This is the fear of marring things already sufficient to themselves; it is the fear of miscounting one's steps and straying into forbidden zones; it is the fear of penetrating wrongly.

We can find the grounds of the novel, I argue, those grounds that seem to be there before the novelist ever arrives upon the scene, hovering in the shaded background or the shimmering underneath of James's metaphors of terrain, horizon, earth, sky, canvas, surface, continuity: ground the vehicle, ground the tenor, ground the ground that allows their comparison, ground the actual ground upon which I, James's reader and critic, sit now, writing.[2]

It's ground all the way down.

I have been making a claim at best implicit in the preceding chapters about the capacities of the reader, and perhaps especially of the critic, for movement in and upon the novel's ground. In the present chapter, I wonder whether the ground upon which my reading stands, or upon which James's reflexive rereading rests, is the same as the ground upon which Hardy's Fanny Robin walks. Or if I and James and Fanny take the same ground as our ontological foundation when we live inside a fiction, as I think we do, then what is the nature of our sharing? If the ontological grounds of the novel are often an aching mystery to the fictional characters they support, they need not be a mystery to the critic's or the novelist's eye. We still, of course, struggle to see these grounds directly; such is the nature of ontology, which deals in the kind of knowledge that is bigger or deeper than the human. But we can reason them out. We can construct a picture, through close reading, of the blank basis of the novel.

It's not only that the critic makes their way within a fictional world in imagination, as any reader does. Rather, it's that the critic rereads and retreads the ground, cultivating their wish, perhaps, to wander slightly off course as only the rereader can, to investigate the curiosities, markings, and patterns that emerge only when the really salient details have become familiar enough to allow us to ignore them. The ground itself is one such curiosity. What James is afraid of as a critic of his own work—that he might find he has done wrong to the pristine ground he was given, that he might no longer know the terrain—we as critics must approach in a different mood, following his metaphors to their vanishing points. As I've already suggested, James's figurations of the ontological ground of fiction might obfuscate more than they elucidate. They float away from the ground, they make what is immaterial material, and finally they prompt us critics and theorists of the novel to get to the root of things, without fear that the immensity, the continuity, the boundlessness of the novel's ground will cast us adrift.

What is at stake in this chapter is the idea of "standpoint," which we've already encountered in Moten's idea of blackness as representing the possibility of an ontology "without standpoint," and perhaps in Austen's image of "the spot." As we'll see, the idea of standpoint is central to James's way of imagining the relationship between novelist, reader, and fictional world. How does metaphor offer us places to stand in an unreal world? I say that this argument, about the critic's (i.e., my own) standpoint in the novel, has so far been implicit in the argument of this book because my focus has been on how the ontological conditions of groundedness are made by novelists to cohere as if self-sufficiently, the foundation of an alien ontology made up somehow of figural language, not necessarily sustained in its being by any link to the ontology of the actual world. Instead of a mere copy of my own ontology that I test for trueness, the world of the novel is a world that I enter without already knowing what might ground it, or what might come to unground it—a world, in short, in which grounds are never as guaranteed as I feel them to be in my world, and in which part of the work of interpretation is the sounding of depths to find what supports and makes possible the world I've entered.

I've also focused my attention frequently on how it feels to be a character in a fictional world, especially for those characters who stand apart for their all too acute awareness of the strange ground upon which they stand and the ways in which that ground, or the underground beneath it, conditions their freedom of movement and their claim to existence. The smoothness of groundwork that can make movement seem a fantasy, the pulsating tug of the underground and its broken promise of access to ontological insight: these work upon and around characters but also, I remain aware, upon me. And the gambit of a work of literary criticism is that I desire these subtle feats of figuration to begin to work more actively upon you, *my* reader, and for you to see how the ontological terraforming of the novel is the precondition for our tentative entry into its carefully configured world.

I want the rhyme between "figuration" and "configuration" to resonate here. In the first place, that means taking the etymology of "configuration" literally, as a "figuring together" that occurs in the relation between the author's figuration of the grounds of the novel (which, just like the ontological grounds of our actual world, can never be seen directly but only speculated upon) and the more trivial and less textured philosophical figure of ontological grounds that such novelistic figuration echoes. In the second place, it means understanding the figuration of the grounds of the novel, for example in metaphors of groundwork or underground, as a practice of arrangement and shaping that demands a flexibility of ontological imagination. We need to be attuned to the moments in fiction when *description* of fictional landscape, earth, tomb, dirt, work-ground, shifts registers and becomes metaphor, becomes an object of philosophical speculation about the forms and edges of being rather than simply a catalog of descriptive detail.

When I talk about the reader's or the critic's entrance into an alien ontology, configured in unexpected ways, or a defamiliarization of the ground as it becomes a figure for something else, I call upon Eve Kosofsky Sedgwick's somewhat throwaway description in *Epistemology of the Closet* of "the inexplicit compact by which novel-readers voluntarily plunge into worlds that strip them, however temporarily, of the painfully acquired cognitive maps of their ordinary lives (awfulness of going to a party without knowing anyone) on condition of an invisibility that promises cognitive exemption and eventual privilege." This plunge into "a space of high anxiety and dependence," Sedgwick goes on to argue, leads the reader into an "overidentification with the novel's organizing eye," and an "almost vindictively eager" willingness to accept the "modes of categorization" offered to them by the novel's narrator. Sedgwick is concerned about the insidious effects of such an overidentification, which might dampen our critical acuity and autonomy. The "worldly" and "urbane" narrator exerts power over the passive reader who only trusts and follows.³ In her metaphor there is an echo of James's anxiety about reentering the world of *Roderick Hudson*; we can think of him as arriving perhaps at a party taking place in a house that used to belong to him, but which seems different now after all these years, everything the same but the decor now feeling dated and the logic behind the arrangement of furniture no longer clear.

The reader might, however, have something more to offer, even in Sedgwick's scenario of the odd party guest, the belated attendee, the one who hasn't mapped the terrain and who scarcely knows where to begin. The ontological ground of the novel, I've been arguing, might first be discovered by the novelist (who often assigns to the narrator the labor of finding or marking its limits and communicating them to the reader), but it might also be somehow finished, or at least productively modified, in the act of close reading, or in James's act of delayed rereading, as the reader or critic explains (to themselves or to others) the conditions of existence that hold in this configured fictional world. Later in the preface to *Roderick Hudson*, when James compares himself to the painter looking upon an old forgotten artwork, seeing it anew, and says of such reseeing that "it helps him to live back into a forgotten state, . . . it breathes upon the dead reasons of things, buried as they are in the texture of the work, and makes them revive," he is, I argue, wondering how exactly we might "live back into" the "continuity of things," the metaphysical abstraction that for him constitutes the ground of the novel. There's a worry here too: not all works of art stand up to such scrutiny, or to the work of "the painter making use again and again of the tentative wet sponge" with the aim of exposing "the sunk surface," "the buried secrets" that James knows are there to be found. An anxious conditional hovers over the whole enterprise, with James admitting that what he says of reading, rereading, and revising holds true only "if the case will wonderfully take any such pressure, if the work doesn't break down under even such mild overhauling." It might turn out in the end that those sunk surfaces and buried secrets "are buried too deep to rise again, and were, indeed, it would appear, not much worth the burying" (*AN* 11). Secrets and surfaces are only worth burying if we can still find them later, if they don't range too far beyond our keen readerly perception, if they remain in the barely underneath position that we have seen associated, for example, with Hardy's metaphor of the painterly groundwork.

It seems, indeed, that in my own idiosyncratic way of reading I have happened upon the grounds of the novel that are buried only so deeply, in shallow enough graves that a little brushing away of accumulated dirt will reopen them. I have shown them to you, have shown novelists showing them to you. They are right there, after all, for us to see, if we know how to look behind metaphor, to track James's journey in reverse to its starting point, and if we are willing to press at the limits of what we take "existence" to signify when it comes to fiction. Close reading is the name we give, I think, to the practice by which I might convince you that such things are there to be seen—*if* the novel can "take any such pressure," if it doesn't "break down" under my "mild overhauling"—and by which James tells us the story of what he has had to contend with in ontologizing fictional worlds.

Some difficulties crop up, however, as soon as we take this argument about James's prefaces seriously. James is often concerned with the story of what Kevin Ohi calls "inception," a concept that we have already encountered in the introduction, the beginning or origin or founding of a literary text that helps us to apprehend "the text's own conditions of possibility," its "self-reflexivity," and especially its "self-grounding quality." Ohi's reading is deconstructive in its sensibility: he is interested in the ways that a fiction might come into being through the "linguistic act" of "positing," which "invokes a text's power to found itself and to reach its outside," or the "fiat" by which "texts as if call themselves into being." I might say that I spatialize what Ohi temporalizes in James, or that my reading is nondeconstructive, Wittgensteinian, investing more faith in the possibility of an ultimate ontological ground or at least feeling satisfied when my spade is turned; but it's not as easy as that to tease apart these strands of metaphysical thinking in James's prefaces. Ohi and I share an interest in how James conceives of the fraught claim to "self-grounding" that literary texts enact. Ohi's reading of inception helps us, for example, to understand James's obsessive concern in the prefaces with "retrospective reconstructions," with "belatedness" and the persistent feeling that "consciousness arrives too late to perceive the emergence of its own ideas," with revision, and with the realization or nonrealization of potentiality. In this version of the story, the urge toward the smooth, open continuity of things that held before the novel's beginning rhymes, I think, with the Freudian death drive. It is a fantasy about a state of preexistence and what it might look like to recover, even if only in memory, its state of pure potentiality, except that as Freud teaches us, such a fantasy of return can only play out in actuality, in our time-bound world, as a drive forward toward death, a state of postexistence that only mirrors preexistence, in which all is hindsight and no potentiality remains. For Ohi, such a drive toward inception makes visible the problem of "the formal contingency of the work," the "arbitrary" and "provisional" quality of such a self-positing form: if the work of art simply grounds itself, arising as if on its own volition, why does it arise this way and not that way?[4]

I am indebted to my feeling of having been in dialogue with Ohi's reading as I composed this chapter, but diverge from his line of thinking in that I don't understand James to argue that the world of a novel is self-grounding or self-positing. Perhaps more mysteriously, I argue that James takes the ground of the novel as an ontological problem rather than a speech-act problem. It is something that itself preexists him and his writing, an object of discovery and working-over rather than an object of creation.

I've claimed, for example, that in James's preface to *Roderick Hudson* the image of the "continuity of things," and the related image of the immense embroidery canvas waiting to be pierced, pierceable anywhere and everywhere, are metaphors for the novel's ontological ground rather than metaphors for the novel's inception. Inception is what happens when the needle finds its perhaps arbitrary or contingent starting point; it's the deciding where; it's James's metaphors of "the seed sprouted," "the precious particle," and the "fruitful essence"; it's "his germ, his vital particle, his grain of gold," "the growth of the 'great oak' from the little acorn" (*AN* 99, 119, 140). And James does fret in his prefaces over these seeds of inception, wondering often where they come from, how they find their way into his brain. The ground of the novel is not this mysterious act of beginning but rather the canvas itself, the soil where seeds get planted and under whose shelter they germinate, a waiting and yet indifferent emptiness. In my reading of the prefaces, I am less interested, then, in James's story about memory, the creative process, and origin, the "idea" that needs "working out" and so is "dropped . . . into the deep well of unconscious cerebration: not without the hope, doubtless, that it might eventually emerge from that reservoir, as one had already known the buried treasure to come to light, with a firm iridescent surface and a notable increase of weight" (*AN* 22–23).[5] I am more interested in disentangling the creative seed of the novel (the "germination" that is for James "a process almost always untraceable") from the ontological ground of the novel to which James feels he *can* find his way, the better to understand how James envisions the dimension of the novel's reality that seems to precede his own involvement (*AN* 24).

In chapter 1, we saw how the groundwork of the novel sometimes shows through its finish in Hardy's fiction. In James's prefaces, the question is how the novelist discovers and approaches this alien ground, this division of above and below, in the first place. What are the conditions that allow for the novelist's crossing over from actuality to fiction, and what does he find already awaiting him when he finally makes his way into that other dimension? It might be that such a leaving-behind of actuality is a *petite mort*, a temporary ascent to a paradise in which an "intenser experience" becomes available, not as a danger to the coherence of the self but as a "sublime security like that enjoyed on the flowery plains of heaven" (*AN* 32). This metaphor comes from James's preface to *The American*, in which the concern is not precisely with the line between reality and fiction but with the related tension in the novelist's art between reality and romance. For James, reality is "the things we cannot possibly *not* know, sooner or later, in one way or another." If we haven't *yet* experienced any of these things it's only "one of the accidents of our hampered state ... that particular instances have not yet come our way," whereas "the romantic stands ... for the things that, with all the facilities in the world, we never *can* directly know; the things that can reach us only through the beautiful circuit and subterfuge of our thought and desire" (*AN* 31–32). The image of reality presented here is difficult and maybe even paradoxical: reality is "things," all the things that vastly exceed my limited view but which are nevertheless clearly limited in number. As I've written elsewhere, James is fascinated throughout his career by the pronoun "everything," and often takes it as an outlet for "the beautiful circuit" of erotic desire.[6] And the endless reach of everything almost always stands in James's work in tension with its various alternatives, some of which we saw were important to Hardy too: something, nothing, anything. I haven't yet encountered all of the fundamental things of reality (only some of them) but I certainly will. It's in the nature of reality to run out. It's in the nature of the romantic, however, to look beyond the knowable, thinkable edges of reality to an intenser experience elsewhere, as the curious and terrified children of Schreiner's fiction peer into the terrifying void, imagining giants' graves underground, and we peer along with them. The romantic, ecstatic knowledge they all seek is knowledge of the underpinning of reality, the metaphysical ground that holds in place this array of things, making them possible.

James makes clear that when he speaks of "the romantic" in fiction, he doesn't speak merely of the exotic. Reality and romance are two aspects of novel-making rather than two distinct genres. Great novelists such as Scott, Balzac, and Zola, he claims, are great in part because of the way they alternate between "the warm wave of the near and familiar and the tonic shock, as may be, of the far and strange," but "I suggest not," he clarifies, "that the strange and the far are at all necessarily romantic: they happen to be simply the unknown," those things *over there* that I haven't known yet, but will, still very much part of reality (*AN* 31). No, James argues, while the romantic does always concern itself with the far and the strange, the far and strange is not always the romantic. I'm arguing that James has a philosophical kind of farness and strangeness in mind here when he talks of the romantic attunement to the things beyond the limits of knowledge itself. The function of the romantic energy that runs through realism is to free us from our exclusive attachment to reality: romance gives us "experience liberated, so to speak; experience disengaged, disembroiled, disencumbered, exempt from the conditions that we usually know to attach to it and . . . drag upon it" (*AN* 31, 33). The ascent to a higher plane of intenser experience made available to us in fiction is the characteristic upward and outward movement of romance, an antigravitational force always in tension with the gravity of the real, which pulls us to the known or at least knowable contours of our actual ontological grounds.

James helps us to see that if we imagine a fictional ontology as entirely separate from an actual ontology, that doesn't necessarily mean that "things" in these two spheres will appear so different. Realist novels do look an awful lot like reality. Whatever detachment from the real is achieved by the novelist works at the level of the metaphysical conditions and criteria that guarantee being. Shifting to a new metaphor, James describes how the novelist can remain safely tethered to a reality made more and more distant, or alternatively how the novelist might sometimes choose the more dangerous course of action, to detach from the real entirely and float free:

> The balloon of experience is in fact tied to the earth, and under that necessity we swing, thanks to a rope of remarkable length, in the more or less commodious car of the imagination; but it is by the rope we know where we are, and from the moment that cable is cut we are at large and unrelated: we only swing apart from the globe—though remaining as exhilarated, naturally, as we like, especially when all goes well. The art of the romancer is, "for the fun of it," insidiously to cut the cable, to cut it without our detecting him. (*AN* 33–34)

The rope that ties imagination to earth serves also as a point of orientation, or what we'll see described later on as "standpoint": "it is by the rope we know where we are," no matter how remarkably long the rope is, and no matter how distant the ground of reality becomes as we move further into the outer space of fiction. The cord-cutting romancer is an extreme possibility on the novelistic continuum James imagines here, the artist who ceases to recognize the "necessity" of reality as the collateral of the fictional gambit and opts instead to become "unrelated," "exhilarated"—at least as long as their gambit succeeds, "when all goes well," one can only assume by satisfying a set of criteria that James doesn't quite enumerate.

I've inserted a metaphor of my own into the previous paragraph, that of the romancer's journey into the realm of fiction as a journey to outer space. In the preface to *The American*, however, James doesn't go there. The cord cut, the balloon rising freely, his analogy reaches its ambiguous conclusion. The scene seems like it could go on, but how? It might itself be reimagined as the first scene of a longer fiction: just think, for example, of the drama of a rogue balloon that begins Ian McEwan's *Enduring Love* (1997), a novel that presses at the boundary between realism and romance that so interests James. "What idiocy," the narrator of that novel says as he runs toward a hot air balloon that has become unmoored with passengers still aboard, "to be racing into this story and its labyrinths," conflating the action of the novel with the hazards of fictionality itself, a reckless and too hurried break from the stability of the actual world. "We were running toward a catastrophe," he says, "a kind of furnace in whose heat identities and fates would buckle into new shapes."[7] McEwan's lethally high-flying balloon perhaps gives us the opposite of James's "when all goes well," romance running too hot and threatening to warp the very fabric of being.

But James doesn't tell us where his romancer's balloon goes after it's cut insidiously loose. When I imagine that it goes to the outer space of the fictional, I'm doing what all the novelists I analyze do: looking to metaphor to make vivid what is actually unknowable in other terms. James himself doesn't stick with one metaphor long enough to make it cohere into a story about the grounds of the novel. Instead, he knits different metaphors together, and I argue that even if we can't assemble a story out of the series of shifting metaphors that we find as we move from preface to preface, I can nevertheless assemble a reading. As I've implied already, James's distinction between reality and romance does not map perfectly onto the distinction between reality and fiction; fiction always floats away from the ground of the real, but it can do so while keeping reality in view, even remaining tethered to it for a kind of basic orientation, or it can do so with the more radical and insidious "fun" of the romancer who liberates experience fully from the conditions of groundedness in the actual that usually "drag" upon us.

Turning now to the preface to *The Portrait of a Lady*, we can see James narrating there how the ground of fiction's alien ontology comes into view; but the question remains, was it always there, somehow hidden, or is it an artifact of hindsight, a metaphor that we invent as readers in order to find our footing, or, as Ohi might put it, to locate (if only arbitrarily) the novel's inception? We've already seen that for the romancer to break into unreality might mean finally emerging from below onto the plains of paradise. Instead of sailing off into the vacuum of outer space, onward and upward forever, the artist who is at the center of James's narrative eventually gains ground and finds a new standpoint. This preface is one of James's most famous and often cited, but our attention has almost always been focused on its "house of fiction" metaphor rather than on the ground upon which the house is built.[8] One of the central problems of the preface is that of how the character of Isabel Archer first emerged into James's consciousness strangely ungrounded—the novel began not with "plot," James says, nor with "a set of relations," nor with "any one of those situations that, by a logic of their own, immediately fall, for the fabulist, into movement, into a march or rush, a patter of quick steps." Rather, as he traces the novel back to "the germ of my idea," he finds "the sense of a single character, . . . to which all the usual elements of a 'subject,' certainly of a setting, were needed to be super-added" (*AN* 42). James is puzzled by this backward story in which Isabel in her first appearance echoes the image of the loose balloon that organizes the previous preface. She is "at large" and unrelated (that phrase, "at large," reappears here), and all the more exhilarated and exhilarating for her characteristic romantic freedom; but there's a deeper ontological question here about how to account for her groundless existence (*AN* 47). Where is she situated? What is the logic, the set of relations, that would place her somewhere, allow her to move as if pattering her feet upon a solid floor? To James's mind, these grounding conditions seem always to have come first, even before his work begins—the fascination of Isabel is that she seems so fundamentally without foundation.

It's as if, James goes on, he feels compelled to recover in memory the ground that only seemed not to be there in the first place. It *seems* to James as if Isabel came into being out of nowhere, sui generis, much as he later describes the emergence of his first idea of Hyacinth Robinson, the protagonist of *The Princess Casamassima*, as he explored the "thick jungle" of the city: "he sprang up for me," James says, "out of the London pavement" (*AN* 60). Although a character is often the initial "germ" of a James novel, that fictional person must, it seems, emerge in relation to a support: a garden to grow in, a pavement on which to stand, a canvas on which to be embroidered. James's acolyte Percy Lubbock claimed that "the work of imagination" was for James "the highest and most honourable calling conceivable, being indeed nothing less than the actual creation of life out of the void," and he's right insofar as James sees fictional existence as in its own peculiar way "actual." But he's wrong, I think, to say that James envisions the actual existence of a fiction as arising out of "the void," a concept that we don't find in James's theory of the novel. We might even say that James obsessively avoids the void. Instead, we find plentiful images of grounds and supports for the world of the novel. Yes, this ground is as mysterious as any void: the novelist reckons, as we've seen, with its forbidding blankness and immensity. James is careful, however, to imagine the ground of the novel as strikingly solid, and even to imagine the novelist's work as bound to the ground by a force akin to gravitational pull. Lubbock was perhaps closer to the mark when in an earlier essay on the New York Edition he described "the scene form" as "the ground-work of the novel as Mr. James has finally elaborated it" in his prefaces, or when he recounted his discovery of James's notes for a novel never completed and described them as "the rough notes in which he casts about to clear the ground."[9]

Even in his conversation, it seems, James was fond of using ground metaphors to illustrate he laid the foundations of his novels: in her memoir of her time working as James's amanuensis, Theodora Bosanquet reports that in the early stages of conceptualizing a novel, "he 'broke ground,' as he said, by talking to himself day by day about the characters and construction."[10] In the case of Isabel Archer, he tries to account for the deeper "motive" of *The Portrait of a Lady* or what he calls, with some palpable ambivalence about the problem, "this projection of memory upon the whole matter of the growth, in one's imagination, of some such apology for a motive" (*AN* 42). James is uncertain whether what grounds Isabel is in fact a "motive" or only an excuse for one, grown under the light of memory and its peculiar desire to make sense of things, even if that means assuming a ground for Isabel that may or may not have existed. "These are the fascinations of the fabulist's art," he continues, these lurking forces of expansion, these necessities of upspringing in the seed, these beautiful determinations, on the part of the idea entertained, to grow as tall as possible, to push into the light and the air and thickly flower there; and, quite as much, these fine possibilities of recovering, from some good standpoint on the ground gained, the intimate history of the business—of retracing and reconstructing its steps and stages. (AN 42)

If Isabel is the seed of *The Portrait of a Lady*, then what makes the novel finally sprout and grow and "thickly flower"? As I suggested earlier, one way to read this passage would prioritize narrative, time, and chronology: James is "retracing and reconstructing" here how the novel developed in "steps and stages," with the image of Isabel as its mysterious initial leap into existence.

But another way to read the passage is ontologically. James contextualizes the metaphor of the protagonist, his "vivid individual," as novelistic seed, by figuring a ground for its growth that isn't created by James himself but is simply there to be "gained," not only a place for Isabel to stand but also a prerequisite for the novelist's own "standpoint" in relation to her and her world. Whether or not he was aware of it at the time, he thinks that there *must* have been some ground to support his fiction. A person, even a fictional one, can't be self-sufficient in ontological terms. James is puzzled, as he puts it, by the question of how Isabel came to be vivid to him "in spite of being still at large, not confined by the conditions, not engaged in the tangle, to which we look for much of the impress that constitutes an identity. If the apparition was still all to be placed how came it to be vivid?—since we puzzle such quantities out, mostly, just by the business of placing them" (AN 47). Isabel's grounding in a context or a set of "conditions" or a "tangle" that not only supports her ontologically but also serves to "impress" her into existence, is (again) perhaps only constructed after the fact, in memory or in rereading. It is a ground "gained" in both senses of that verb: a destination arrived at as the novel's idea passes from darkness into light, from beneath to above a sacred horizon; and also an object finally secured, which seems as if it only comes into being and into the novelist's possession as the seed erupts through its surface.

The question of infinite regress, however, continues to rankle: where does this seed, and the ground it grows in, come from? One might always ask another question, seeking for some more fundamental ground, perhaps finally arriving, like Lubbock, at "the void." Once we reach what we take to be the ultimate foundation, what then? Whereas in those early prefaces James goes to the image of the blank canvas or the smooth "continuity of things" to figure the groundwork that seems to him to preexist the novel, providing the preconditions for its existence, the problem for James in the preface to *The Portrait of a Lady* is slightly different. Many novels, he reflects, seem to begin not with the empty groundwork that awaits the novelist's touch but rather with the single character who needs to be given a ground upon which to stand, and upon which the novelist might stand beside her. James quotes Ivan Turgenev, who described to him how characters "hovered before him, soliciting him": "As for the origin of one's wind-blown germs themselves," Turgenev goes on in James's recounting of their conversation, "who shall say . . . where *they* come from? We have to go too far back, too far behind, to say. Isn't it all we can say that they come from every quarter of heaven, that they are *there* at almost every turn of the road?" (*AN* 43). Perhaps it's best, James thinks along with Turgenev, to stop retracing and reconstructing at some point. If *the* ultimate ground of the novel can't finally and securely be gained, we can at least include in our picture of the novel's metaphysical structure *a* ground, provisional as it may be. Speculation is the fundamental mode of metaphysical inquiry.

Gaining ground might be one metaphor, then, for what Ohi calls the novel's inception, but it is more broadly an ontological figure aimed at making vivid the novel's ground and the "standpoint" it affords. This standpoint is necessary for telling the story of inception; it is the secure position that allows for the "recovering" of that knowledge. What begins as an occult image—the seed that seems to grow of its own accord, propelled by "lurking forces of expansion" and "necessities of upspringing"—develops into an image of ordinary supportive relations and the everyday "business of placing." As James puts it elsewhere, "To 'put' things is very exactly and responsibly and interminably to do them" (*AN* 347). The seed grows from underground to aboveground, and in that sense this metaphor recalls Schreiner's interest in the novel's underground depths. But perhaps more importantly, the growth of the germinating plant and its springing into the open air allows us to find the horizon that separates these two realms, below and above, in the first place. The parable of the novel's ground relies on that basic ontological question that Jonathan Schaffer phrases as "What grounds what?" And such questions are always asked and answered belatedly, from within the situation of an already established universe whose edges we are trying to discover, as James captures in his description of this novel's flowering. Only after the fact, in the act of rereading, recovering, reconstructing, tracking the novel's growth from seed to maturity, do we see clearly that horizon. The ground finally gained, James the rereader then finds a place to stand and look.

But already I've gone a bit too far. I wonder if it is really *James* who stands alongside Isabel on the ground gained in retrospect, or if it is instead one of the many emissaries James figures in the prefaces as going forth into fictional worlds on his behalf like holographic projections, or like the personification of experience with which we began? He describes in the preface to *The Golden Bowl*, for example, "my preference for dealing with my subject-matter, for 'seeing my story,' through the opportunity and sensibility of some more or less detached, some not strictly involved, though thoroughly interested and intelligent, witness or reporter," or, in other words, "not as my own impersonal account of the affair in hand, but as my account of somebody's impression of it" (*AN* 327). Some witness, some report, somebody: an indefinite person, a fungible body, stands in for the definite James, by necessity of course. He himself can't breach the boundary between the actual and the fictional despite being a creator of fictions. Like Sedgwick's disoriented party guest, he must rely upon his host to make him at home, and is himself afforded the "invisibility" afforded to any reader. He might offer "an impersonal account" of the goings on in that other world, but prefers to refract that account through the perspective of somebody on the ground. If this somebody is "more or less detached," "not strictly involved," he is nevertheless able by virtue of his nearness, his footing on the ground of the novel, to become "interested," intelligently alert, impressionable. I want to emphasize that the "somebody" who figures here as James's narrator is the same kind of hopelessly indefinite entity who earlier figured as James's rereading self, the personification of experience who enters the old novel.

But as James continues to develop this running theme of the novelist's surrogates, those who are able to enter the fictional world from which he as an actual person is barred, it begins to seem that he is getting things backward when it comes to who is concrete and who is abstract, who is embodied and who is spectral. "This somebody," he goes on, "is often ... but an unnamed, unintroduced and (save by right of intrinsic wit) unwarranted participant, the impersonal author's concrete deputy or delegate, a convenient substitute for the creative power otherwise so veiled and disembodied" (*AN* 327). How could a somebody, who may as well be nobody, thoroughly negated as they are, unnamed, unintroduced, and unwarranted, be figured as the concrete being in this extended metaphor, a substitute for the very real Henry James who sees himself as disembodied, "impersonal" now in a more profound sense? We're thrown back to the question we encountered in Quine's theory of metaphysics: Who has the "right" to exist in the world of the novel? Whose footsteps can find some traction on that ground? What does concreteness mean when it comes to unreality?

These are the questions that preoccupy James in the preface to *The Golden Bowl*, which functions not only as an introduction to that novel in particular but also as a conclusion to *The Art of the Novel* in general. Somewhat like Hardy, who imagines how a character moves step by step (or indeed fails to move, fails ever to arrive) across the ground of the novel, one of James's key figures in this final preface is that of the footstep. To find a standpoint on the ground gained, to move with decisiveness in the novel: such things are not available to James himself. It's as if, in order to imagine the novel's world as real, to find its ontological ground, he must sacrifice (at least temporarily) his conviction of his own actuality. He must be willing to disembody himself, to substitute for his actual self a somebody who can be recognized as concretely existing on the terms of the novel's fictionality. Such a substitution is the only way to become, as he puts it, truly "responsible" for the work of art.[11] It's best, James thinks, to swap himself out and thereby avoid "the mere muffled majesty of irresponsible 'authorship,'" but this involves a difficult and circuitous approach to his fictional delegate's standpoint:

> Beset constantly with the sense that the painter of the picture or the chanter of the ballad (whatever we may call him) can never

be responsible *enough,* and for every inch of his surface and note of his song, I track my uncontrollable footsteps, right and left, after the fact, while they take their quick turn, even on stealthiest tiptoe toward the point of view that, within the compass, will give the most instead of the least to answer for. (*AN* 328)

James identifies responsibility for the world of the novel, for every inch of its pristine ground, with a point of view (or perhaps we can now describe it as a standpoint of view), a secure position that James can only reach with clumsy desperation, his "uncontrollable footsteps" zigging and zagging across disorienting terrain. He wants intensely to be able to "answer for" this world, as much as he possibly can—he can never, as he says, be responsible enough for it—but can only do so through this stealthy, reckless movement, cutting himself loose for a moment from the actual, seeking out the delegate who can help him with the "business of placing" himself firmly on the novel's ground.

The distance and the difficulty of this journey lessen, James finds, as he reaches the later volumes of the New York Edition, those novels, "my final things" he calls them, composed and published in more recent years (*AN* 335). The ground he finds awaiting him there, the shaping work he has done upon it—they are fresher in memory. Returning to metaphors of the footstep, he writes that to reenter these newer novels is "to become aware ... that the march of my present attention coincides sufficiently with the march of my original expression; that my apprehension fits, more concretely stated, without an effort or struggle, certainly without bewilderment or anguish, into the innumerable places prepared for it" (*AN* 335). James the author has "prepared" the ground for James the reader, and the two Jameses are in this case close enough for that preparation to remain felicitous. It's a fantasy of attunement between reader and author, a comfortable meeting of minds on the terrain of the novel's ground, that I argue we might extrapolate into a more general theory of the relationship between reader, author, and fictional world. The novel simply works best when we find the ground successfully prepared for us, when the guides and surrogates and representatives we find there can remain intelligent and interested enough to function across centuries. But I for one am rankled by something in this image, a question that James drops but leaves unresolved: What could it possibly mean for a reader to fit his apprehension into "innumerable" places? And how could those places ever have been prepared for him, infinite as they are, like all those endless holes in the canvas waiting to be pierced?

It is, after all, a fantasy, and perhaps that explains this obtrusive word, "innumerable," which suggests a magic at work in the novelist's art, a capacity for unending responsibility and the forging of uncountable paths for the footsteps of the reader. From the single standpoint on the ground gained that seems to make our access to fiction possible, we arrive in James's conclusion at a more diffuse and branching image of a novel in which all paths are always at the ready, a novel in which, wherever I move, I find a place prepared for me. It's this kind of idea, I think, that Lukács has in mind when he elaborates at the opening of *The Theory of the Novel* his own fantasy of the age of the ancient Greek epic: "Happy are those ages when the starry sky is the map of all possible paths—ages whose paths are illuminated by the light of the stars. Everything in such ages is new and yet familiar, full of adventure and yet their own. The world is wide and yet it is like a home."[12] For Lukács, the novel and the modern age that invented it represent the broken remnant of this happy past, a world in which the soul's "home" is lost beyond recovery, and "philosophy, as a form of life or as that which determines the form and supplies the content of literary creation, is always a symptom of the rift between 'inside' and 'outside.'" But for James, the novel can yet promise the same kind of comfort, the feeling that in its world we walk on a ground "new and yet familiar" and inhabit a mode of being that is strange and yet somehow still our own.

As he enters these happier novels, the ones that still feel right, he feels that rift between inside and outside that Lukács laments beginning to fade away. His "intelligence, as a reader" becomes in relation to "the historian of the matter" (that is, the narrator, or the novelist's fictional delegate) "passive, receptive, often even grateful; unconscious, quite blissfully, of any bar to intercourse, any disparity of sense between us." Maybe, James reflects, there can be a way of inhabiting the novel's unfamiliar kind of existence that prioritizes passivity instead of responsibility, a pleasurable sinking into the ground that feels as if it has been made for me to alight upon it: "Into his very footprints the responsive, the imaginative steps of the docile reader that I consentingly become for him all comfortably sink; his vision, superimposed on my own as an image cut in paper is applied to a sharp shadow on a wall, matches, at every point, without excess or deficiency" (*AN* 335–36). This is on the one hand an erotic scenario of submissive roleplay, James consenting to become the docile and responsive reader "for him," the novel's creator, and it's the pleasing symmetry of the dominant-submissive scenario that at least momentarily allows for the blissful melting away of boundaries, bars, disparities, between the actual and the fictional. But this is also a more banal image of "comfort." It is the soft sinking of feet into well-worn tracks; it is the comfort of discovering the perfect fit; it is the satisfaction of finding that the shape of another's vision matches with absolute perfection the shape of my own.

Reading this section of the preface, J. Hillis Miller gets stopped short by a difficult question: "just how the line of footprints or the silhouette can be said to be an accurate report, account, or representation of the ground on which it is inscribed is puzzling, to say the least." How can we possibly be expected to reckon with the blankness at the heart of these images, "the wall itself" upon which the silhouette and the paper cut-out are placed, or the "vision of that undifferentiated field across which he walks"? How can we begin to understand the claim that "the story itself is a patterned or differentiated representation of the unpatterned and undifferentiated, the clear matter in the sense of a field without marks or discriminations"?[13] One of my aims is to try to sort through Miller's nonplussed reaction to this passage. His questions are, I think, answerable if we take the literary metaphor of the ontological ground as doing serious philosophical and formal work in the prefaces.

Hovering in the background of James's fantasy, however, is the persistent image of those times when all doesn't go so well in finding one's way across the snow-covered plain, or in fitting the paper cut-out quite so perfectly to the shadow on the wall. James still remembers the discomfort of living in those older novels, the ones that he feels less successful, from which he is alienated by the distance of decades and the evolution of his own talent. In those cases, he says, "It was . . . as if the clear matter still being there, even as a shining expanse of snow spread over a plain, my exploring tread, for application to it, had quite unlearned the old pace and found itself naturally falling into another, which might sometimes indeed more or less agree with the original tracks, but might most often, or very nearly, break through the surface in other places" (AN 336). I can't help but see the echo here of Hardy's image of a snow-bleached landscape, those "forms without features" that are all we have left when orienting details fade away, and the difficulty of finding our way or even moving on such a forbiddingly empty ground. It's as if in revisiting those novels James struggles to see the work he has done, his eye stripping things down to the blankness of the canvas underneath it all, looking for the "clear matter" that might offer the possibility of retracing his steps. But instead, we return to the "uncontrollable footsteps" that haunted James in the preface to *The Portrait of a Lady*, which try to find the innumerable places prepared for them but instead find themselves just missing the mark, stepping instead into those equally innumerable "other places."

In my own reading of the preface to *The Golden Bowl*, I find myself at this point frazzled and dismayed. I've been offered a beautiful fantasy of what it feels like to submit consentingly to the conditions of a novel's existence. To sink into a novel that way: yes, that is what I long for. But James offers me that fantasy only to snatch it away, reminding me that, for the most part, fiction is an ontological wilderness where I am more often at large and exhilarated, not always pleasurably. There's a final twist in store, however, that I think redeems what can seem this irredeemable tension between the comfort and the terror of novelistic ontology. (We must remember, too, Hardy's conviction, reading Hegel skeptically in the British Library, that we're mistaken to think that any ontology has our comfort in mind.) "No march," James writes, "I was soon enough aware, could possibly be more confident and free than this infinitely interesting and amusing *act* of re-appropriation" that comes with foraging across the snowy tundra of the uncomfortable novel, "shaking off all shackles of theory, unattended, as was speedily to appear, with humiliating uncertainties, and almost as enlivening, or at least as momentous, as, to a philosophic mind, a sudden large apprehension of the Absolute" (*AN* 336).

Forget sinking into well-worn steps. Forget passivity and submission. Forget comfort! In this liberatory conclusion, James identifies all of these with the "shackles of theory," with the reader plagued by "humiliating uncertainties," unable or unwilling to plant his feet and move. This is another version of Sedgwick's party guest, terrified by the removal of all his comforting cognitive maps as he plunges into a novel, but James suggests, as does Sedgwick, that maplessness is also a privilege. Without a map, I am (or can choose to be) "confident and free," the strange place in which I'm lost, and which I desire to reappropriate, to own for myself, suddenly "infinitely interesting and amusing." Heedless of whether I get my footing right or wrong, heedless of the imagined authority that has laid those paths and sharp footprints in the first place, I am at liberty to realize that the right places really *are* "innumerable."

A happy age indeed.

The aim of this chapter has been to show how reading, and especially the kind of reading we call "close," brings into view the novel's ontology. Literary criticism can in this sense "do" philosophy in its own language and with its own tools of analysis rather than only seeing its objects through the lens of philosophical theories of ontology that might take up fiction as a problem but are ill-equipped to see how particular fictions work. This claim runs underneath this entire book, as all performances of literary criticism make implicit arguments about the nature of close reading, about what close reading can or should do, about what kinds of questions it can answer and what kinds of secrets it can reveal. I've been using the techniques of close reading in my analysis of novels to show how authors use metaphor to lay bare the ontological basis of their fictional worlds, leaving the traces of the novel's groundwork, or underground, for us readers to discover. And so the difference in this chapter is perhaps only that here I have taken as my object an exemplary work of novel theory rather than a work of fiction. James's *The Art of the Novel* has significantly shaped the modern enterprise of theorizing the novel, and my own sensibilities and sensitivities as a critic of the novel. As so many critics before me have done, I've been trying to mine it for a particular vein of figuration chosen from among its many glistening channels. I've been wanting to show how James's reigning metaphor of "the ground gained" by the reader shapes my own understanding of what close reading means and does.

But if grounds are so important to James's conception of the novel's being, then wouldn't it stand to reason that his fiction must include, like Hardy's, Schreiner's, and Whitehead's, some ontological excursions, some reigning figure for the ground of fictional existence? Certainly James's fiction is full of images of characters finding themselves "placed" and "fixed" and even "pinned," and I often wonder to what surface or substance they are supposed to be fixed or pinned in these metaphors; I sometimes thought those metaphors would come to the center of this chapter. And in my own previous work on James, it might be that I was seeing the pronoun "everything" and its antecedent, what philosophers call the domain of "absolute generality," not only as an object of erotic desire for characters in James's fiction but also as an image of the "immense continuity of things" that grounds their universe in its being. For now, these ideas remain a glimmer around this chapter's edges, hopeful of another reader who will take them up.

James is the ideal case study for this chapter because his figuration of the ground of the novel is so interestingly specific to his theorization of his own labor as a writer, a reader, and especially a reviser. He can see the ontological grounds of the novel as fundamental only when he looks at a completed novel with a reader's eye, and so he offers us an example of how ontological grounds support not only the existence of a fiction but also the reader's entry (sometimes reentry) into that fiction. I have in mind here Kate Stanley's claim that in the prefaces James's goal is the establishing of "vital new connections" between past and present, author and reader: "The medium of connection between the novel's 'productive germ' and its realized form will also, ideally, serve as the medium of transmission between author and audience.... The gaps that seemed to divide the reader and writer are recast as the sites where they are most likely to meet."[14] I share Stanley's feeling that James believes in the ground of the novel. For him, it is a place where the actual and the unreal can meet.

I think also of Alicia Mireles Christoff's broader account, so resonant with Stanley's analysis of James and my own, of reading novels through the lens of object relations psychoanalysis. This theoretical vocabulary, Christoff argues, "resignifies presence and absence. It makes presence more complex and multiple, a dappled light, and it makes absence a condition of possibility rather than one of loss or absolute limitation. . . . What this means for novel reading," she reasons, "is that we can believe in the power of our relationships to literary figures of various kinds (characters, narrators, authors, and readers), allowing their own fictionality to be productive and enriching rather than somehow disqualifying."[15] Speaking ontologically rather than psychoanalytically (though the two fields of thought are not by any means mutually exclusive), novelistic grounds allow us a real standpoint even in an unreal existence. When we worm our way across the boundary between the actual and the fictional, sometimes in the best version of that process feeling the boundary momentarily dissolve, we also need to feel ourselves firmly supported in our newly redoubled existence. We also need to find a standpoint on the ground gained by such a reckless and painful crossing, in which we disembody ourselves, cutting loose the cord that moors us to the actual, to become differently concrete elsewhere.

FOUR

Meeting Grounds

How is it possible for Virginia Woolf to assert that "there is no 'I' in *Wuthering Heights*"? It's a remarkable claim to venture about a novel with more than one first-person narrator, but it's none of those "I"s Woolf has in mind; rather, it's the "I" of Emily Brontë herself, somehow left outside of her own creation. As opposed to her sister Charlotte, who fills *Jane Eyre* with the vehemence but also the narrowness of an impassioned "I," "The impulse which urged [Emily] to create was not her own suffering or her own injuries. She looked out upon a world cleft into gigantic disorder and felt within her the power to unite it in a book."[1] Emily Brontë recognizes the novel's capacity for ontological critique, Woolf argues. The novel can unite and order in fiction what is cleft and disordered in actuality, but only by creating a different kind of chasm: that which cleaves Brontë's world from the world of her novel, a chasm she does not cross. Or if she must cross it in order to write, as James suggested to us in the last chapter—if she must gain that other ground—Woolf suggests that she is careful to retreat to actuality after she is finished with her fiction, and, more importantly, that she leaves no traces, no Jamesian footprints in the snow, to mark her short-lived presence there.

About a century after Woolf's essay, Zadie Smith's lecture "The I Who Is Not Me" takes up the same problem, but whereas Woolf analyzes the work of another novelist, Smith analyzes her own craft. She describes what it looks and feels like to ensure that there is no "I" in one's fiction, and what it might mean to discover that "I" has sneaked in and buried itself there anyway. Reflecting on the writing of *Swing Time* (2016), her fifth novel but the first to be narrated in the first person, Smith wonders why she has been so averse to "I." "I started writing very young," she says, "at an age where I felt that any reader who picked me up would be well within their rights to say: now, who exactly does this girl think she is? My answer to that was: 'no one.'" It's a defense mechanism, Smith admits, this muting or even erasure of selfhood, but an attractive one, because it squares with so many myths of the novelist's gift of impersonality. Isn't the novelist, Smith's younger self thinks, supposed to suspend her own identity, to become that phantom and nonspecific "no one" so that she can enter into the mind of anyone? Like Shakespeare, she wants to be "simultaneously everywhere and nowhere, . . . like a gnomic god." She describes her "strange pride" in the refusal of the first person, "as if it proved I was less self-preoccupied or vain than the memoirist or the blogger or the *Bildungsroman*-er. No one could accuse me of hubris if I wasn't there."[2] Virginia Woolf would seem to agree, commending Emily Brontë for keeping "I" out of it while Charlotte seems narcissistically to make Jane Eyre speak in nothing more than Charlotte's own voice.

"But after my book was finished," Smith continues, "and I had a chance to reflect upon it I could see more clearly how the I who is me ran through it all in a subterranean way." The object-subject enacted in that swerve between pronouns, "the I who is me," serves as a proxy here for a larger problem about the line that separates the fictional from the actual. The "I who is me" gets in unintentionally and must bring something of actuality along with them, but they don't quite break out into the open, nor do they tip the balance from "not-I" to "I"; they remain lodged in that underground of the novel that Schreiner found so compelling as a metaphor for fiction's peculiar kind of being. Or it might be that Smith's metaphor is closer to Whitehead's: the underground of the novel through which "I" can run as if digging surreptitious and fugitive tunnels, all the while building the novel's infrastructure from beneath.

It's not however the "I" I'm after as I read Woolf's and Smith's essays, at least not for its own sake. I'm somewhat more interested in the pronoun's relation to the prepositions that attach to it. As long as I remain firmly here, while the novel takes shape, I-less, there, the recklessness of Smith's "hubris" morphs into the success of what Woolf calls Brontë's "gigantic ambition."[3]

One goal of this book has been to elucidate what "there" might point to in Woolf's and Smith's formulations. We've seen novelists' various attempts to point to the ground of the novel's fictional existence through the work of metaphor: it's the blank groundwork barely underneath the novel's finish; it's the underground where novelistic existence roots or tunnels; and finally, it's the ground that somehow preexists the novel, which the novelist "gains," however temporarily. After all of that, the simplicity of "there" refreshes. Smith is "here," giving her lecture (she points out that in essays, e-mails, birthday cards, and lectures, she has never had a problem speaking in the first person), and the world of her debut novel *White Teeth* (2000), for example, is "there." But doesn't there need to be some path from here to there and back again for the writing of a novel to happen? Smith isn't describing the real act of writing, after all; she's describing an anxious and self-conscious claim, her desire to appear as if "I wasn't there" to preclude the charge of hubris that threatens, it seems, from all directions, or from the potential, nonspecific "no one" she has been hoping herself to become: "*No one* could accuse me of hubris if I wasn't there."

Even more recently, the novelist and memoirist Akwaeke Emezi has described yet a different approach to the problem of the novelist entering the world of their novel as if shifting into another register of being. But where Woolf speaks of the desirability of keeping the actual and the fictional separate, and where Smith speaks of the sometimes accidental ways that the actual intrudes upon the fictional even as we try our best to keep these worlds apart, Emezi writes of their own work as using the materials of selfhood while "writing into the unknown."[4] They borrow the phrase from a fellow writer who tries to follow Emezi's suggestion that a novel falls short if it offers only "a reflection of known things" (*Dear* 49). Emezi instead wants fiction to go further, and they echo Hardy in their insistence that realism can only be art if it takes defamiliarization as its primary aim: "I want reflections that are alive, that shift things for me instead of showing me the familiar" (*Dear* 51). It's not that writing into the unknown doesn't use the novelist's self and their own experiences, "excavating my own self," as Emezi puts it, but rather that the novelist can't in the first place take the self and the actual existence that grounds personal identity as a given. If the novel merely copies the actual world, using its ontology as its model and sharing the limits of that ontology, then the novel's ground can only sustain and support some of us, those who share a set of philosophical assumptions rooted in a Western tradition. The novelist must begin instead with "questions about existence," and the process of writing into the unknown then becomes a "casting out into unformed space, tracing blindly, discovering something through the writing of it," much as James feels that to make a novel he must gain some other, mysterious ground that preexists him (*Dear* 52).

Describing this process of writing into the unknown while nevertheless excavating the self, Emezi has in mind their debut novel *Freshwater* (2018), which they have described as a novel about "metaphysical dysphoria" (*Dear* 16). *Freshwater* draws upon Emezi's own experience of dysphoria as they came to identify as trans and nonbinary, and also as an ọgbanje, "an Igbo spirit that's born to a human mother" (*Dear* 15). As Emezi puts it, "The possibility that I was an ọgbanje came to me years before I wrote *Freshwater*, around the time I began calling myself trans, but it took me a while to collide and connect the two worlds," to be able to use Igbo cosmology as a frame through which to understand transness and vice versa (*Dear* 16). If a cosmology is about wholeness and totality—a metaphysical theory that can account for the entire universe—then Emezi aims for syncretism, the possibility and indeed the "dysphoria" of "inhabiting simultaneous realities that are usually considered mutually exclusive" (*Dear* 15). By means of that syncretism, Emezi thinks, they might begin the work of decentering the Western and cisnormative metaphysics that define for many novelists and readers the absolute horizon of realism. Framed differently, a novel about a young woman populated by spirits, wandering between realms, who comes to discover that she is an unfortunately embodied god might be understood as realism rather than as fantasy: not an easy reflection of known things, at least for some readers, but nevertheless "a reflection for those of us living in shifting realities, worlds framed as madness, bordered by unknowns" (*Dear* 52). Reality is relative, and therefore realism is relative. Smith, along similar lines, writes that "what I try to concern myself with in fiction" is "the way of things in reality, as far as I am able to see and interpret them, which may not be especially far."[5] The novel chastises our ontological hubris, by asking us to think about how different and even competing ontologies adjoin, communicate, overlap, and collide, so that Emezi's *Freshwater*, for example, is both about a character's experience of metaphysical dysphoria and about the novel as a genre of metaphysical dysphoria.

Having read James's prefaces in chapter 3, and having now begun to analyze Woolf's, Smith's, and Emezi's reflections upon the difficulty of the novelist who tries to put "I" into the novel or to keep "I" out, we might say that all of these authors examine a broader aesthetic problem, which Adorno describes in language that resonates with our competing images of the sealed or the ontologically porous novel: "The communication of artworks with what is external to them, with the world from which they blissfully or unhappily seal themselves off."[6] Adorno offers us a choice of adverbs—blissfully or unhappily—and in that choice recognizes a range of possibilities for the artwork's complex metaphysical relation to the world outside of it. We've seen that for James, the kind of "communication" Adorno wonders about is most possible and most potent in the act of rereading and the process of revision, when the configuration of the fictional world and its relation (blissful or unhappy) to actuality sharpen in retrospect. In Woolf and Smith, we see the problem considered from the other side and with agency ascribed differently: not the artwork that seals itself off from reality but the artist who seals themself out of the artwork, thinking that the ground of the novel cannot sustain their existence in all its uncompromising actuality. In Emezi, we see a novelist who tries to put multiple ontologies in tense juxtaposition, to open up what they call elsewhere in their autobiographical writing "a space between spaces," between realms not quite here and not quite there, syncretic, simultaneous, colliding (*Dear* 22). All four novelists share with Adorno a question about how, despite the artwork's completion, closure, or sealing off, communication between its world and ours might continue. As I suggested in the previous chapter, "close reading" is one name we give to the possibility of such ongoing communication between this world and that.

For his part, Adorno argues that artworks communicate with what is external to them by way of a cryptic silence, "through noncommunication; precisely thereby [artworks] prove themselves refracted."[7] Adorno may at first seem paradoxical here, but anyone who's been given the cold shoulder, or longed for an answer that did not come, knows how noncommunication communicates. The artwork wants to get away from us, to turn its back on us, to drift as far as it can into outer space. Or maybe it laments the necessity of separating from us as an adolescent reaching adulthood might mourn their newfound independence. But in any event its silence speaks volumes. From James's point of view, as the creator of his own novels, revision and reshaping of the artwork is still possible, although we have seen that such labor raises a host of questions. For us as ordinary readers or even professional literary critics, however, no matter what we ask of the novel or how we address it, taking it to pieces in our close readings, it will not respond, nor will it sanction our efforts.

Something does get through the sealed boundary between the actual and the fictional in Adorno's image, and in James's theory of the novel; and Emezi claims along similar lines that as a novelist you can "bend your desires into reality." But in all three cases that something—a ray of light, an emissary, a yearning—is inevitably refracted, bent out of shape by the prismatic angles at which these two worlds meet. (Refraction is a bending, but also a way of revealing an underlying reality, the spectrum of light, more clearly.) Adorno sees that quintessentially aesthetic but famously slippery quality we call "form" as the key to art's "rejection of the empirical world," but later on in *Aesthetic Theory* he intensifies the image of the bent artwork as he reckons with art's struggle to free itself from actuality: "In the utopia of its form," he writes, "art bends under the weight of the empirical world from which, as art, it steps away." Here is the double bind of art as Adorno sees it: to become fully itself, it must detach from the empirical world that first gave it being. Yet at the same time, even as it "steps away" from the real, art retains an imprint of its pressure; as it pretends a utopian, liberatory indifference to the laws and limits of reality, art nevertheless carries reality on its shoulders.

We might say that Adorno, like Emezi, describes art's metaphysical dysphoria, tracing "dysphoria" to its Greek root: "hard to bear."[8] Could we imagine a fiction, even a realist fiction, that relinquishes the weight of the actual and becomes truly itself, unbent? If form initially promises such a possibility, the promise is soon broken. Form is really just "sedimented content," Adorno insists, using a metaphor of ground and gravity that helps connect his ontology of art to our concern with the ontological grounds of the novel.[9] Form is what settles to the bottom, accumulating upon art's barely perceptible ground, helping us to see its contours if only we can clear away the silt and muck. We might at this moment recall Hardy reading Hegel in the British Library, wondering how anyone could presume "that the world must somehow have been made a comfortable place for man." I suggested in chapter 1 that Hardy refuses the model of the groundless novel, which would offer us a respite from an uncomfortable reality by rebuilding it all from nothing, preferring to imagine the grounds of the novel as almost unbearably real and alive.

The present chapter takes up the idea of the novel as a meeting ground that sustains multiple kinds of existence—fictional, actual, and what we might call other, between, trans, nonbinary—although as we'll see, the gaining of this kind of novelistic ground is fraught with difficulty and marked by the dysphoria to which Hardy, Adorno, and Emezi in their different ways gesture. This chapter's central metaphor carries two meanings: first, the metaphor of the meeting ground aims to illuminate the way in which novelists imagine fictionality and actuality coexisting on the ground of the novel; second, the metaphor of meeting grounds points our attention to the joining or at least adjacency of two incommensurate ontological frameworks, each with its own vocabulary for describing metaphysical foundations, and the possibilities of movement (often uncomfortable, painful, dysphoric) between these realms.

Just as Quine in the field of metaphysics concerns himself with policing the boundary between the sparsely populated world of what there is and the overcrowded slum of what exists only in possibility, I argue that novelists must often reflect upon their own practices of cordoning off different metaphysical frameworks. They concern themselves with what and who is allowed existence in the novel (whether, for example, the "I" of the author is granted admission), and with the conditions that need to be met for incommensurate ontologies to connect or overlap. As Jacob Romanow asks in his analysis of Anthony Trollope's fiction, "What... if fiction's realism inheres in its thematic and formal awareness of the imbrication between the fictive and the real; if fiction becomes realistic by rejecting the poetic illusion of a discrete world-of-the-text?"[10] Very much unlike Quine, novelists cannot be in the business of keeping intruders out. The novel must by its nature (as something to be read) maintain an opening between actual and fictional worlds, and so must imagine a metaphysical ground that can support a fictional character or place but that can equally support an author's or a reader's more temporary and fraught inhabitation.

―――

Why read a realist novel? What do we achieve by leaving our own reality behind only to be confronted by a stultifyingly exact copy of it? After all, as Woolf argues in her essay "On Re-Reading Novels," the problem is that "novels,... besides being so long and badly written, are all about old familiar things; what we do, week in, week out, between breakfast and bedtime; they are about life, and one has life enough on one's hands without living it all over again in prose."[11] There is such a thing as too much devotion to the actual, even in realist fiction. It's a familiar complaint for Woolf that extends to her argument in "Modern Fiction" that the Edwardian novel—represented by the work of Arnold Bennett, John Galsworthy, and H. G. Wells—has ushered in an era of novelistic hyperrealism, or "materialism" as she calls it, devoted to cataloging in fiction the solid objects of the world, "unimportant things, . . . making the trivial and the transitory appear the true and the enduring."[12] Attempting to *get* the reality of the thingly world with perfect observational finesse (and not even succeeding at that dubious goal), these novelists end up alienating those of us who already live in reality and need a mysterious something more, a twist, an opening, to allow us or even invite us to cross that boundary between real and fictional worlds.

Of her three examples of the materialist authors then dominating the field, it is Bennett who comes in for the most serious critique. He is a "workman," Woolf says, and what his novels gain in solidity they lose in vivacity: "He can make a book so well constructed and solid in its craftsmanship that it is difficult for the most exacting of critics to see through what chink or device decay can creep in. There is not so much as a draught between the frames of the windows, or a crack in the boards. And yet—if life should refuse to live there?"[13] Life here is preserved, but perhaps only as the undead are preserved. Immune to decay, even immortal, and in this sense not really, flourishingly alive. The "well constructed and solid" novel looks like nothing so much as a sealed coffin in which the reader has been buried alive. Entering that world of undead copies of actuality, we might not feel welcomed by a familiar atmosphere; we might instead long for the sustenance of fresh air.

Writing of Charlotte Brontë, Woolf arrives at a similar but perhaps more detailed image of how the novel borrows from actuality and of how that borrowing might turn out to be a burden, something like the heavy weight of the empirical world that Adorno describes art as longing to escape. "A novelist, we must reflect," Woolf writes, "is bound to build up his structure with very much perishable material which begins by lending it reality and ends by encumbering it with rubbish."[14] Woolf has been relating what she expected to find in *Jane Eyre*—a typically Victorian novel encumbered by rubbish heaps of actuality—before she read it and found it instead to be marked by a scrupulous order and selectivity in its relation to the real world from which it borrows its materials. Woolf hits upon the fine balance the novelist must achieve if they wish to be successful: just enough of the perishable material of the actual world to lend reality to the fiction, but not so much that the novel comes to resemble a suffocating pile of objects that seem to have been discarded there.

The word "reality" does a great deal of work in Woolf's formulation: How do we come to imagine reality as a quality that the "perishable material" of actuality seems to promise to the novel, but whose true foundation lies elsewhere than that mere rubbish pile? Reading Woolf more precisely, it's not even the novel or its depicted fictional world that wants to borrow reality from the world of things, it's the novel's "structure." A failed effort after a structural verisimilitude, predicated upon the concreteness of things, might describe something like what Barthes would later name "the reality effect," that is, a devotion to material description which seems to be woven into the fabric of realist fiction but could be better described as a set of "structurally superfluous notations" that signify nothing more than reality itself and so exert a powerful "resistance to meaning."[15]

In "Modern Fiction," Woolf admits that novelists' talk about "reality" is hopelessly fuzzy, and perhaps as fuzzy as the other term, "life," that Woolf often uses as an analogue. The question of how we circumscribe such metaphysical concepts is central to the essay, and Woolf uses Bennett as a cautionary example of how such circumscription can go wrong when it is imagined as an effort to immobilize and suffocate our concepts rather than let them breathe and wander:

> Can it be that . . . Mr. Bennett has come down with his magnificent apparatus for catching life just an inch or two on the wrong side? Life escapes; and perhaps without life nothing else is worth while. It is a confession of vagueness to have to make use of such a figure as this, but we scarcely better the matter by speaking, as critics are prone to do, of reality. Admitting the vagueness which afflicts all criticism of novels, let us hazard the opinion that for us at this moment the form of fiction most in vogue more often misses than secures the thing we seek. Whether we call it life or spirit, truth or reality, this, the essential thing, has moved off, or on, and refuses to be contained any longer in such ill-fitting vestments as we provide.[16]

Woolf's "confession of vagueness" attaches to the necessity of figuration for making her point—"to have to make use of such a figure as this"—but do those metaphors, of the novel as "an apparatus for catching life" and of life as something that can "escape," aim to remedy confusion, or does metaphor in this essay step bravely into the risk of uncertainty, to "hazard the opinion" that the kind of novel exemplified by Bennett's work misses an indispensable *something*, whatever that something might be called? It is a something that can only be explained by pointing ("this"); it is a something that we "seek" in the novel and that the novel desires to "secure"; it is a something that can be caught by the novel's apparatus, or perhaps its structure; it is a something that doesn't want or need us, that doesn't particularly desire to be held in one place, that moves off, or on, indifferent.

It seems so easy to miss this something that I start to sympathize with poor Bennett, who after all only misses it by "an inch or two." But then, I think, I might be reading Woolf's criticism of Bennett somewhat wrongly. He does secure a great deal with his magnificent apparatus, and it's clear that Woolf doesn't think his failure is anything so uncommon. What's more uncommonly bad for Woolf is how tightly Bennett seals that apparatus, so that even if life is just an inch or two to the other side of its walls, even if life is banging upon its doors, asking for admission, it cannot find a place to enter. Perhaps it's only out of frustration, then, that life's essential something has moved on from the novel, seeking a friendlier reception elsewhere. Life refuses to live there, as Woolf says, and although this refusal protects the novel against decay, it also makes it into a forbidding or at least boring place, a warehouse stuffed with unmeaning things.

Bennett is in the business of catching and securing, while Woolf seems to favor opening and widening, fitting the novel with the right kinds of apertures, or allowing it to crack in places, so that life can find its own way in. Life is for Woolf that "luminous halo," that "semi-transparent envelope surrounding us from the beginning of consciousness to the end." In her figural vocabulary, it is something difficult to isolate, perhaps impossible to catch—not "a series of gig lamps symmetrically arranged" but rather a diffusive and translucent aura, "varying," "unknown and uncircumscribed," whose boundaries are much more permeable than all that thingly dross of the actual world.

Woolf wants to know how reality can lend something of itself to the novel, but something more than its dead husk. She wants to know how the novel can let life in without killing it. Is it possible for the novel to provide a ground upon which something of the actual world, even its most essential something, can flourish and grow in unpredictable new directions? Life descends from elsewhere, "an incessant shower of innumerable atoms," and the novel's duty, it seems, is to allow it all a place to settle. Although James Joyce stands in Woolf's essay as the possible antidote to Bennett's extreme materialism, he is not without his faults, and those faults are in some sense the mere reverse of Bennett's. Yes, he is a "spiritualist." Yes, he gives us "life itself" and so signals a path forward for the modern novel. But for all that, he doesn't surpass the novelist who to Woolf's mind represents the very best of Victorian realism, Thomas Hardy. Reading Joyce, we can't escape "our sense of being in a bright yet narrow room, confined and shut in, rather than enlarged and set free"; his work has upon us "the effect of something angular and isolated." Trading Bennett for Joyce, we trade one confined space for another; neither has figured out how to allow for free movement across the boundaries that structure the relationship between the novel and the actual world.

By contrast, Emezi imagines the novelist's journey from the *here* of actuality to the *there* of fiction as a "spell," a magic wrought out of the power of imagination to destabilize the line between the real and the unreal. "We want the work to sustain itself," they write of themself and their fellow novelists, "we want it to feed us and keep us safe, but sometimes it feels like we're missing a map. How can we get to where we want to be? What is the hack strategy to make it happen? What words do you chant into the space between spaces, to bend your desires into reality?" (*Dear* 22). Emezi is thinking here not only about the novelist's work across ontological frameworks, the magic of finding one's way through that space between spaces, but also of the novelist's concrete labor and remuneration. Novel-writing is a way of bringing a new world into being; it is also, for Emezi, a way of bringing their own desired future into being, a different way of actualizing what is at present unreal or, in other words, lending something of unreality (the dream, the fantasy) to reality, rather than lending reality to fiction as in Woolf's image. "I wanted a book deal," Emezi writes, "I wanted to be able to write full time, and I wanted a Nigerian visual artist to design the book's cover. . . . I wanted to be able to afford to keep making my work. I wanted to wear pink faux fur to my book launch, and I wanted to stunt at awards" (*Dear* 22). The spell, it turns out, is a minor variation on the pop magic of "manifestation." As *The Secret* would have it: "Ask, believe, and receive."[17]

Novel-writing creates a new existence, but that existence is also a commodity. It can be bought and sold, and the novelist's crafting of a fictional existence can therefore, in turn, shape the novelist's actual existence: "I drew a map of the future I wanted, then I took those defined lines and pulled them across time, dragging them into the present." Understood this way, the relationship between the novelist and the novel and the marketplace in which the novel becomes a commodity is almost painfully clear: "All you have to do is write," Emezi insists. "You refine your spells, adjusting a touch here, a sacrifice there, but the work is a spell on its own; it does its magic once executed" (*Dear* 23).

Let's call it metaphysical confinement, the very unmagical state that Woolf describes of being trapped either in the narrowly material or the narrowly spiritual novel, unable to complete the spell that would open a circuit between imagination and actuality—something like what Karen Zumhagen-Yekplé, in her reading of *To the Lighthouse*, describes as Woolf's abiding "sense of metaphysical finitude," or what Dora Zhang calls "the challenge of describing what is not material or visible" that is a frequent subject of Woolf's fiction and her theorization of fiction.[18] If we desire a more capacious understanding, a novel that comprehends the material and the spiritual, the actual and the imagined, we need to spend some time investigating the border areas between these ontological frameworks, as we've already seen Meinong arguing as he urges us to look to the neutral zones, or what Emezi might imagine as speaking into "the space between spaces," the reality of those living in "shifting realities ... bordered by unknowns," where different fields of inquiry into being overlap or gape apart.[19]

Woolf's fiction narrates this problem too, of what I earlier called the feeling of metaphysical confinement or dysphoria that comes from trying to keep seemingly incompatible realms apart rather than allowing for the possibility of a "neutral zone" or "meeting ground" that might support multiple kinds of existence. Think, for example, of Mrs. and Mr. Ramsay in Woolf's *To the Lighthouse* (1927), each in their different way concerned about keeping worlds separate, and about what happens when one kind of tenuously held ground (the island, the home) threatens to be engulfed by another (the sea, the wet). The novel's characters frequently draw upon the seashore and the seafloor as metaphors for the kind of metaphysical dysphoria Woolf describes in her essays on fiction: Is it possible from my position here, on solid ground, to face and even embark upon what lies out there, in the fluidity and chaos of moving water? But just as often, the novel's characters are simply anxious about the sea and its encroachment, and about the erosion of the land upon which they stand.

At the very outset of the novel, for example, as her son James begs to cross the water to visit the lighthouse perched on a small island, Mrs. Ramsay describes to her children with some dismay the lighthouse keeper's existence out in the ocean "upon a rock the size of a tennis lawn": "to see the same dreary waves breaking week after week, and then a dreadful storm coming, ... and the whole place rocking, and not to be able to put your nose out of doors for fear of being swept into the sea."[20] Later on, we see how Mrs. Ramsay's image of the lighthouse keeper's constant vulnerability to drowning is a hyberbolic projection of her own fear of oceanic invasion. She wishes her house were less permeable to the ocean and that those living in it would show more respect and help her to seal it up in the right ways: "If they could be taught to wipe their feet and not bring the beach in with them—that would be something.... If every door in a house is left perpetually open, things must spoil.... That windows should be left open, and doors shut—simple as it was, could none of them remember it?" (25–26). Mrs. Ramsay offers us a maxim—if doors are left open, things must spoil—that could be dropped into Woolf's metaphoric description of Bennett's fiction as a space so tightly constructed that no decay can creep in. In *To the Lighthouse*, the sea is Woolf's reigning figure for the dangerously unstable boundary between incompatible realms—and especially for the forces of erosion and decay that eat away the very ground we stand on, until we're left with an island beneath our feet no larger than a tennis lawn. Again, one could almost sympathize with Bennett in light of these passages from *To the Lighthouse*: Who doesn't fear the creep of decay?

Later, as Mrs. Ramsay's family and their houseguests gather for dinner, that fear of watery instability obtrudes again. But this time it is expressed entirely through figuration. Mrs. Ramsay thinks how "the night was now shut off by panes of glass" as the party assembles itself around the candlelit table, and that the windows, "far from giving any accurate view of the outside world, rippled it so strangely that here, inside the room, seemed to be order and dry land; there, outside, a reflection in which things wavered and vanished, waterily" (79–80). The final adjective, "waterily," makes the sentence wobble suddenly between the figural and the literal: it's only a trick of perception being described, the way the light plays upon the glass so that the sheer darkness outside seems to ripple like water. But what is outside *is* water, as the novel has reminded us again and again. When the next paragraph begins, this strange mixture of reality with the "as if" of the fictional imagination persists: "Some change at once went through them all, as if this had really happened, and they were all conscious of making a party together in a hollow, on an island; had their common cause against the fluidity out there" (80). It's an odd metaphor given that the novel does in fact take place upon an island, although on an island somewhat larger than the house itself, and that there really is fluidity out there, although a little bit farther away than the other side of the window. In some sense the content of that metaphoric "as if" description *had* "really happened" and in another sense the metaphor shrinks the scope of the novel's setting so that it can represent a more abstract problem about what it means to maintain order and dry land in the face of a fluidity that peers in at the windows, threatening to make everything waver and vanish if we allow it entry.

Where Mrs. Ramsay's fear of the ocean is quite literal—the ocean heaves and surges; it threatens to drown us; its wet and salt and sand decays our homes—in this dinner party scene, and in Mr. Ramsay's philosophical meditations, this fear morphs into a metaphor for the problem of incommensurate but adjoining metaphysical grounds. (Or it might be better to say the adjoining of a solid ground with the hungry energy of groundlessness.) Mr. Ramsay often turns to metaphors of standpoint and firm grounds when thinking about his philosophical positions in general. When he thinks of the progress of reasoned thought as progress through the alphabet from A to Z, and laments his inability so far to reach R, he reflects that "Here at least was Q. He dug his heels in at Q. Q he was sure of." As he makes an almost physical effort to move his mind on toward R—"He braced himself. He clenched himself."—we are told that "qualities that would have saved a ship's company exposed on a broiling sea with six biscuits and a flask of water—endurance and justice, foresight, devotion, skill, came to his help. R is then—what is R?" (30–31). The narrator figures this impossible transition for thought, the transition from Q to R, as a movement from solid land, a spot where Mr. Ramsay can simply dig in his heels and plant himself, to the peril of the "broiling sea." It seems Mr. Ramsay possesses all the "qualities" necessary for the voyage—or is it that these qualities aren't quite enough for smooth sailing, only enough to save himself from drowning? Something more would be required to take the step from dry land to that moving, aqueous ground.

Mr. Ramsay's parable is quite like the parable we encountered in Schreiner's *The Story of an African Farm*, about the hunter who becomes obsessed with catching the beautiful white bird called Truth. (Reading Woolf's "Modern Fiction," we might say that the bird could just as easily be called Reality, or Life, or merely Something.) Just as the hunter in that parable pursues Truth toward the summit of a great mountain until the moment of his death, Mr. Ramsay, accepting that he likely doesn't have the genius required to get past Q to R, vows that nevertheless "he would not die lying down; he would find some crag of rock, and there, his eyes fixed on the storm, trying to the end to pierce the darkness, he would die standing" (31). At least, he thinks, one can fully claim the ground upon which one has found firm footing, while refusing to look away from the stormy dark that lies on the other side of that forbidding line separating R from Q. The very idea of alphabetizing the movement through phases of philosophical knowledge returns us to Zeno's paradox, and the comfort of dividing what is in fact smooth and continuous into discrete and countable steps. Woolf has already hinted to us in her theory of the novel that she doesn't like the idea of such dividing lines, which lead us to the hermetically sealed novel, borrowing from reality while also paradoxically trying to ward it off. Mr. Ramsay is only another tragic image of the errant thinker who places too much faith in the support of solid ground.

Woolf dramatizes this problem in a later passage in which we again see Mr. Ramsay sitting on his terrace working out an extended metaphor that compares his philosophical rumination to a long ride on horseback. It is like "foraging and picnicking" in "familiar" territory, he thinks, "like a man who . . . ambles at his ease through the lanes and fields of a country known to him from boyhood. . . . Hours he would spend thus, with his pipe, of an evening, thinking up and down and in and out of the old familiar lanes and commons" (38). This bucolic journey doesn't last, however. A "but" interrupts Mr. Ramsay's pleasant trip, and we realize that this sour turn, his arrival at an "edge," the precipice that separates land from sea, is as predictable as the rhythms of the walk itself: "but at length the lane, the field, the common, the fruitful nut-tree and the flowering hedge led him on to that further turn of the road where he dismounted always, tied his horse to a tree, and proceeded on foot alone. He reached the edge of the lawn and looked out on the bay beneath" (38). No matter where he goes in thought, Mr. Ramsay at some point encounters such an edge over which it would be dangerous to venture. He might be the grown-up version of Schreiner's young philosopher Waldo, himself so attuned to forbidding edges and the danger of tipping into the void that lies beyond the limits of the universe.

It's a peculiar feature of this extended metaphor, at least in my own reading experience, that as it goes on and on, I can easily forget that it's a metaphor, especially because the earlier meditation on the movement from Q to R takes place while Mr. Ramsay actually is out on a walk, stopping here and there to admire the geraniums. At some point I lose track, immersed in Woolf's descriptive detail and the concreteness of these landmarks—"the lane, the field, the common, the fruitful nut-tree and the flowering hedge"—and it is with some feeling of being jarred that I enter the paragraph that follows, which returns more clearly to figuration as it describes in free indirect style the tragedy of Mr. Ramsay's constrained movement:

> It was his fate, his peculiarity, whether he wished it or not, to come out thus on a spit of land which the sea is slowly eating away, and there to stand, like a desolate seabird, alone. It was his power, his gift, suddenly to shed all superfluities, to shrink and diminish so that he looked barer and felt sparer, even physically, yet lost none of his intensity of mind, and so to stand on his little ledge facing the dark of human ignorance, how we know nothing and the sea eats away the ground we stand on—that was his fate, his gift. (38)

Here at last is the simple fact about ground meeting sea: ground doesn't survive the encounter. Or more precisely, it does survive, but it is deluged and made invisible, or it is eaten away, pulverized by the incessant movement of water. Mr. Ramsay can dig in his heels or amble at his ease. He can enjoy all the comforts that solid ground affords. But there is always the edge, and it approaches mercilessly. Better to imagine it as fate, even as a gift, at least to possess the knowledge of this eating edge and to find some glory in one's desolation.

Having been lulled by Mr. Ramsay's extended metaphor into forgetting that it's only a fictional representation of the workings of his mind, having returned to a full awareness that this is all figuration, that Mr. Ramsay is all the while sitting on his terrace and smoking his pipe, and that he's "thinking up and down," not really walking up and down, any old familiar lanes, nothing can prepare me for what comes next in this scene. When Mr. Ramsay arrives at that image of himself as a desolate seabird, we're told that "it was in this guise that he inspired . . . in his wife now, when she looked up and saw him standing at the edge of the lawn, profound reverence, and pity, and gratitude too" (38). It feels something like catching a continuity error, or hearing an uncanny skip in a record that reminds you of the artificiality of sound. Everything becomes jumbled here when we come to know that Mr. Ramsay's fable of his own wandering mind has been partly but not entirely true. There was no *horse*, surely, I think. But I should have noticed that after he ties up the horse in his imagination and proceeds on foot, he does really proceed on foot. He is really standing upon a ground being eaten away by the sea. "He reached the edge of the lawn," we're told, and yet on my first reading of this scene I missed entirely the protrusion of that more manicured and domestic ground, the lawn, into the scene of fields and nut-trees that precedes it. Woolf shows us in this scene how tenuous is the line that keeps fiction apart from reality and reality apart from fiction. We're asked to be mindful of the moments when the "actual" ground becomes a fictional or at least figural ground, and when the "actual" ground returns to support us. It's doubly complicated that all of this happens within a novel, where my use of "actual" in the previous sentence must be marked by scare quotes: actual for the Ramsays, but not for me.

"Suddenly to shed all superfluities," Mr. Ramsay imagines as he stands at the edge of the lawn, to become nothing more than "intensity of mind": here is a little return to Woolf's theory of the novel as a different kind of encounter between two universes—that of fiction and that of actuality—that can seem strangely incompatible. Strangely, that is, because one is supposed to be a mirror for the other, transmuting it, formalizing it, defamiliarizing it, whatever term we might choose to describe the main function of mimesis—in any event, borrowing from the actual world to populate that bare ground of the novel. The question for the Ramsays and for Woolf is, what is superfluous and what essential? Where can one find one's footing—what James called a standpoint on the ground gained by the novelist—and to what extent might the intrusion of that other place, or even its very persistent existence, over there, across the edge that approaches, uproot me?

We've seen some of the various ways these questions might be answered, whether by Woolf's characters or by Woolf herself.

Mrs. Ramsay imagines the lighthouse keeper who fears that to stick even his nose outdoors he risks being swept into the sea; the house that rapidly decays as the sea finds its way in; and the fluidity somewhere *out there*, against which she and her circle steel themselves. Mr. Ramsay imagines himself a noble seabird perched upon a quickly eroding spit—but a bird can also take to the air once the ground finally disappears, and so his metaphor is perhaps more optimistic or more forgiving. (I think here of Hardy's Mrs. Yeobright and the heron that ungrounds itself as she watches, dying and awestruck.) Woolf in her essays imagines the novel as built upon a ground similarly eroding, especially in its relation to actuality, overly constrained, bounded on all sides by an airtight seal, and herself, the theorist of the novel, trying to find a standpoint of her own, "On the flat, in the crowd, half blind with dust, ... for down in the plain little is visible. We only know that certain gratitudes and hostilities inspire us; that certain paths seem to lead to fertile land, others to the dust and the desert."[21] We can only plant ourselves in the thick of it, Woolf decides, and see what we can see.

As she stares at her husband filled with reverence and pity and gratitude, Mrs. Ramsay offers her own metaphor of grounding, and it resonates with Woolf's picture of herself as the heroic theorist, standing still amid the fray and trying to aid us in seeing the something that could become a fertile ground for the modern novel. Mrs. Ramsay thinks to herself that her husband inspires gratitude in her "as a stake driven into the bed of a channel upon which the gulls perch and the waves beat inspired in merry boatloads a feeling of gratitude for the duty it has taken upon itself of marking the channel out there in the floods alone" (39). To Mrs. Ramsay, her husband is not the seabird itself but rather its perch. He has in some sense become a tiny offshoot of the hidden ground, a miniscule island made of wood, a way of marking the presence of the ground underneath that water cannot in the end destroy. It's a happy image of a kind of communion between the water, the earth, and the air, and of the tiny heroism of staking a position in relation to all three, orienting those sailors in their navigation just as Woolf tries to aid us in finding our way to the Promised Land and out of the unforgiving desert.[22]

Novels and novelists are always following paths, it seems. We'll remember Lukács and his description of the novel's "paths of adequation" from chapter 1. Here we have Woolf trying to find those "certain paths" for the modern novel that will lead it to greener pastures. Zadie Smith writes in 2008 about a choice, represented by the work of Joseph O'Neill and Tom McCarthy, between "Two Paths for the Novel," before changing the essay's title a year later for its inclusion in *Changing My Mind* to "Two Directions for the Novel," as if deciding that as a metaphor the path is too earth-bound. ("Directions" might include, for example, upward.) In "The I Who Is Not Me," Smith seems to clarify her position on paths when she writes that in her theorization of the novel and in her own fiction, "I am trying to counter the narrow path with the wide-open road."[23] But whatever paths the novel might follow or the novelist might identify, and however they try to widen them, those paths still cannot take me, in all my solidity and fleshiness, from the *here* of actuality to the *there* of fiction. Some part of me can get there; the bulk of me is left behind.

This problem presents itself to me (the reader, the critic), and also to the novelist, as we've already seen in Woolf's and Smith's meditations upon how much of the "I" can really get into a novel. Smith thinks that despite all its difficulties and pitfalls, the attraction of first-person narration lies its generation of a "reality effect" that "is so strong, immediate." But while this effect "utilizes the flesh-and-blood self, mining it for information, stripping it for parts and re-presenting it . . . that flesh-and-blood self can never actually appear on the page. . . . Echoes, shadows, inversions, fragments—this much writing can do. But the whole enchilada lives on a different plane."[24] James seems to have understood this planar metaphor too—his own alternative to the "path" is after all the hot-air balloon that takes him to heaven. Smith's enchilada is something different, though, emphasizing as it does the limitations of our movement into and out of fictional worlds. Like Woolf's rubbish heap, like Emezi's self-"excavation," Smith's flesh-and-blood self must be *used* by the novelist, mined and disassembled, but only in a carefully limited way. As much access as one can get to a shadowy echoey world, "refracted" in relation to our world in just the way Adorno described, one doesn't get to eat anything there. Such possibilities are always elsewhere. But the twist of Smith's metaphor is its insistence that the whole enchilada *is there*, that the plane upon which it lives *is somewhere*. As a reader I become like Mr. Ramsay on his eroding spit, staring out upon the sea that seems so unable to support his existence in the way that the ground can, or like Mrs. Ramsay peering through the window at a world that ripples, waterily, aware that its fluidity must remain on that side of the window and she must remain on this side if she hopes to avoid obliteration.

It might be, Smith thinks, that through the creation of fictional characters, the novelist finds an opening into fiction, not simply placing the "I" into the novel but rather mining its resources, allowing the self to remain "subterranean," in order to perform the ultimate metaphysical trick: making another "I" where one didn't exist before. She clarifies that she is not "expressing contempt for this autobiographical instinct in readers and in myself," by which they seek to identify the first-person narrator with the author's entire self. The instinct is more complex than mere prurience. "I want to try to find a place," she writes, "to reconcile the 'I-who-is-not-me' of the writer with the 'I-whom-I-presume-is-you' that the reader feels they can see." To accomplish this reconciliation, and therefore "to appreciate fiction fully," she continues, "it helps to conceive of a space that allows for the writer's experience and the reader's simultaneously, a world in which Portnoy is at once entirely Philip Roth and not Philip Roth at all. That sounds like an impossible identity, but literature, for me, is precisely the ambivalent space in which impossible identities are made possible."[25] The metaphors of "place" and "space" to describe the metaphysical work of fiction here help me to clarify what I mean by my own metaphor of the novel as a "meeting ground." When Smith describes a place where the impossible becomes possible, where ambivalence finds support, where a fictional character can be both the author and not the author, where my experience and the novelist's experience are both "allowed," and allowed even at the same time, she points me to the thing I named in the very first sentence of this book as the object of my own seeking: a ground upon which I can know that fictions are real.

One might object that Smith's point about the creation of fictional characters is more ethical or even political than it is metaphysical. Surely the novel's ambivalence and ambiguity, its power to create impossible identities, are qualities meant to teach us lessons about empathy across difference and about the endless contradictions of human psychology and embodiment. I think, for example, of George Eliot in "The Natural History of German Life" insisting that if only Dickens's characters had more depth and plausibility, more "psychological character" to complement their "external traits," then "his books would be the greatest contribution Art has ever made to the awakening of social sympathies."[26] This model of fictional character is familiar enough: that impossibility Smith describes, of making unreal people real, awakens us to the complexity of others. But as Alex Woloch has argued, the formal constraint of the novel—it only has so much space—puts a hard limit on its capacity to represent humanity as fully as Eliot might like. The "character-space," Woloch argues, "marks the intersection of an implied human personality—that is, as Dostoevsky says, 'infinitely' complex—with the definitively circumscribed form of a narrative. The implied person behind any character is never directly reflected in the literary text but only partially inflected."[27] As Smith would say, the novel can do echoes, shadows, fragments, inversions—or in other words partial inflections of reality—but the whole enchilada is beyond our grasp.

We can start to see in Woloch's own metaphors of space and circumscription, placed against Smith's argument about the ambivalent space of the novel, how the problem we face here is metaphysical—perhaps in addition to being ethical and political, depending on the goals of our reading. "We occasionally speak of Sarrasine," Barthes argues, referring to the title character of the Balzac novella that is the subject of *S/Z*, "as though he existed, as though he had a future, an unconscious, a soul." (I might interrupt here and say, as if he had a ground to stand on.) But Barthes insists that "what we are talking about is his *figure* (an impersonal network of symbols combined under the proper name 'Sarrasine'), not his *person* (a moral freedom endowed with motives and an overdetermination of meanings)."[28] Woloch and Smith each echo Barthes's argument in their different ways. All three think of ontology as the central problem in thinking about fictional character and the paradox of a character's very existence. *Where* is a fictional character, they ask? If a fictional character is unreal, impossible, partial, figural, impersonal in relation to reality and real people, then how can fiction lay a groundwork for the reality, the possibility, the fullness of fictional existence?

It's not, Smith insists, that Philip Roth offers us a "role model" when he creates Portnoy. We can't find such an obvious opening between fiction and reality, an opening by which the character can finally "become" real when I, the reader, incorporate him into myself or, as Woolf might say, I "lend" him something of reality. Smith argues that "The offer was not: *You, too, can be like Portnoy.* The offer was: *Portnoy exists! Be as you please.*" Smith wants to understand better what I described earlier as the metaphysical trick by which fictional characters emerge into being. The mere existence of Portnoy, and especially the emphatic, exclamatory, piercing insistence upon his existence—Portnoy exists!—is enough, she argues, to give us the sense that *all* metaphysical grounds are fictional, insofar as the partially inflected, provisional quality of fictional existence might serve as a model by which to understand our own being in the actual world. Roth's "final and greatest lesson," she argues, "is to insist on the fictional status of identity itself." This insight leads Smith on to her metaphor of the wide-open road, which she offers as a substitute for the narrow path of the novel: "For what is impossible about any real-life identity," she writes, "is its narrowness. Not to take yourself as a natural, unquestionable entity can lead you in turn to become aware of the radical contingency of life in general."[29]

As Thom Dancer has argued, Smith's method as a critic is itself characterized by provisionality and contingency. "In contrast to the analytic ambition of strong theories," he writes, "Smith prefers a criticism whose interventions are less direct and more intimate, fallible, and indeterminate."[30] And we can see this intimate, fallible, indeterminate method at work in what we might call the occasional theory of the novel that she develops across her essays and lectures. Smith homes in again and again on fiction as a resource for thinking not only ethical, aesthetic, and political indeterminacy (the main focuses of Dancer's reading of her work) but also what I'm describing as the ontological indeterminacy required to move freely in and out of fictional existence. Or, as Alexandra

Kingston-Reese argues, "in reaffirming the value of the novel" in the "Two Paths" essay, "Smith does so by refracting it through its negations and refusals of the aesthetic—advocating not for the smooth surface of lyrical realism, but for the meaning that is found in ethical and aesthetic disturbance."[31] Similarly, Dancer and Chris Holmes argue that Smith understands the novel not as aspiring to a Lukácsian totality but rather as a genre attuned to "the necessity of accepting limitation" in its relation to reality, or as "a process, an exercise, which allows the limitations of the genre to take center stage."[32] Heather Houser makes a similar point about Smith's work in her recent reading of *White Teeth*. She points out Smith's tendency in passages of description to mark the limits of description, showing us landscapes and people while expressing how impossible it is to make description complete or exhaustive or confident. This "tension between evoking and revoking" that characterizes Smith's descriptions, "the paradoxical give-and-take that structures it," is a way to "defer, render absent, or withhold grounding," to "confer an unstable ontological status onto the fictional world as well as the reader's positioning."[33]

All of these readings emphasize that as Smith imagines the novel's relationship—ethical, aesthetic, ontological—to the world outside of it, expressing what Peter Boxall describes as "a desire to re-apprehend the real, a desire to find new forms with which to examine reality," she ascribes special significance to the relative positionality of the reader and the novelist, something like the problem of "standpoint" that we saw at work earlier in James's theory of the novel.[34] The ontological status of a fictional world coheres only in this relation between standpoints and the possibility of movement or identity between them, which is why Smith is so concerned about where the "I" moves, where it buries itself, where its grounding or undergrounding in the novel allows it to bring forth new existences like James's Isabel Archer, sprouting from the novel's earth.

But despite all their emphasis on the contingency of fictional realities, Woolf and Smith share a conviction that the self named "I" really does exist. If creating a fiction can feel destabilizing or can generate uncertainty about how we enforce the boundaries between the real and the unreal, the novelist can presumably step away from the work of novel-writing for a moment and feel secure in their actual existence. Emezi, however, takes no such solace, and their theory of the novel begins from the premise that what some call "reality" is itself dysphoric, inhospitable to trans and nonbinary being, to ọgbanje being and the Igbo metaphysics to which that idea of being belongs, to all kinds of being that fall as if bereft of support into the unstudied "neutral zone" between frameworks. In this scenario, the creation of fictions and the merging or overlapping of existences that it requires function as a comfort for the subjectivity not entirely at home in the metaphysical framework that has been built to surround them.

I turn now to a fuller reading of Emezi's *Freshwater* and of their broader theory of metaphysical dysphoria because Emezi helps us to think more clearly about what the grounds of the novel signify to the novelist who feels pulled toward the neutral zone, toward the meeting grounds—who desires neither to gain ground nor to maintain the boundary between the solid ground here and the other ground that ripples outside the window, waterily, but rather to lose ground, to cast out into fiction's unformed space.

Emezi's conviction about the novel's relation to metaphysical dysphoria is the opposite of Hardy's. Hardy exhorts us to remain uncomfortable, even when the ground of being feels alien, because after all, the world is not made for our comfort, and even fiction can be no respite from the dysphoric feeling of living in an ill-configured reality. Emezi insists that even if reality is uncomfortable, a fiction need not reproduce the conditions of that discomfort:

"These humans are so loud," they write, "in how they press down, in how they enforce their realities. What would it look like if we took up our own space, *all* of our space, planets and planets worth of it?" (*Dear* 60). If we don't have available to us in reality the planets and planets of space needed to accommodate our existence, then novels, those "portals into other constructed worlds," might function as a multiplier of metaphysical grounds (*Dear* 49). After all, for Emezi "nowhere seems real," and "my search for somewhere to be is really a search for self, and the only self I feel at home with is one that doesn't exist" (*Dear* 2). Later in their memoir, they go further: "I am not real. . . . I belong only in the worlds I create," those "quarantined godquarters" where unreal being feels at home (*Dear* 147). Whereas so many of the novelists I've examined in this book try to understand fictional being by looking to concrete metaphors of ground, earth, canvas, and underground, Emezi finally revels in the novel's unreality. They celebrate the novel's offering of planets and planets of space to house, finally, Wyman's slum of possibles and Meinong's unduly populous realm of being—its capacity to make nowhere a place rather than a negation, so that the nowhere that seems most real to them might become a "somewhere to be."

Freshwater works to make these metaphysical arguments in tandem with Emezi's autobiographical theory of the novel by thematizing, as Woolf does, the problems of metaphysical constraint and dysphoria, although I'll argue that Emezi's novel finds a way out of that dysphoria in its protagonist Ada's arrival at a syncretic understanding of the multiple realities she inhabits. By the end of this novel of painful dysphoria, Ada learns that realities—human and nonhuman, real and unreal—can and must coexist on the same ground. To "know where the ground is," as Ada puts it late in the novel—that is the goal. In both the novel and Emezi's autobiographical writing, the metaphor of "gates" between worlds allows Emezi to think about points of access that can be opened or barred, or in some cases can malfunction and get stuck. Just as she worries while writing the novel about the "gatekeepers" of the publishing industry who might refuse the novel entry into the literary marketplace, who might see it as "stepping out of place" in the traditions of Black and African fiction with its focus on "metaphysical selves" (*Dear* 49), the ọgbanje spirits who populate the novel's protagonist and serve as our narrators describe the painful process by which "we were wrenched, dragged through the gates" that allow movement between their world and ours but are meant to open and close at the right moments.[35] The gates are meant, they explain, to be "a temporary channel, . . . a thing that is sealed afterward, because the gates stink of knowledge" of what lies on the other nonhuman side, "they cannot be left swinging wide like a slack mouth, leaking mindlessly. That would contaminate the human world—bodies are not meant to remember things from the other side" (*Freshwater* 33). There are echoes of Woolf here in the concern of the ọgbanje with erecting barriers between different kinds of being. The gates, left open, allow too much knowledge to waft across that barrier, like the bad breath of that slack mouth. The gates, left open, leak "mindlessly," a failure of the reason that can keep realities compartmentalized, confident that here is real, there unreal.

I opened this chapter by noting that in Woolf's description of Emily Brontë's work, we get an image of a novelist who enters into fictional existence only to retreat back to her own territory, leaving no trace of herself on the other side. (This in contrast to James, who returns to *The Golden Bowl* to find his own footprints marking its snowy ground.) And yet in Woolf's wider theory of the novel, what seems more important to her is that the novel maintains an opening for something or someone, even "decay," to "creep in." There is a double bind here—on the one hand, keep the lines between fiction and reality clear when it comes to the selfhood of the novelist, but on the other hand take care not to seal the world of the novel so tightly that nothing and no one can enter—that Emezi's novel takes up as its central metaphysical premise. What happens when one kind of being intrudes upon another and fails or forgets to return to the place they belong? The question is metaphysical, but it's also a miniature allegory of colonial invasion and occupation. It's important, as Emezi themself points out, that we as readers can comprehend these two kinds of being as equally "real," rather than seeing the novel as bifurcated between, on one hand, a realist mode that would diagnose Ada with dissociative identity disorder and, on the other, a gothic phantasmagoria of Igbo religion that functions as a coping mechanism. Emezi made a point, they write, of insisting during their promotion of the novel, in interviews and readings, on "Igbo ontology as a valid reality made unreal only by colonialism. I cannot give ground or go to them," they continue, speaking of those who would dismiss their argument and perpetuate this colonial erasure of Igbo ontology, "I must hold" (*Dear* 79). Reading this novel as part of a realist tradition, I aim to honor Emezi's argument and also to honor their account of how the novel, as a literary form invested in the coexistence of fictionality and reality, works to dismantle hard ontological boundaries between the real and the unreal, the embodied and the immaterial.

Rooted to the ground of "Igbo ontology as a valid reality," the novel narrates how in the haphazard, painful, stalled movement between worlds, an in-between reality opens up that can itself come to feel like a prison, with seemingly incompatible beings stuck together there, each longing to separate and return home. "There are limitations in the flesh that intrinsically make no sense," the plural ọgbanje narrator of *Freshwater*'s opening sections laments, "constraints of this world that are diametrically opposed to the freedoms we had when we used to ... dip in and out of bodies at will" (12). And so they experience their stuckness in physical reality as a punishment made all the worse by their memory of the immaterial reality from which they came: "We were sentenced to those yawning gates between worlds, left wild, growing in all directions but closed. Open gates are like sores that can't stop grieving: they infect with space, gaps, widenings. Room where there should be none" (35). The ọgbanje experience their new mode of being as a constant exercise in body horror—slack yawning mouths, bad smells, weeping sores, infection—and a state of deep unease with the insidious widening of these bleeding stinking breathing gaps. The ọgbanje understand how their dysphoria becomes Ada's dysphoria too: "Reality was a difficult space for her to inhabit, unsurprisingly" they tell us, "what with one foot on the other side and gates in between" (27). Later on, in one of the novel's few chapters narrated by Ada herself, Ada says that "I don't even have the mouth to tell this story.... In many ways, you see, I am not even real.... I am not even here" (94). Ada's mouth cannot, she thinks, serve as a gate. Her mouth cannot be the one to tell her story and in doing so bridge the gap between her world and, for example, mine. Spoken by a fictional character, those words that cancel themselves out, "I am not even real," "I am not even here," seem filled with pathos: How can I address myself to reality when I and my mouth are fictions, unreal, nowhere? What Ada doesn't yet know is that she is real, and she is somewhere. Not only that, she succeeds in addressing me, the reader, across the gap that separates the fictional and the actual.

Ada eventually begins to experiment with the blending of realities, or what I was earlier calling a metaphysical syncretism, through the emergence of another individualized spirit within her, the one she names Saint Vincent. Unlike the spirits who feel themselves hopelessly mired in embodiment, Saint Vincent moves freely in Ada's dreams, "when she was floating in our realm, untethered and malleable. He molded her into a new body there, a dreambody with reorganized flesh and a penis complete with functioning nerves and expanding blood vessels, tautening easily into an erection" (122). Saint Vincent reverses the ontological hierarchy by which embodiment is fundamental and the immateriality of dreams merely derivative and mimetic, and allows Ada to understand unreality as what Hardy might call the work-ground upon which new realities and even new embodiments can take shape.

Ada associates Saint Vincent with her own history of gender dysphoria—her childhood excitement at being seen as a boy, and her horror at the onset of puberty. The ọgbanje recount how "the hormones redid her body, remaking it without consent from us or the Ada. We were distressed at this re-forming of our vessel, ... because it was nothing other than a cruel reminder that we were now flesh, that we could not control our form, that we were in a cage that obeyed other laws, human laws" (123). Saint Vincent's "dreambody," however, the compound word itself marking the linking of two separate ontologies, one fictional and one real, helps Ada and the ọgbanje to imagine reality otherwise. They can now understand that the shaping of the body by hormones, while unwilled and constraining, might also be reversible or at least alterable with the help of medicine: "we discovered that humans had medical words—terms for what we were trying to do—that there were procedures, gender reassignment, transitioning" (189). Gender dysphoria and what Emezi elsewhere calls the "flesh dysphoria" or "nonhuman dysphoria" of being a god immured within a human body—these experiences overlap for Ada, and surgery aims to remedy both. Saint Vincent's dreambody functions not exactly as a template for what Ada hopes to accomplish. She does not pursue a phalloplasty, for example. But it does function as a template for how unreality might be made real, how the given body that seems so heavy in its actuality might yet be drawn closer to a vision of another mode of embodiment first glimpsed in dreams.

I don't want to sound naive, and neither I think does Emezi. Saint Vincent's "dreambody" remains a vision for Ada, a fantasy of the endlessly plastic body that might draw upon the tradition of trans thought that understands trans* to stand, as Kadji Amin puts it, for "the plastic and generative capacities of matter," a "quasi-mystical force that generates being," an "unpredictable movement that destabilizes taxonomy, selfhood and ontology." Amin wants to problematize that idea of trans* as "preontological," pointing out that if we imagine trans* as a set of vital energies that in some sense produce "ontological differentiation" itself, then we cannot imagine those as also exempt from the concepts and pressures of ontology, "an unambivalent antidote."[36] Emezi's novel echoes Amin's critique in its depiction of the dreambody as a fantasy. The dreambody is unreal and Ada's body is real. Ada must involve doctors and surgery to undo some of the unwilled changes of puberty because her body is her body, and breasts don't in reality just disappear; while the dreambody changes of its own accord, again and again, grounded upon nothing and beholden to no constraints.

Ada does not desire to have a dreambody because she knows she cannot have one: such things do not exist where she lives. But its image stands in her mind for the possibility of in-between ontologies, nonbinary and nonhuman, that would refuse the finality of a single and unmalleable reality. As the ọgbanje put it,

> it was too late for the Ada to do anything except try to keep up with us, try not to be drowned in the liminal fluid we swam in. It tasted sharp as gin, metallic as blood, was soaked in both, down past the red into the deep loam. Ọgbanje space. We could rest in it like the inside curve of a calabash; we could turn in on ourself, wind back to our beginning, make those final folds. Sometimes they call this the crossroads, the message point, the hinge. It is

also called flux space, the line or the edge—like we said, resurrection. (193)

Ada does not want to drown in the liquid liminality that characterizes existence for the ọgbanje, awash in gin and blood. It's perhaps that "deep loam" she seeks, a ground that is beyond even the red of flesh and blood, a hinge, line, or edge out of which a new existence might sprout, or out of which an existence thought hopelessly dead and buried might rise again, resurrected.

Emezi's Ada stands in this sense opposed to Smith's reading of Portnoy. Smith begins with an exclamation (Portnoy exists!) and proceeds to an argument on behalf of the questionability of all existence claims (don't be too confident that you are an unquestionable entity; even the being of life in general is contingent). Ada is a study, perhaps, in what Sara Ahmed has described as the dysphoric state of "being in question." "To be in question," she writes, "is to try to be; to be in question makes being trying."[37] And indeed we've already seen that for Ada reality is a difficult space to inhabit because her feet are planted in at least two realities. The pluralization of reality, the moving between them, makes being trying. I've been arguing that the novel itself performs such a pluralization of reality, in which not only characters but writers and readers too must learn to move on multiple grounds.

I must be clear: I don't want to advance the cavalier claim that inhabiting trans or nonbinary identities is analogous to any reader's inhabitation of a novel, or that the experience of reading a novel allows me, the cisgender critic, a special kind of empathy with the lived experience of trans and nonbinary people. My claim is something more complex. Thinking carefully about what it means to understand a fiction as "real" and to see the novel as a meeting ground that can sustain fictional and actual realities helps us to think carefully about what it means to understand sexed embodiment as "real" and to see the body as its own kind of ontological meeting ground where what is given as actual can abut or overlap with what is as yet imagined and unreal. Cáel M. Keegan points to this very problem as he recounts the development of trans studies as an academic discipline, caught between the fields of women's studies and queer studies and their competing claims about the ontology of sex and gender:

> To the extent that women's studies seeks the liberation of women and others (gay men, lesbians) who are oppressed by sex "like women," trans* studies must perform a *but* . . . , saying *but* gender is *not real like that*. However, in response to queer studies' investment in deconstructing the gender binary (M/F) to unravel heteronormativity, trans* studies must turn inside out, articulating a constative *but* that asserts *but* gender is *real like this*.[38]

Gender is not real, in other words, but it's also not unreal. If the field of trans studies can only be articulated in relation to these incommensurable metaphysical claims, it can only go in circles, Keegan argues. If the question is always about *whether* gender is real or unreal, trans studies can only respond with a *but*.[39] If the question might be, however, what are the textures of gender's unreal being, we have a place for trans studies to articulate its proper metaphysical claim. I've tried to make a similar argument in this book about the history of metaphysical arguments over the existence of fictional beings. When the focus is population control, trying to keep the field of being sparse, we lose the opportunity to argue that fictional being might not be competing for space with actual being. The two modes of existence might adjoin and cooperate. They might in special cases overlap.

Keegan suggests, like Ahmed, that this state of being caught between, of always answering *but*, but never being allowed to state one's own case or lay one's own grounds, makes being difficult. As he puts it, "to find oneself in such a situation might feel impossible—or, rather, it might produce the feeling that one is being made into an impossibility."[40] We might say that *Freshwater* is about being made difficult, being made impossible. And as Grace Lavery argues in elaborating a theory of "trans realism" focused on the work of George Eliot and Sigmund Freud, the work of the realist novel might be "to persuade . . . readers to relinquish a beautiful fantasy and face a discomforting truth about the reality of their own material existence."[41] For Ada, that discomforting truth *is* that her material existence is real, despite her conviction that she is not a woman and also not a human. How to map the border areas, meeting grounds, neutral zones that lie beyond binary gender, between human and nonhuman, between real and fictional, is the question that drives the novel's resolution, as Ada finally turns away from Western medicine and toward Igbo metaphysics, looking for other ontological categories: the deep loam, the message point, the hinge, the line, the edge, the flux space. A being elsewhere and otherwise.

Ada begins to investigate the conditions of her own existence. Or to borrow the terms of C. Riley Snorton, she is "seeking to understand the conditions of emergence of things and beings that may not yet exist." In Snorton's case, those beings are the Black trans people whose existence is not allowed metaphysical consideration, because it is an existence too often foreclosed by and identified with death, or what Keegan calls the "impossibility" of being.[42] As opposed to this backward-looking cancellation, by which it's only after the killing of Black trans existence that it becomes the object of serious metaphysical inquiry, Snorton imagines a forward-looking "emergence" of Black trans being into existence.

When Ada finally begins to learn about ọgbanje existence from an Igbo historian, she appeals to Ala, the python mother goddess who is the progenitor of the ọgbanje, and she hears a response echo in her mind: *"Find your tail"* (224). Being might be self-grounding, the kind of turning inward upon the self that the ọgbanje themselves earlier described, "the final fold." "If I don't know where my tail is," Ada realizes, "then I don't know anything. I don't know where I'm going, I don't know where the ground is, or where the sky is, or if I'm pointing away from my head. The meaning was clear. Curve in on yourself.... You will form the inevitable circle, the beginning that is the end. This immortal space is who and where you are, shapeshifter" (224). To find where the ground is means to orient oneself toward it but not necessarily to take it as the only possible support. Circling in on herself, Ada comes to know where the ground is, where the sky is, where her head is, but she also comes to know that none of this orientation in material reality is the guarantee of her being. As Susan Stryker has said of the metaphysical theory behind the theory of gender performativity, "the biologically sexed body guarantees nothing; it is necessarily there, a ground for the act of speaking, but has no deterministic relationship to performative gender."[43]

Ada can be her own guarantee, beginning and end, immortal and plastic. "I had surrendered," she says as the novel concludes, "and the reward was that I knew myself.... Like the historian said, you have to know your place on this earth.... I am here and not here, real and not real, energy pushed into skin and bone. I am my others; we are one and we are many" (226). I've argued for understanding this novel as realist, following Emezi's insistence that realism means something different to those whose inhabitation of reality is complicated, painful, dysphoric. "Writing into the unknown" serves as a model for how this novel resolves the question of impossible being, being at the edge, using the unique quality of fictional being to elaborate a meeting ground that might support the kind of in-between existence that isn't always allowed to inhabit reality comfortably.

Novels that think about the grounds of fiction might also (at least sometimes) be seeking ways to imagine metaphysical grounds for the sexed or racialized body that are not absolute, constraining, unmalleable. As Keegan argues, we want to be able to say that the sexed body, the human body, is something real without saying that we must simply be satisfied with the one we get, or that the trans body is any less real than the cis body. We want similarly to be able to say that the racialized body is something real without saying that race is deeply determinative of identity, status, or standpoint at the level of ontology. Exploring the ways in which the novel crafts a world that is not quite real, but not quite not real, might help us here. I've grouped together in this chapter three novelists who are also theorists of the novel and who share a conviction that the novel makes space—*must* make space—for being. Despite their differences, Woolf, Smith, and Emezi all write from marginalized positions and wonder about how tightly the novel must be bound to the actuality that limits their movements and exerts undue pressure upon their being. That "I" that stands upon the ground of actuality: How can they use the novel to access another ground, a meeting ground where existence is at least somewhat more multiple, somewhat more flexible, than it is in reality? Not a row of gig lamps but a luminous halo, an endless rain of brilliant atoms. Not an island eroding from beneath our feet but a stake plunged bravely into the invisible seabed underneath, allowing for the navigation of a liquid ground. Not a narrow path but an open road, a space of contingent and improvisational being. Not a binary opposition of being and nonbeing, human and nonhuman, but a neutral zone between. Not a sharp and wounding edge, but a circle that grounds itself in immortal space.

AFTERWORD

Basement

I believe I have found what I sought: a ground upon which to know that fictions are real.

I can't quite say I stand upon it, although I have tried so earnestly and in so many ways to say exactly that. I don't stand upon it, but when I read I sometimes feel it pressing up from beneath the world I read about. I sometimes feel it pressing up from beneath me.

I can't quite say I stand upon it, because it is only a metaphor; because it is frictionless; because it is nothing at all but white or brown or black; because it is beneath the beneath, out of my sight; because it is unreal—actualized only fitfully as I read; or because it is watery and dreamy and heaving and plastic.

It might be that I've been seeking the ground of the novel because I am the ground of the novel, or at least *a* ground of the novel's temporary actualization. I make it real in my head, and when I put the book away, my mind's turning to other things is the novel's de-actualization.

But sometimes, in those moments I've collected here, I feel that fictional being is indifferent to me, speaking its own language, satisfied with blank grounds and deep undergrounds, satisfied with blinking on and off, satisfied with the nonbinary.

It's as if I'm not really in the novel when I'm in it, but rather I am one aspect of a pulsation that sustains it, running along an electrically charged edge beneath, beyond, around. Maybe that edge, that energy of beneathness and beyondness and aroundness, is the ground of the novel that I sought and found, the ground of the novel that becomes charged with my presence when I find my way into a fiction.

Walter Pater called this metaphysical edge the basement: another metaphor of ontological grounding. He thought that even those who claim to stand outside of the world—"The saint, the artist, the speculative thinker"—are nevertheless recognized by the world as "moral types, or categories" and regarded as having "the right to exist."[1] That idea again, "the right to exist," which we've seen at play in Quine, in Meinong, in Adorno, in Emezi. What does it mean for works of art, or nonexistent beings, or nonbinary or queer or racialized or nonhuman people, to lay claim to such a right? What does it mean when such a right is no longer regarded as "self-evident" in Adorno's terms?

The saint, the artist, the speculative thinker: "out of the world's order as they are," Pater writes, they "yet work . . . in and by means of the main current of the world's energy" (215). Perhaps seeking that edge that I'm figuring as the ground of the novel is like seeking another current altogether, not the main current of the world's energy but the subsidiary or minor current that is the energy of nonbeing.

When I think of Pater's saints and artists and speculative thinkers, wishing they could see the world from a position outside of actuality, I think of Schreiner's Waldo, lying awake and wishing he could stop the ticking of the clock and thereby halt the inexorable march of the living into death. I think of Undine, listening for the night's comforting whisper. I think of Emezi's Ada, caught between incompatible realities. These are fictional instantiations of the type Pater has in mind, the type whose unworldliness makes them sensitive to the shapes and the boundaries of being, but who is nevertheless stuck in the world, unable to stop the clock, terrified to open the window that separates the indoors from the dark night and watery movement beyond, embodied but not yet dreambodied. They have the right to exist, but not easily, wholly, comfortably.

What would it mean for one to exist and to persist in existing without being regarded by the world as having the right to exist? For after all, Pater says, "there is another type of character," which he calls the "basement type." Here is how he describes basement being:

> There is another type of character.... It does not take the eye by breadth of colour; rather it is that fine edge of light, where the elements of our moral nature refine themselves to the burning point. It crosses rather than follows the main current of the world's life. The world has no sense fine enough for those evanescent shades, which fill up the blanks between contrasted types of character.... For this nature there is no place ready in its affections. This colourless, unclassified purity of life it can neither use for its service, nor contemplate as an ideal. (215–16)

The pure being of this type takes shape at the place where our moral nature refines to the burning point, or in other words the place where a moralized version of ontology—concerned with the question of what has the right to exist and what doesn't—gives way to a different kind of metaphysical question, which deals with the colorless purity of being, a kind of existence that is unintelligible to the "moral world" and which yet fills its negative spaces, transmits itself at right angles across its currents.

Pater's image of the "purity" of colorless being, its existence beyond the "contrasted types" of the world, or, we're invited to imagine, even beyond the foundational opposition of blackness and whiteness, is another instance of the racialized metaphors that appear again and again in these fantasies of access to ontological truth.

When a basement is at odds with the edifice it supports, everything should fall. But "basement" also has a double meaning, or it did for Pater. In addition to the underground level of a building, "basement" also denotes a more abstract kind of foundation, "an underlying or essential element of something complex."[2]

The "basement type" is, on the one hand, a recluse, or perhaps a prisoner, trapped in the underground space from which they wait to become a "majority," Pater says in the essay's final sentence: "A majority of such would be the regeneration of the world" (222).[3]

But the basement type is, on the other hand, "foundational" in that more abstract, metaphysical sense: the fundamental type, not an aspiration but an already existing metaphysical essence, waiting to serve as our common ground if only we could find it underneath all the accidents of the solid world.

As Carolyn Williams argues, Pater often wants to draw our attention to the ground *as* a figure, standing for a "principle of continuity" or for "the amorphous soil out of which new figures 'rise.'" For Pater, the figure of the ground is "metafigural, second-order, self-reflexive."[4] The ground is not a perfect and transcendent truth in Pater's thought. It is the truth of fertile earth.

In *The Renaissance,* Pater says that metaphysics, or more specifically "the commonplace metaphysical instinct," is nothing more than a bad habit. "A taste for metaphysics," he writes, "may be one of those things which we must renounce if we mean to mould our lives to artistic perfection." He's thinking of a particular, "commonplace" tradition of Platonic metaphysics, which asks us to see through or past the actual world to locate a purer and more perfect form elsewhere.

"For us," he says, collecting around him a community of the like-minded, the "necessity" that makes being possible "is not as of old an image without us, with whom we can do warfare; it is a magic web woven through and through us, like that magnetic system of which modern science speaks, penetrating us with a network subtler than our subtlest nerves, yet bearing in it the central forces of the world."[5]

Rather than an ideal realm of forms, rather than an entirely separate realm of nonbeing with which we are at war, we seek an electromagnetic field, or another invisible dimension that runs at crosscurrents to our own. (There's that metaphor again of the main current and the central forces of the world, and that question again about what other subtler currents might branch off in unexpected directions.) Pater's electromagnetic field is something like Meinong's third order of being, an energy that shoots through existence and subsistence alike: a different kind of ground, a different version of ontological "necessity."

It's more difficult to imagine extricating ourselves from this ground, like imagining how to pull the basement out from underneath the house. Pater's metaphysical ground is of us and in us, the basement type that moves perpendicularly across the fibers of our world, only metaphorically "underneath."

Plato sought "a standard of unchangeable reality," a set of "ideas or ideals" by which "we come in contact . . . with the insoluble, immovable granite beneath and amid the wasting torrent of mere phenomena."[6] Beneath and amid: even in describing Plato's theory, Pater wants to emphasize its uncertainty about background and foreground. Is it that Plato's forms are the solid foundation underneath the roiling waters of phenomena, more immovable and therefore more real? Or is it that this hard granite itself only takes shape against the background, in the midst of, the moving phenomena that erode its soft places, seeking the point at which its hardness becomes insolubility?

"Hereafter, in every age," Pater warns, "some will be found to start afresh quixotically, through what wastes of words! in search of that true Substance, the One, the Absolute, which to the majority of acute people is after all but zero, and a mere algebraic symbol for nothingness." Pater laments the lasting influence of this aspect of Plato's metaphysics: "By one and all it is assumed, in the words of Plato, that to be colourless, formless, impalpable is the note of the superior grade of knowledge and existence, evanescing steadily, as one ascends toward that perfect (perhaps not quite attainable) condition of either, which in truth can only be attained by the suppression of all the rule and outline of one's own actual experience and thought."[7]

From Pater's goal of "moulding" our lives to artistic perfection—a task that requires us to renounce the taste for metaphysics—we arrive at Pater's critique of a metaphysical theory that sees perfection as a matter of evanescence, a suppression of actuality in favor of transcendence. But how do we square this critique of Plato's metaphysics with the colorless and pure existence of that "basement type" that seems to promise the world's regeneration from below?

The basement type underlies our world, but only just barely, hovering at the refined edge of the moralized right to exist, and promising that it might, if it could multiply, serve as the ground for a new and yet real world, regenerated. We might say that Pater's basement type is what Quine's fictional philosopher Wyman would have called an "unactualized possible," a fictional being who could change the world if only they became real, if only they could move from Quine's "slum of possibles" into the community of the actual.

The basement type finds its position on the charged borderline between the pure and the impure, the colorless and the variegated, remaining painfully on that disorienting queer periphery—what we've already seen Sara Ahmed describing as "a way of inhabiting the world at the point in which things fleet"—whereas Plato and his followers aim for the heaven of pure being, ascribing to colorless, transparent nothingness the supreme "right to exist."

Living in his brilliantly illuminated, electrified basement, the narrator of Ralph Ellison's *Invisible Man* (1952) tells us that when the world can't or won't see you, when you become invisible, "you often doubt if you really exist. You wonder whether you aren't simply a phantom in other men's minds. . . . You ache with the need to convince yourself that you do exist in the real world."[8] With Pater in mind, with *The Grounds of the Novel* in mind, I can't help but think of Ellison's narrator as describing simultaneously a problem of racialized being and a problem of fictional being.

Ellison's narrator insists that even though no one seems to see him, "I am a man of substance, of flesh and bone, fiber and liquids" (3). I began this book with the fictional Wyman mounting a defense of fictional being. I conclude now with Ellison's fictional narrator mounting a defense of Black existence that is the same time a claim to the substance, the flesh-and-blood fibrous actuality, of fictional being. These two aspects of his claim cannot, I think, be prized apart.

It's not any deficiency or anomaly in *him* that makes him invisible, he tells us. He is not a "spook," not "one of your Hollywood-movie ectoplasms." His invisibility has nothing to do with "a biochemical accident to my epidermis." It is a matter of others' inability to see rightly, "a peculiar disposition of the eyes of those with whom I come in contact. A matter of the construction of their *inner* eyes, those eyes with which they look through their physical eyes upon reality" (3).

But Ellison's narrator, having embraced his quality of invisibility, has "found a home—or a hole in the ground, as you will." Something like Isabel Archer breaking through the ground from underneath as she emerges into fictional existence, but gone topsy-turvy, or something like Cora mapping the Underground Railroad as she navigates its entrances, its exits, and the tunnels that connect them, he cultivates invisible being in the place where the ground opens toward another ground below. Don't assume that he's deprived, he warns us, don't assume that because he lives in a "hole" it must be "damp and cold like a grave; there are cold holes and warm holes. Mine is a warm hole."

He does not sink into nonexistence: he hibernates. He urges us to "remember, a bear retires to his hole for the winter and lives until spring; then he comes strolling out like the Easter chick breaking from its shell" (6).

I always think of Pater's basement type when I read those lines. "A majority of such would be the regeneration of the world." It's a matter of waiting to emerge. "A hibernation," Ellison's narrator says, "is a covert preparation for a more overt action" (13).

So much of being is a fiction. So much of being is being invisible, being made invisible. So much of seeing and knowing being is a matter of the inner eyes, not the physical ones.

Until he can be seen, light will have to stand in for others' inner eyes. Ellison's narrator drains off "a hell of a lot of free current" from the electric company, wiring his basement with over one thousand light bulbs (5, 7). "Light confirms my reality, gives birth to my form," he says. "Without light I am not only invisible, but formless as well; and to be unaware of one's form is to live a death" (6–7). Basement being is self-sufficient being, imagining a ground for one's own being elsewhere, deeper, warmer. If light is what's needed (because inner eyes, the keen sense for reality, are lacking), then the current can be redirected to the "border area" of Harlem where this fictional man hibernates.

Even when there are no eyes to see it, being makes a home for itself.

Being settles into holes in the ground. Being resourceful, being illuminates its own form.

Being figures itself in light, in earth, in groundwork, in underground, in groundbreaking, in seabeds, in colorlessness and in Blackness, in flesh and in blood and in dreambody.

Being waits in the basement, biding time.

ACKNOWLEDGMENTS

Thank you to the trusted colleagues and friends who read chapter drafts or even the entire manuscript along the way, and whose responses helped determine the direction and final shape of the book: Thom Dancer, Josh Gang, Kara Gaston, Melissa Gniadek, Rijuta Mehta, Anjuli Raza Kolb, Anna Thomas, and Marshelle Woodward.

I am ever thankful for the administrative staff in the Department of English and Drama at the University of Toronto Mississauga and in the Graduate Department of English at the University of Toronto, all of whom have helped me in countless ways: at UTM, Rob Eberts, Merrylee Greenan, Megan Janssen, Cecilia Konney, Sabrin Mohammed, and Waffa Saleem; and in the Graduate Department, Elly Choi, Benjamin Eldridge, Kelly Hayward, Cristina Henrique, Tanuja Persaud, Marguerite Perry, Jason Phillips, Wajiha Rasul, and Elizabeth Wulf.

The writing of this book was made possible thanks to an Insight Grant from the Social Sciences and Humanities Research Council of Canada. For invaluable help in the grant application process, thanks to Carla DeMarco and Mark Bold. During the years I was working on this book, I also had the generous support and mentorship of several department chairs and associate chairs at UTM and the Graduate Department: thank you to Alex Gillespie, Dan White, Rick Greene, Terry Robinson, Jacob Gallagher-Ross, Paul Stevens, Tom Keymer, Paul Downes, and Naomi Morgenstern.

My work on this book benefited immensely from conversations with audiences at Harvard's Mahindra Center for the Humanities, Queen Mary University of London, the Society for Novel Studies, the North American Victorian Studies Association, and the American Comparative Literature Association. I thank those who attended and engaged so generously with my work, and especially Deb Gettelman, Aeron Hunt, Chunlin Men, Kathleen Frederickson, Jonathan Farina, David Kurnick, and Yoon Sun Lee for their invitations and their organizational labor.

Many others have helped me in my work on this book, whether offering enlivening, encouraging conversation; or useful reading suggestions; or mentorship; or much needed resources; or simple gestures of friendship and support: thank you to Rachel Ablow, Tania Aguila-Way, Carolyn Betensky, Pearl Brilmyer, Alicia Mireles Christoff, Jonathan Farina, Daniel Hack, Audrey Jaffe, David Kurnick, Deidre Lynch, Meredith Martin, Andrew Miller, Carol Percy, Simon Reader, Terry Robinson, Talia Schaffer, Cannon Schmitt, Dana Seitler, Emily Steinlight, Cheryl Suzack, Irena Yamboliev, and Karen Zumhagen-Yekplé.

Teaching an undergraduate course on Thomas Hardy and the graduate seminar "Decadent Natures" was central to my thinking about the project as it blossomed from Hardy outward, and I thank those intrepid students for taking the journey with me.

An early version of chapter 1 appeared as "Thomas Hardy's Groundwork," *PMLA*, vol. 134, no. 5, October 2019, published by the Modern Language Association of America, and the astute reading of two anonymous readers as well as the journal's editorial board had an enormous influence not only on that chapter but the entire book. Thank you to the MLA for permission to reprint.

It has been a privilege to work with the team at Stanford University Press. Caroline McKusick has been a dream editor. Her excitement about this book has been so meaningful to me, and she solicited reports from two truly brilliant anonymous readers, each of whom was a model of peer review at its very best, seeing the book and its aims clearly and suggesting how to make it the fullest iteration of itself. Thanks also to production editor Gigi Mark, to marketing assistant Kapani Kirkland, to the design team, and to copy editor Susan Olin for all of their smart, thoughtful, creative work transforming a manuscript into a book.

My husband, Jeff Campanelli, and our daughter Rose are the two people I am most grateful for, beyond words, beyond measure.

During the time I was writing this book, I lost my father, Brian Wright, but he has remained vividly present to me as a voice in my head and a visitor in my dreams. He and my mother, Lisa, laid the ground upon which my own life has flourished. I wish I could give him a copy of this book. I know he would have been proud.

NOTES

Preface
1. Eliot, *Daniel Deronda*, 125.
2. Pater, *Plato and Platonism*, 115, 118.
3. Pater, 119.
4. Pater, 125.
5. Cather, "The Novel Démeublé," 6.
6. Pater, *Plato and Platonism*, 128.
7. Austen, *Pride and Prejudice*, 164.
8. Austen, 164.
9. Levinas, "There Is," 30.
10. Levinas, 35.

Introduction: On What There Is in the Novel
1. Quine, "On What There Is," 21. Further citations appear parenthetically within the text.
2. As Emily Steinlight has argued in *Populating the Novel*, the fictional imagination of the realist novel actually excels at population control. The wrangling of excess, unmanageable masses, is a fundamental principle of its form, and in the post-Malthusian moment of

the nineteenth century, fiction took on the role of "revealing the accumulation of life perpetually surpassing society proper"; "realist art" in particular, with "its promise to make mass life affectively graspable," takes the unrepresentable, uncountable crowd as a starting point (3, 11).

3. Souriau, *Different Modes*, 150–51.

4. Latour, *Inquiry*, 239.

5. Similarly, proponents of "ontological permissivism" take issue with the conservative approach characterized by Quine, with its tight control over the number of existing objects, arguing instead for the existence of a dizzying plenitude of objects, but they limit their thinking to the material world and are strangely indifferent to the question of fictional being. For an overview of debates between permissivism and conservatism in contemporary metaphysics, with the aim of defending conservatism, see Korman, *Objects*, 13–25. For an overview of the same debate, but with the aim of defending permissivism, see Fairchild and Hawthorne, "Against Conservatism."

6. Gallagher, "Rise of Fictionality," 349.

7. Smith, "The I Who Is Not Me," 346.

8. Foucault, *History of Sexuality*, 101.

9. Schaffer, "On What Grounds What," 348, 347. Further citations appear parenthetically within the text.

10. For an analysis of the problem of the stage as metaphysical ground in the context of theater history, and the development of the raised stage as "emancipation from the ground" (69), see Puchner, "The Problem of the Ground."

11. Ahmed, *Queer Phenomenology*, 160.

12. Chandler, *X*, 21; Keegan, "Getting Disciplined," 6.

13. Moten, "Blackness and Nothingness," 739. In my own prose I generally use "Black" and "Blackness" to refer to people, culture, and identity, but when analyzing the work of other critics and theorists, I mirror them when they use "black" and "blackness." While this makes for some inconsistency, I hope that it also reflects the reality of an ongoing discussion in the field of Black studies.

14. In *The Savage Detectives Reread*, David Kurnick uses the metaphor of "gravity" along related lines to think about Roberto Bolaño's particular kind of reality effect, the "impression of reality" generated by his fiction (13–14) and his way of making the reader feel at home in its fictional world: "part of the gravity effect of his writing was . . . the sense that I too was positioned, geolocated in the world mapped by his imagination" (22).

15. Blumenberg, *Paradigms*, 3, 5, 14, original emphasis. For another engagement with Blumenberg's theory of metaphorology, resonant with my own, to trace the literary and philosophical history of the metaphor of "roots" and "rootedness," see Wampole, *Rootedness*.

16. Blumenberg, *Paradigms*, 14.

17. Blumenberg, "Concept," 513, original emphasis.

18. Blumenberg, "Concept," 513n11.

19. Manley, "Introduction," 1. For another useful overview of the field, see Bliss and Miller, eds., *Routledge Handbook of Metametaphysics*.

20. Blumenberg, "Concept," 522, 524.

21. Elaine Auyoung asks in *When Fiction Feels Real* "how nineteenth-century novels invite readers to feel as though they have come to know unreal persons, places, and incidents in unexpectedly intimate and durable ways" (3), and my reading perhaps focuses on the "unexpectedly . . . durable" part of her formulation. How does it all hang together? What kind of durability sustains fictional being? Timothy Gao has recently argued in his analysis of the Victorian novel's engagement with ideas of virtuality and play that "the famously ordinary realist setting occupies a magical or quantum existence we take extraordinarily for granted," and that fiction in the nineteenth century comes to occupy "an alternative plane of reference, existing non-materially yet concretely, independently yet in parallel to the actual" (*Virtual Play*, 20). Part of my goal here is to cease taking that "magical" existence for granted but also to think in metaphysical terms about what the elaboration and figuration of such an alternative plane means for our understanding of being, whereas Gao wants to

understand the vicarious and virtual quality of fictional "experience" through the history of thinking about play.

22. Beauvoir, "Literature and Metaphysics," 269. For another reading of Beauvoir's essay, much more extensive than mine, in relation to the history and theory of the novel, see Ong, *Art of Being*, especially 38–39 and 79–89. Ong and I share an interest in thinking about the novel's special capacities for thinking about ontology, although her focus on the tradition of existentialism, a specifically "existentialist poetics of the novel" (34), and "the impact of novelistic form on existentialist thought" (35) means that she takes up a rather different set of metaphysical questions than I do, generally focused on "the problematization of aesthetic totalization from the perspective of the demands of first-person authority over existence" (34).

23. Beauvoir, "Literature and Metaphysics," 273, 275, 274.

24. Beauvoir, 274–75.

25. For a particularly nuanced and imaginative account of this seemingly banal observation, that when we read we feel as if we exist in reality and unreality simultaneously, see Plotz, *Semi-Detached*. Plotz examines "the interplay between actuality and aesthetic mimesis" in a range of novels, films, and visual art in order to "shed light on how writers understood what it meant for readers to experience the world of a book as if it were real, while nonetheless remaining aware of the distance between such invention and one's tangible physical surroundings" (3). Plotz is interested less in the metaphysical implications and more in the phenomenological complexities of this paradox.

26. See Parent, "Ontological Commitment," for one example of the view that Quine's Wyman is "Meinong in a thin disguise" (86). Parent also points out that Quine in private correspondence denied that McX and Wyman were meant to stand for any real philosophers (95n4) and in that sense insisted upon their fictionality.

27. Meinong, "Theory," 78. Further citations appear parenthetically within the text.

28. Russell, "My Mental Development," 17.

29. Boxall, *Value of the Novel*, 13.

30. Bewes, *Free Indirect*, 6.
31. Manley, "Introduction," 3.
32. Carnap, "Empiricism," 21.
33. Carnap, 21–23, 24.
34. Quine, "On What There Is," 21.
35. Carnap, "Empiricism," 24.
36. Austin, "Plea," 7.
37. Kramnick, *Paper Minds*, 22.
38. Nersessian, *Calamity Form*, 2, 11. See also Kramnick and Nersessian's cowritten essay, "Form and Explanation," which extends their understanding of ontological pluralism to an argument that "form" can and should have different meanings as it pursues different kinds of explanations in different disciplinary contexts.
39. Carnap, "Empiricism," 23.
40. Bersani, *Thoughts and Things*, 69.
41. I draw the items in this list from Livingston and Sauchelli, "Philosophical Approaches," which offers a detailed overview of several ways philosophers have theorized the ontology of fictional characters. For more on possible worlds as a model for understanding fictional being, including a useful précis of the history of the possible worlds approach in narrative theory, see Ryan, "From Parallel Universes to Possible Worlds," especially 643–51. For foundational work in this field, see Ryan, *Possible Worlds* and Doležel, *Heterocosmica*.

As I've already suggested in my citation of Bersani, my objection to possible worlds approaches lies in their emphasis on fictional being as only "possible" rather than in some important literary sense elaborating an account of its own unique mode of actuality. I agree with Doležel's basic idea that the relation between fictionality and actuality is "a bidirectional exchange," so that while fictional world-making draws upon the materials of reality, "in the opposite direction, fictional constructs deeply influence our imagining and understanding of reality," but I disagree with him when he says, in a Quinean mode, that "we grasp fiction in opposition to reality" (x). That kind of approach, I insist, leads us away from close reading and literary interpretation, insisting on seeing fiction as problematic from the point of view of actuality, rather than trying to understand its being as it is constructed and elaborated in the form and figural language of the novel itself.

42. Adorno, *Aesthetic Theory*, 1.

43. Zhang and Freed-Thall, "Modernist Setting," n.p.

44. Ohi, *Inceptions*, 4, 11, 18. For a similar kind of reading, see Hayot, *On Literary Worlds*, which argues in a Heideggerian vein that in the creation of a literary world, "A world encloses and worlds itself as the container that is identical with its contents and its containing, as a ground for itself that does not exceed or reach outside itself" (24). Although Hayot's concerns extend occasionally into metaphysics, he is most interested in the problem of "world" as it concerns the formulation of a new idea of "world literature." We might also think of Anna Kornbluh's "antimimetic theory of realism," which imagines the realist novel as "a speculative projection of hypothetical social space" rather than primarily a representation bound to the status quo of the actual world (*Order of Forms*, 30, 13). For a further elaboration of this idea of antimimetic realism, focused on the fiction of Vernon Lee, see Yamboliev, "Vernon Lee's Novel Construction."

45. Adorno, *Aesthetic Theory*, 59.

46. Jaffe, *Victorian Novel*, 2.

47. Freedgood and Schmitt, "Denotatively," 3.

48. Freedgood, *Worlds Enough*, 34, 99–100. See also Jones, *Realism, Form, and Representation*, for an argument focusing on the development of realism in the Edwardian period. Jones claims that Edwardian novelists developed a concept of "synthetic realism," or in other words realism "not as the determined reflection of an established reality but instead as the overdetermined representation of unsolvable metaphysical dilemmas that disrupt the integration of reality" (3).

49. For a reading of metalepsis that brings together examples from film and metaphysics, see Kennedy, who points out that in classical metaphysics, metalepsis is a crucial figure for marking the hierarchical relationship between "the natural and the *super*natural, what is

part of human experience and what lies *beyond* it" (228). Metalepsis is about "a separation of realms of being," or what I'm describing as an impulse to analyze one realm of being only by getting fully outside of it to another realm that lies beyond its edges. Kennedy's reading of Christopher Nolan's *Inception* explores the possibility that we might sometimes need to accept the terms of the reality we occupy rather than restlessly seeking confirmation of its actuality by getting outside of it.

50. Wittgenstein, *Philosophical Investigations*, §217.

51. Brooks, "Formalist Critics," 72; Derrida, *Of Grammatology*, 158. My thanks to an anonymous reader of the manuscript for suggesting the term "internalist" to describe my commitments as a reader.

52. Macpherson, "A Little Formalism," 390.

53. Moi, "Nothing Is Hidden," 34–35.

54. See Freedgood and Schmitt, "Denotatively."

Chapter 1: Groundwork

1. Hardy, *Far from the Madding Crowd*, 85. Further citations appear parenthetically within the text.

2. Steinberg, "Other Criteria," 84.

3. For a reading of painterly representations of "ground level" that engages with some of these problems, see Clark, "Painting at Ground Level."

4. Nancy, *Ground of the Image*, 7.

5. Hardy, *Return of the Native*, 41. Further citations appear parenthetically within the text.

6. Casagrande, *Unity in Hardy's Novels*, 7.

7. Hardy, *Life and Work*, 239.

8. Ahmed, *Queer Phenomenology*, 157, 178.

9. Barthes, *The Neutral*, 50.

10. Moten, "Blackness and Nothingness," 739.

11. Brilmyer, *Science of Character*, 107, 106.

12. See Jacobus, "Tree and Machine"; Scarry, "Participial Acts"; J. Hillis Miller, *Topographies*, 9–56, and "Individual and Commu-

nity"; Shires, "Radical Aesthetic"; Irwin, *Reading Hardy's Landscapes*; Ward, "*The Woodlanders* and the Cultivation of Realism"; and Jaffe, *Victorian Novel Dreams of the Real*, 94–116.

13. See Bullen, *Expressive Eye*; Berger, *Thomas Hardy and Visual Structures*; Auyoung, "Sense of Something More."

14. See Kornbluh, *Order of Forms*, 122–38; Cohen, *Embodied*, 86–107; Cohn, *Still Life*, 148–83; Henchman, *The Starry Sky Within*, 129–57; Christoff, *Novel Relations*, 22–45; and Brilmyer, *Science of Character*, 103–143.

15. Hardy, *Under the Greenwood Tree*, 108.

16. Hardy, *Jude the Obscure*, 8. Further citations appear parenthetically within the text.

17. In a dissertation in progress at the University of Toronto, Angela Du reads *Tess of the d'Urbervilles* as elaborating a palimpsestic temporality by which subjectivity can be scraped clean and revised. That metaphor of the palimpsest resonates in my mind with the metaphor of the primed canvas or the blank page that I consider in this chapter.

18. Ward, "*The Woodlanders* and the Cultivation of Realism," 868.

19. See William Cohen's *Embodied* for a reading of *The Return of the Native* and its attention to the face "as a screen onto which thoughts and feelings are projected and as a physiological receptacle for sensory encounters with the world" (88). While Cohen's concern is with problems of characterization, and the human body's sensory relationship to the landscape, I share his sense that "For Hardy, . . . the face is a tissue of interwoven strata" (91), built in layers that both register and resist the straightforward relationship between background and foreground, or between groundwork and finish.

20. J. Hillis Miller, *Topographies*, 9–10, 21, 16, 19.

21. Hardy, *Tess of the d'Urbervilles*, 304.

22. For a different reading of Hardy's interest in the obscurity of nighttime, focusing on Hardy's "lit-window scenes" as "lyric interpolations in his novels' love plots" (162), see Gibson, "Thomas Hardy's Lit Interiors."

23. Elisha Cohn reads scenes such as this one as emblematic of Hardy's interest in portraying "a world without human autonomy, individuality, or agency" (*Still Life*, 153). In describing Egdon Heath, Cohn argues, Hardy "evokes a diminished self-awareness, and in-between existence, that refuses the pressures of self-reflection without invoking individual interiority. The most extraordinary features of the heath are at once super-perceptible and unperceived" (157). Although I'm less interested than Cohn in the implications of this scene for questions of autonomy or agency, I follow her in wanting to emphasize the existential "in-between" that Hardy's groundwork invokes.

24. See Scarry, *Dreaming by the Book*, 77–88.

25. Simplicius, *On Aristotle Physics 6*, 114.

26. Carson, *Eros the Bittersweet*, 81–82.

27. Nancy, *Ground of the Image*, 59, 61–62.

28. For another version of the impossibility of getting anywhere on foot in Hardy, in this case because one tends to move in a circle and end up where one began, see Kolb, "Plot Circles."

29. Lukács, *Theory of the Novel*, 29. Further citations appear parenthetically within the text.

30. As Anna Henchman has pointed out, Hardy is deeply interested across his career with the problems of perspective opened up by techniques and theories of astronomical observation. She focuses on how Hardy compares the observation of celestial bodies to the observation of other minds (*Starry Sky Within*, 129–57). For another reading of the way in which the movements and interactions of celestial bodies model problems of literary form, taking Chaucer's poetry as its central example, see Gaston, "Forms and Celestial Motion."

31. Bersani, *Thoughts and Things*, 69.

32. For readings of the problem of scale in Hardy's fiction, more attuned to ecology and to the measurement of "deep time," see Morgan, "Scale in *Tess* in Scale" and Rosenberg, "Infinitesimal Lives."

33. Hardy, *Life and Work*, 184.

34. Hegel, *Philosophy of Right*, 10.

35. Williams, *Marxism and Literature*, 132, 131.

36. Hardy, "Science of Fiction," 263; Hardy, *Life and Work* 107.

37. Hardy, "Science of Fiction," 263.

Chapter 2: Underground

1. Schreiner, *African Farm*, 1. Further citations appear parenthetically within the text.

2. Ivan Kreilkamp argues that the metaphor of the giant's grave stands for the geography and temporality of settler colonialism: "The present-day living erects itself on the grave of the displaced or vanished formerly living, as if the operations of the human as culturally defined necessitate the killing off of some previous life-form" (*Minor Creatures*, 158). Similarly, Deborah Shapple Spillman identifies the image with a repressed or otherwise occluded Indigenous history that she goes on to identify with Waldo's fraught fascination with cave painting and other traces of Indigenous art (*British Colonial Realism*, 175–216). These readings are helpful in establishing a broader context for Schreiner's racializing metaphors of the underground, whether those metaphors stand for a violently repressed Indigenous presence, for an elusive ontological substrate, or for both simultaneously.

3. J. M. Coetzee argues, for example, that Schreiner's novel helps to establish "one of the *topoi* of South African literature: the veld as the site of the presence of absence," its "topography" as laid out in the opening pages best described as "a limitless plain beneath a limitless sky" ("Farm Novel," 1). Coetzee's reading helps us to see how the novel can verge on the kind of groundlessness we associate with paradox (a present absence) or with the problem of infinite regress.

4. Gage McWeeny argues in *The Comfort of Strangers* that in the nineteenth century, the "social universe" comes to be figured as "invisible dark matter" that exerts "gravitational effects" upon "the sense-making work of realist literary form," and his metaphor seems especially apt for helping us to understand Waldo's anxious, gravitationally inflected night terror of the mass of humanity tipping over into darkness (4, 6).

5. For more on vision as a privileged mode of sensuous experience in *The Story of an African Farm*, which helps to effect a dissolution of the boundary between the body and its environments, see Anne Summers, "Visual Landscapes." This more phenomenological approach to Schreiner's depiction of landscape or ecosystem is exemplified as well by Hannah Freeman, who traces the political implications of "Schreiner's vision of a boundless relationship between her characters and their landscape" ("Dissolution and Landscape," 19); and by Andrew McMurry, who in "Figures in a Ground" examines, from the perspective of ecofeminist theory, the pervasive feeling of the novel's characters of being embedded in the ground.

6. Dickens, *Bleak House*, 20.

7. Schreiner's interest in ontological questions about the nature of existence might be framed not only by philosophy but also by theology, as Kimberly Rodda argues in her recent dissertation, "Doubtful Forms." In her reading of Schreiner, Rodda examines ontological problems, but with a particular focus on the complex relationship between immanence and transcendence that runs through debates about faith, doubt, secularism, and secularization. Religion is beyond the scope of this chapter, but, as Rodda shows, it offers another crucial frame for understanding Schreiner's novel.

8. Moten, "Blackness and Nothingness," 738–39.

9. Warren, *Ontological Terror*, 27.

10. Chandler, *X*, 2.

11. Bradley, *Appearance and Reality*, 2, 38.

12. Ahmed, *Queer Phenomenology*, 172.

13. Schreiner, letter to Betty Molteno, May 24, 1895.

14. Spencer, *First Principles*, 17.

15. Spencer, 71.

16. Spencer, 75.

17. Anahid Nersessian's reading of nescience identifies it as a structuring condition of life under capitalism, located in "the space between fact and hypothesis, where things in the world unevenly graze the thinner stuff of speculation. . . . A standoff between experience

and conjecture, nescience can never quite mend their split" (*Calamity Form*, 48). In this model, nescience is a space between rather than a zone beyond, and yet I think Spencer would like Nersessian's reworking of the spatial metaphor. It is, after all, the vibrating tension between knowledge and its opposite that drives Spencer's argument here.

18. Schreiner, *Undine*, 8–9.

19. Schreiner, 11.

20. Levinas, "There Is," 30.

21. Arata, *Fictions of Loss*, 108.

22. Schreiner, *From Man to Man*, 33–34.

23. Schreiner, 4.

24. This phenomenon of stalled or circular movement aligns with Jed Esty's reading of the novel's plots of stalled or fragmented development, which he maps onto Schreiner's diagnosis of the failure and stagnation of the South African colonial project. "The peculiarly asocial nature and syncopated time of Waldo's development," Esty argues, implies that "he is not subject to everyday realist temporality, but instead models his subjectivity on deep and inhuman forms of zoological, geological, and metaphysical time" (*Unseasonable Youth*, 78). Zarena Aslami similarly traces the "fantasies of wholeness" represented in the novel by a liberal model of the colonial state, which works "to make meaning out of fragments or . . . unattached surfaces of colonial life" (*Dream Life*, 27–28). These readings of the novel's political theory of colonial nationhood or the state, and the way that theory gets bogged down in different forms of fantasy, abstraction, or stasis, run parallel to my own reading of the novel's fantasies of metaphysical gnosis.

25. Cannon Schmitt argues along similar lines that the normative claim of the sentence, and the plural first-person point of view of the chapter as a whole, are grounded in evolutionary theory and its movements between ontogeny and phylogeny: the "we" of this chapter, he claims, "interpellates readers into a shared understanding of evolution as progressive development, offering up specific experiences as universal ones" ("Evolution," 105).

26. Krebs, *Gender, Race, and the Writing of Empire*, 116.
27. McClintock, *Imperial Leather*, 267.
28. Schreiner, *Thoughts on South Africa*, 15–16.
29. Krebs, *Gender, Race, and the Writing of Empire*, 115; Burdett, *Olive Schreiner*, 62.
30. Freedgood, "Fictional Settlements," 399.
31. Freedgood, *Worlds Enough*, xvi.
32. McKittrick, *Demonic Grounds*, xi, x, 5.
33. Souriau, *Different Modes*, 156.
34. Kreilkamp, *Minor Creatures*, 149.
35. Saldívar, "Second Elevation of the Novel," 3–4. Stephanie Li, on the other hand, is deeply critical of the "affront to genre" and "hybrid forms" of *The Underground Railroad* as fundamentally evasive of historical reality, an indulgence in fantasy that offers happy-ending-hungry readers "an escape from history" in its escape from realism ("Genre Trouble," 1, 20).
36. For readings of *The Underground Railroad* that focus on its thematization of infrastructure, see Kornbluh, "We Have Never Been Critical," and Tanaka, "Fossil Fuel Fiction."
37. Whitehead, *The Underground Railroad*, 3. Further citations appear parenthetically within the text.
38. Sharpe, *In the Wake*, 74.
39. Wynter, "Novel and History," 99–100.
40. There's a resonance here with Lara Langer Cohen's analysis of the underground as it appears in the genre of the "city mystery" in US literature. Cohen argues that in the US context especially, the underground represents a unique conflation of literal and metaphoric registers: "[The actual underground's] relationship to the figurative underground presents a particularly dizzying example of how difficult it is to read any literal underground metaphorically, because the figurative underground is itself a metaphor—making the literal underground of the city mysteries a metaphor of a metaphor. Vehicle and tenor become images of one another in a kind of subterranean hall of mirrors" ("Depths," 7).
41. Moten, *Stolen Life*, 158; Best and Hartman, "Fugitive Justice," 3.

42. Dubey, "Racecraft," 368, 369.

43. Jackson, *Becoming Human*, 1, 4.

44. Eliot, "Natural History," 51–52.

45. For another reading of this chapter and how it functions as "a discrepant kind of structural compensation" (31), see James, *Discrepant Solace*, 30–33.

Chapter 3: The Ground Gained

1. James, *Art of the Novel*, 3. Further citations appear in parentheses in the body of the text, with the title abbreviated as *AN*.

2. It's exactly this jumbled quality of Jamesian metaphor that Sianne Ngai identifies with a kind of gimmickry at work in James: "Oversimplistic words for complex things; lavish words for impoverished things; too much for too little and too little for too much. The disproportion between James's tenors and vehicles, between his overworked and underperforming, ostentatious yet impoverished images, elicits a feeling of aesthetic suspicion opening a portal to the gimmick as form" (*Theory of the Gimmick*, 278).

3. Sedgwick, *Epistemology of the Closet*, 97.

4. Ohi, *Inceptions*, 4, 18, 30, 38, 17, 30.

5. Like Ohi, Sedgwick reads the prefaces with an eye to the creative process and its blockages, focusing on a family of anal and digestive metaphors—the rectum, constipation, fisting—that allow James to connect the problem of creativity to the problem of queer shame. See Sedgwick, "Shame, Theatricality, and Queer Performativity: Henry James's *The Art of the Novel*," in *Touching Feeling*, 35–66.

6. See Wright, *Bad Logic*, 142–76.

7. McEwan, *Enduring Love*, 1, 3.

8. For a reading focused on James's dizzying array of architectural metaphors, including the house of fiction, as central to his formalist theory of the novel, see Kornbluh, *Order of Forms*, 33–55. As Kornbluh puts it, "Jamesian architecture invites us to think form spatially" (38).

9. Lubbock, introduction to *Letters*, xv, xix.

10. Bosanquet, *Henry James at Work*, 36.

11. For more on "responsibility" as an ethical problem in the preface to *The Golden Bowl*, see J. Hillis Miller, *Ethics of Reading*, 101–127.

12. Lukács, *Theory of the Novel*, 29.

13. J. Hillis Miller, *Ethics of Reading*, 113.

14. Stanley, *Practices of Surprise*, 114–15.

15. Christoff, *Novel Relations*, 192–93.

Chapter 4: Meeting Grounds

1. Woolf, "Jane Eyre and Wuthering Heights," 188–89.

2. Smith, "The I Who Is Not Me," 333.

3. Woolf, "Jane Eyre and Wuthering Heights," 189.

4. Emezi, *Dear Senthuran*, 52. Further citations appear parenthetically within the text.

5. Smith, "Notes on *NW*," 248.

6. Adorno, *Aesthetic Theory*, 5.

7. Adorno, 5.

8. *Oxford English Dictionary*, 2nd ed., s.v. "dysphoria."

9. Adorno, *Aesthetic Theory*, 5.

10. Romanow, "Metafiction," 1081.

11. Woolf, "On Re-Reading Novels," 122.

12. Woolf, "Modern Fiction," 159.

13. Woolf, 158–59.

14. Woolf, "Jane Eyre and Wuthering Heights," 185.

15. Barthes, "Reality Effect," 146.

16. Woolf, "Modern Fiction," 159–60.

17. Byrne, *The Secret*, 68.

18. Zumhagen-Yekplé, *Different Order*, 139; Zhang, *Strange Likeness*, 117.

19. My reading of Woolf does not claim any particular philosophical influence, although it's been well established by critics before me that Woolf would have been acquainted with the ideas of some of the major philosophers who were her contemporaries. See Banfield, *Phantom Table*, for a thorough accounting of Woolf's approach to epistemology and the ways that resonates with the work of Bertrand

Russell, G. E. Moore, and Ludwig Wittgenstein, among others; and see Quigley, *Modern Fiction*, 63–102, for a reading of Woolf's fiction in relation to Bertrand Russell's writing on the philosophical problem of vagueness, a problem particularly relevant to her interest in blurry border areas between frameworks.

20. Woolf, *To the Lighthouse*, 8. Further citations appear parenthetically within the text.

21. Woolf, "Modern Fiction," 157–8.

22. We might think here about the work of literary critics who have written about the deep affinities between the history of the novel form and the history of seafaring. Margaret Cohen, for example, argues in *The Novel and the Sea* that the history of sea adventure fiction might offer us a counternarrative to Lukács's story of the novel as a genre all about "the disenchanted cosmos.... Unmoored from divine authority as well as assistance, the heroes of sea fiction perform their capacity to negotiate the edges of an unknown, expanding, chaotic, violent, and occasionally beautiful sublunary realm" (3). Her description of the negotiation of edges between realms might easily describe Mr. Ramsay's metaphorized relationship to the sea as much as it does the actually seafaring heroes of the eighteenth and nineteenth centuries that are her focus.

Cannon Schmitt argues in "Tidal Conrad (Literally)" that Conrad's attention to the technical details of nautical life (tides, winds, sails, masts, etc.) helps us to develop a reading practice that values "unwonted attention to the literal in literary texts" (10) as opposed to conventions of close reading that value "the deep and the figurative" (9). In some ways my reading of Woolf stands in contrast to Schmitt's reading of Conrad, since I'm claiming that for Woolf the sea is a locus of the figural rather than of the literal. But in other ways the two readings resonate, since Woolf's interest is fundamentally in the sea as a figure through which we work out the relationship between the fictional and the actual.

23. Smith, "The I Who Is Not Me," 340.

24. Smith, 345.

25. Smith, 337.
26. Eliot, "Natural History," 55.
27. Woloch, *The One vs. the Many*, 13.
28. Barthes, *S/Z*, 94.
29. Smith, "The I Who Is Not Me," 338, 340.
30. Dancer, *Critical Modesty*, 82.
31. Kingston-Reese, *Contemporary Novelists*, 43.
32. Holmes and Dancer, "Novel at the Limit," 377.
33. Houser, "Shimmering Description," 1, 3.

34. Boxall, *Value of the Novel*, 45. See also James, "In Defense of Lyrical Realism," which argues that for Smith, the problem of "lyricism" in the novel represents a deeper problem: that of locating "narrative sites where style both stages and solicits reflections on fiction's affective and ethical capacities" (71). We might also think here of Holmes's identification in "The Novel's Third Way" of "a touchstone in Smith's critical work, a refrain on the interiority of the novel as analogous, or at least hospitable, to the interiority of the mind," a hospitality we might describe as "architectural" (142). Holmes's metaphors are different than mine, but he at least implies a similar set of ontological questions about how something like "mind" (whether the writer's or the reader's mind, or both) can enter into the "interiority" of the novel and find a hospitable environment there.

35. Emezi, *Freshwater*, 4. Further citations appear parenthetically within the text.

36. Amin, "Trans* Plasticity," 50, 51.
37. Ahmed, *Living a Feminist Life*, 115.
38. Keegan, "Getting Disciplined," 4.

39. See also Keegan, "Against Queer Theory," for a related argument about the tense adjacency between the fields of trans studies and queer studies. Keegan argues in that essay that "trans studies is against queer theory" in the sense that "queer theory is the disciplinary surface against which trans studies must constantly narrate itself, the field against which trans studies finds itself pressed in a stipulated intimacy" (349).

40. Keegan, "Getting Disciplined," 6. For another approach to this problem, see Lavery, "Egg Theory's Early Style," which argues "that the construction of queer universalism" (or what Lavery also calls "foundationalist gayness") "in a certain thread of queer theory" exemplified by the work of Eve Sedgwick "has been predicated on the impossibilization of transition" (395).

41. Lavery, "Trans Realism," 721.

42. Snorton, *Black on Both Sides*, xiv.

43. Stryker, "(De)subjugated Knowledges," 10.

Afterword: Basement

1. Pater, "Diaphaneitè," 215. Further citations appear parenthetically within the text.

2. *Oxford English Dictionary*, 2nd ed., s.v. "basement."

3. In *Place for Us*, D. A. Miller describes a similar kind of queer basement fantasy in relation to the Broadway musical, the fantasy of the gay boy who imagines his suffering and isolation transformed into a kind of emotional victory. In a chapter titled "In the Basement" (and in an interlude within the chapter titled "Life down a hole"), Miller describes how, in the 1950s, "the boys destined, as it was said, to be *musical*, would descend into the *basement* of their parents' home . . . , and there they would sing and dance to recorded Broadway music . . . under the magical belief that, having lent the score the depth of their own abjection, they might then borrow all its fantastic hope that their solitary condition would end in glory and triumph."

4. Williams, *Transfigured World*, 9.

5. Pater, *The Renaissance*, 117.

6. Pater, *Plato and Platonism*, 21.

7. Pater, 32, 33–34.

8. Ellison, *Invisible Man*, 4. Further citations appear parenthetically within the text.

BIBLIOGRAPHY

Adorno, Theodor. *Aesthetic Theory*. Edited by Gretel Adorno, Rolf Tiedemann, and Robert Hullot-Kentor. Translated by Robert Hullot-Kentor. New York: Continuum, 2002.
Ahmed, Sara. *Living a Feminist Life*. Durham, NC: Duke University Press, 2017.
———. *Queer Phenomenology: Orientations, Objects, Others*. Durham, NC: Duke University Press, 2006.
Arata, Stephen. *Fictions of Loss in the Victorian Fin-de-Siècle: Identity and Empire*. Cambridge: Cambridge University Press, 1996.
Aristotle. *Metaphysics*. Translated by Hugh Lawson-Tancred. New York: Penguin, 2004.
———. *Physics*. In vol. 1, *The Complete Works of Aristotle: The Revised Oxford Translation*. Edited by Jonathan Barnes. Princeton, NJ: Princeton University Press, 1984.
Aslami, Zarena. *The Dream Life of Citizens: Late Victorian Novels and the Fantasy of the State*. New York: Fordham University Press, 2012.
Austen, Jane. *Pride and Prejudice*. 3rd ed. Edited by Donald Gray. New York: Norton, 2001.

Austin, J. L. "A Plea for Excuses: The Presidential Address." *Proceedings of the Aristotelian Society* 57 (1956–57): 1–30.

Auyoung, Elaine. "The Sense of Something More in Art and Experience." *Style* 44, no. 4 (Winter 2010): 547–65.

———. *When Fiction Feels Real: Representation and the Reading Mind*. Oxford: Oxford University Press, 2018.

Banfield, Ann. *The Phantom Table: Woolf, Fry, Russell, and the Epistemology of Modernism*. Cambridge: Cambridge University Press, 2000.

Barthes, Roland. *The Neutral: Lecture Course at the Collège de France (1977–78)*. Edited by Thomas Clerc and Eric Marty. Translated by Rosalind Krauss and Denis Hollier. New York: Columbia University Press, 2007.

———. "The Reality Effect." In *The Rustle of Language*, edited by Françoise Wahl, translated by Richard Howard, 141–48. Berkeley: University of California Press, 1989.

———. *S/Z: An Essay*. Translated by Richard Miller. New York: Hill and Wang, 2000.

Beauvoir, Simone de. "Literature and Metaphysics." Translated by Veronique Zaytzeff and Frederick M. Morrison. In *Philosophical Writings*, edited by Tricia Wall, 269–77. Champaign: University of Illinois Press, 2004.

Berger, Sheila. *Thomas Hardy and Visual Structures: Framing, Disruption, Process*. New York: New York University Press, 1990.

Bersani, Leo. *Thoughts and Things*. Chicago: University of Chicago Press, 2015.

Best, Stephen, and Saidiya Hartman. "Fugitive Justice." *Representations* 92, no. 1 (Fall 2005): 1–15.

Best, Stephen, and Sharon Marcus. "Surface Reading: An Introduction." In "The Way We Read Now," edited by Stephen Best and Sharon Marcus. Special issue, *Representations* 108, no. 1 (Fall 2009): 1–21.

Bewes, Timothy. *Free Indirect: The Novel in a Postfictional Age*. New York: Columbia University Press, 2022.

Bliss, Ricki, and J. T. M. Miller, eds. *The Routledge Handbook of Metametaphysics*. New York: Routledge, 2021.

Blumenberg, Hans. "The Concept of Reality and the Possibility of the Novel." In *History, Metaphors, Fables: A Hans Blumenberg Reader*, edited and translated by Hannes Bajohr, Florian Fuchs, and Joe Paul Kroll, 499–524. Ithaca, NY: Cornell University Press, 2020.

———. *Paradigms for a Metaphorology*. Translated by Robert Savage. Ithaca, NY: Cornell University Press, 2016.

Bosanquet, Theodora. *Henry James at Work*. Ann Arbor: University of Michigan Press, 2006.

Boxall, Peter. *The Value of the Novel*. Cambridge: Cambridge University Press, 2015.

Bradley, F. H. *Appearance and Reality: A Metaphysical Essay*. 6th ed. London: Allen and Unwin, 1916.

Brilmyer, S. Pearl. *The Science of Character: Human Objecthood and the Ends of Victorian Realism*. Chicago: University of Chicago Press, 2022.

Brooks, Cleanth. "The Formalist Critics." *Kenyon Review* 13, no. 1 (Winter 1951): 72–81.

Bullen, J. B. *The Expressive Eye: Fiction and Perception in the Work of Thomas Hardy*. New York: Oxford University Press, 1986.

Burdett, Carolyn. *Olive Schreiner*. Horndon, UK: Northcote House, 2013.

Byrne, Rhonda. *The Secret*. Hillsboro, OR: Atria Books, 2018.

Carnap, Rudolf. "Empiricism, Semantics, and Ontology." *Revue Internationale de Philosophie* 4, no. 11 (Jan. 1950): 20–40.

Carson, Anne. *Eros the Bittersweet: An Essay*. Princeton, NJ: Princeton University Press, 1986.

Casagrande, Peter. *Unity in Hardy's Novels: "Repetitive Symmetries."* London: Macmillan, 1982.

Cather, Willa. "The Novel Démeublé." *New Republic* 30 (April 12, 1922): 5–6.

Chandler, Nahum. *X: The Problem of the Negro as a Problem for Thought*. New York: Fordham University Press, 2014.

Christoff, Alicia Mireles. *Novel Relations: Victorian Fiction and British Psychoanalysis*. Princeton, NJ: Princeton University Press, 2019.

Clark, T. J. "Painting at Ground Level." In *The Tanner Lectures on Human Values*. Salt Lake City: University of Utah Press, 2002. https://tannerlectures.utah.edu/_resources/documents/a-to--z/c/clark_2002.pdf.

Coetzee, J. M. "Farm Novel and 'Plaasroman' in South Africa." *English in Africa* 13, no. 2 (October 1986): 1–19.

Cohen, Lara Langer. "The Depths of Astonishment: City Mysteries and the Antebellum Underground." *American Literary History* 29, no. 1 (February 2017): 1–25.

Cohen, Margaret. *The Novel and the Sea*. Princeton, NJ: Princeton University Press, 2010.

Cohen, William A. *Embodied: Victorian Literature and the Senses*. Minneapolis: University of Minnesota Press, 2008.

Cohn, Elisha. *Still Life: Suspended Development in the Victorian Novel*. New York: Oxford University Press, 2015.

Dancer, Thom. *Critical Modesty in Contemporary Fiction*. Oxford: Oxford University Press, 2021.

Derrida, Jacques. *Of Grammatology*. Translated by Gayatri Chakravorty Spivak. Baltimore: Johns Hopkins University Press, 1997.

Dickens, Charles. *Bleak House*. Edited by Nicola Bradbury. New York: Penguin, 2003.

Doležel, Lubomir. *Heterocosmica: Fiction and Possible Worlds*. Baltimore: Johns Hopkins University Press, 1998.

Du, Angela. "Not Yet: The Victorian Novel's Untold Futures." PhD dissertation in progress, University of Toronto.

Dubey, Madhu. "Racecraft in American Fiction." *Novel: A Forum on Fiction* 50, no. 3 (November 2017): 365–74.

Eliot, George. *Daniel Deronda*. Edinburgh: Blackwood, 1876.

———. "The Natural History of German Life." *Westminster Review* 66 (July 1856): 51–79.

Ellison, Ralph. *Invisible Man*. New York: Vintage, 1995.

Emezi, Akwaeke. *Dear Senthuran: A Black Spirit Memoir*. New York: Riverhead, 2021.

———. *Freshwater*. New York: Grove, 2018.

Esty, Jed. *Unseasonable Youth: Modernism, Colonialism, and the Fiction of Development*. Oxford: Oxford University Press, 2011.

Fairchild, Maegan, and John Hawthorne. "Against Conservatism in Metaphysics." *Royal Institute of Philosophy Supplements* 82 (July 2018): 45–75.

Foucault, Michel. *The History of Sexuality. Vol. 1: An Introduction*. Translated by Robert Hurley. New York: Vintage, 1990.

Freedgood, Elaine. "Fictional Settlements: Footnotes, Metalepsis, the Colonial Effect." *New Literary History* 41, no. 2 (Spring 2010): 393–411.

———. *Worlds Enough: The Invention of Realism in the Victorian Novel*. Princeton, NJ: Princeton University Press, 2019.

Freedgood, Elaine, and Cannon Schmitt. "Denotatively, Technically, Literally." In "Denotatively, Technically, Literally," edited by Elaine Freedgood and Cannon Schmitt. Special issue, *Representations* 125, no. 1 (Winter 2014): 1–14.

Freeman, Hannah. "Dissolution and Landscape in Olive Schreiner's *The Story of an African Farm*." *English Studies in Africa* 52, no. 2 (October 2009): 18–34.

Gallagher, Catherine. "The Rise of Fictionality." In *The Novel, vol. 1: History, Geography, and Culture*, edited by Franco Moretti, 336–63. Princeton, NJ: Princeton University Press, 2006.

Gao, Timothy. *Virtual Play and the Victorian Novel: The Ethics and Aesthetics of Fictional Experience*. Cambridge: Cambridge University Press, 2021.

Gaston, Kara. "Forms and Celestial Motion in Chaucer's *Complaint of Mars*." *PMLA* 133, no. 2 (March 2018): 282–95.

Gibson, Lindsay Gail. "Thomas Hardy's Lit Interiors." *Thomas Hardy Journal* 30, no. 3 (Autumn 2014): 161–84.

Hardy, Thomas. *Far from the Madding Crowd*. Edited by Suzanne B. Falck-Yi and Linda M. Shires. Oxford: Oxford University Press, 2008.

———. *Jude the Obscure*. Edited by Patricia Ingham. Oxford: Oxford University Press, 2008.

———. *The Life and Work of Thomas Hardy*. Edited by Michael Millgate. London: Macmillan, 1984.

———. *The Return of the Native*. Edited by Simon Gatrell. Oxford: Oxford University Press, 2008.

———. "The Science of Fiction." In *Selected Poetry and Non-Fiction Prose*, edited by Peter Widdowson, 261–64. London: Palgrave Macmillan, 1996.

———. *Tess of the d'Urbervilles*. Edited by Juliet Grindle and Simon Gatrell. Oxford: Oxford University Press, 2008.

———. *Under the Greenwood Tree*. Edited by Simon Gatrell. Oxford: Oxford University Press, 1985.

Hayot, Eric. *On Literary Worlds*. New York: Oxford University Press, 2012.

Hegel, G. W. F. *Philosophy of Right*. Edited and translated by Thomas Malcolm Knox. Oxford: Oxford University Press, 2015.

Henchman, Anna. *The Starry Sky Within: Astronomy and the Reach of the Mind in Victorian Literature*. New York: Oxford University Press, 2014.

Holmes, Chris. "The Novel's Third Way: Zadie Smith's 'Hysterical Realism.'" In *Reading Zadie Smith: The First Decade & Beyond*, edited by Philip Tew, 141–53. London: Bloomsbury, 2014.

Holmes, Chris, and Thom Dancer. "The Novel at the Limit." In "The Novel at Its Limits," edited by Chris Holmes and Thom Dancer. Special issue, *Critique: Studies in Contemporary Fiction* 62, no. 4 (August 2021): 374–85.

Houser, Heather. "Shimmering Description and Descriptive Criticism." *New Literary History* 51, no. 1 (Winter 2020): 1–22.

Irwin, Michael. *Reading Hardy's Landscapes*. New York: St. Martin's, 2000.

Jackson, Zakiyyah Iman. *Becoming Human: Matter and Meaning in an Antiblack World*. New York: New York University Press, 2020.

Jacobus, Mary. "Tree and Machine: *The Woodlanders*." In *Critical Approaches to the Fiction of Thomas Hardy*, edited by Dale Kramer, 116–34. London: Palgrave Macmillan, 1979.

Jaffe, Audrey. *The Victorian Novel Dreams of the Real: Conventions and Ideology*. New York: Oxford University Press, 2016.

James, David. *Discrepant Solace: Contemporary Literature and the Work of Consolation*. Oxford: Oxford University Press, 2019.

———. "In Defense of Lyrical Realism." *diacritics* 45, no. 4 (2017): 68–91.

James, Henry. *The Art of the Novel: Critical Prefaces*. Chicago: University of Chicago Press, 2011.

Jones, Charlotte. *Realism, Form, and Representation in the Edwardian Novel: Synthetic Realism*. Oxford: Oxford University Press, 2021.

Keegan, Cáel M. "Against Queer Theory." In "Trans* Studies Now," edited by Susan Stryker. Special issue, *TSQ: Transgender Studies Quarterly* 7, no. 3 (August 2020): 349–53.

———. "Getting Disciplined: What's Trans* about Queer Studies Now?" In "25 Years On: The State and Continuing Development of LGBTQ Studies Programs," edited by K. G. Valente, Molly Merryman, and Warren J. Blumenfeld. Special issue, *Journal of Homosexuality* 67, no. 3 (October 2018): 1–14.

Kennedy, Duncan. "Metalepsis and Metaphysics." In *Metalepsis: Ancient Texts, New Perspectives*, 223–46. Edited by Sebastian Metzner and Gail Trimble. Oxford: Oxford University Press, 2020.

Kingston-Reese, Alexandra. *Contemporary Novelists and the Aesthetics of Twenty-First Century American Life*. Iowa City: University of Iowa Press, 2020.

Kolb, Margaret. "Plot Circles: Hardy's Drunkards and Their Walks." *Victorian Studies* 56, no. 4 (Summer 2014): 595–623.

Korman, Daniel Z. *Objects: Nothing out of the Ordinary*. Oxford: Oxford University Press, 2015.

Kornbluh, Anna. *The Order of Forms: Realism, Formalism, and Social Space*. Chicago: University of Chicago Press, 2019.

———. "We Have Never Been Critical: Toward the Novel as Critique." *Novel: A Forum on Fiction* 50, no. 3 (November 2017): 397–408.

Kramnick, Jonathan. *Paper Minds: Literature and the Ecology of Consciousness*. Chicago: University of Chicago Press, 2018.

Kramnick, Jonathan, and Anahid Nersessian. "Form and Explanation." *Critical Inquiry* 43, no. 3 (Spring 2017): 650–69.

Krebs, Paula M. *Gender, Race, and the Writing of Empire: Public Discourse and the Boer War.* 1999; reprint, Cambridge: Cambridge University Press, 2004.

Kreilkamp, Ivan. *Minor Creatures: Persons, Animals, and the Victorian Novel.* Chicago: University of Chicago Press, 2018.

Kurnick, David. *The Savage Detectives Reread.* New York: Columbia University Press, 2022.

Latour, Bruno. *An Inquiry into Modes of Existence: An Anthropology of the Moderns.* Translated by Catherine Porter. Cambridge, MA: Harvard University Press, 2013.

Lavery, Grace. "Egg Theory's Early Style." In "Trans* Studies Now," edited by Susan Stryker. Special issue, *TSQ: Transgender Studies Quarterly* 7, no. 3 (August 2020): 383–98.

———. "Trans Realism, Psychoanalytic Practice, and the Rhetoric of Technique." *Critical Inquiry* 46, no. 4 (Summer 2020): 719–44.

Levinas, Emmanuel. "There Is: Existence without Existents." Translated by Alphonso Lingis. In *The Levinas Reader*, edited by Seán Hand, 29–36. Oxford: Blackwell, 1989.

Li, Stephanie. "Genre Trouble and History's Miseries in Colson Whitehead's *The Underground Railroad*." *MELUS: Multi-Ethnic Literature of the U.S.* 44, no. 2 (Summer 2019): 1–23.

Livingston, Paisley Nathan, and Andrea Sauchelli. "Philosophical Perspectives on Fictional Characters." *New Literary History* 42, no. 2 (Spring 2011): 337–60.

Lubbock, Percy. *The Craft of Fiction.* London: Jonathan Cape, 1921.

———. Introduction to *Letters of Henry James*, by Henry James, xiii–xxxi. Edited by Percy Lubbock. New York: Scribner's, 1920.

———. "The Novels of Mr. Henry James." *Times Literary Supplement*, no. 391 (July 8, 1909): 249–50.

Lukács, György. *The Theory of the Novel: A Historico-Philosophical Essay on the Forms of Great Epic Literature.* Translated by Anna Bostock. Cambridge, MA: MIT Press, 1971.

Macpherson, Sandra. "A Little Formalism." *ELH* 82, no. 2 (Summer 2015): 385–405.

Manley, David. "Introduction: A Guided Tour of Metametaphysics." In *Metametaphysics: New Essays on the Foundations of Ontology*, edited by David Manley, David J. Chalmers, and Ryan Wasserman, 1–37. Oxford: Oxford University Press, 2009.

McClintock, Anne. *Imperial Leather: Race, Gender, and Sexuality in the Colonial Context*. New York: Routledge, 1995.

McEwan, Ian. *Enduring Love*. London: Penguin, 1997.

McKittrick, Katherine. *Demonic Grounds: Black Women and the Cartographies of Struggle*. Minneapolis: University of Minnesota Press, 2006.

McMurry, Andrew. "Figures in a Ground: An Ecofeminist Study of Olive Schreiner's *The Story of an African Farm*." *English Studies in Canada* 20, no. 4 (December 1994): 431–48.

McWeeny, Gage. *The Comfort of Strangers: Social Life and Literary Form*. New York: Oxford University Press, 2016.

Meinong, Alexius. "The Theory of Objects." Translated by Isaac Levi, D. B. Terrell, and Roderick M. Chisholm. In *Realism and the Background of Phenomenology*, edited by Roderick M. Chisholm, 76–117. New York: Free Press, 1960.

Mill, John Stuart. "What Is Poetry?" In *The Broadview Anthology of Victorian Poetry and Poetic Theory*, edited by Thomas J. Collins and Vivienne J. Rundle, 1212–27. Peterborough, ON: Broadview Press, 1999.

Miller, D. A. *Place for Us: Essay on the Broadway Musical*. Cambridge, MA: Harvard University Press, 1998.

Miller, J. Hillis. *The Ethics of Reading: Kant, de Man, Eliot, Trollope, James, and Benjamin*. New York: Columbia University Press, 1987.

———. "Individual and Community in *The Return of the Native*." In *Communities in Fiction*, 93–138. New York: Fordham University Press, 2015.

———. *Topographies*. Stanford, CA: Stanford University Press, 1995.

Moi, Toril. "'Nothing Is Hidden': From Confusion to Clarity; or,

Wittgenstein on Critique." In *Critique and Postcritique*, edited by Elizabeth S. Anker and Rita Felski, 31–49. Durham, NC: Duke University Press, 2017.

Morgan, Benjamin. "Scale in *Tess* in Scale." *Novel: A Forum on Fiction* 52, no. 1 (May 2019): 44–63.

Moten, Fred. *Black and Blur*. Durham, NC: Duke University Press, 2017.

———. "Blackness and Nothingness (Mysticism in the Flesh)." *South Atlantic Quarterly* 112, no. 4 (Fall 2013): 737–80.

———. *Stolen Life*. Durham, NC: Duke University Press, 2018.

Nancy, Jean-Luc. *The Ground of the Image*. Translated by Jeff Fort. New York: Fordham University Press, 2005.

Nersessian, Anahid. *The Calamity Form: On Poetry and Social Life*. Chicago: University of Chicago Press, 2020.

Ngai, Sianne. *Theory of the Gimmick: Aesthetic Judgment and Capitalist Form*. Cambridge, MA: Harvard University Press, 2020.

Ohi, Kevin. *Inceptions: Literary Beginnings and Contingencies of Form*. New York: Fordham University Press, 2021.

Ong, Yi-Ping. *The Art of Being: Poetics of the Novel and Existentialist Philosophy*. Cambridge, MA: Harvard University Press, 2018.

Parent, Ted. "Ontological Commitment and Quantifiers." In *The Routledge Handbook of Metametaphysics*, edited by Ricki Bliss and J. T. M. Miller, 85–99. New York: Routledge, 2021.

Pater, Walter. "Diaphaneitè." In *Miscellaneous Studies: A Series of Essays*, edited by Charles L. Shadwell, 215–22. New York: Macmillan, 1895.

———. *Plato and Platonism: A Series of Lectures*. London: Macmillan, 1893.

———. *Studies in the History of the Renaissance*. Edited by Matthew Beaumont. Oxford: Oxford University Press, 2010.

Plotz, John. *Semi-Detached: The Aesthetics of Virtual Experience since Dickens*. Princeton, NJ: Princeton University Press, 2018.

Puchner, Martin. "The Problem of the Ground: Martin Heidegger and Site-Specific Performance." In *Encounters in Performance*

Philosophy, edited by Laura Cull and Alice Lagaay, 65–86. Basingstoke: Palgrave Macmillan, 2014.

Quigley, Megan. *Modern Fiction and Vagueness: Philosophy, Form, and Language*. Cambridge: Cambridge University Press, 2015.

Quine, W. V. O. "On What There Is." *Review of Metaphysics* 2, no. 5 (September 1948): 21–38.

Rauschenberg, Robert. *White Painting* [three panels], 1951. Latex paint on canvas., 72 × 108 inches. San Francisco Museum of Modern Art. http://sfmoma.org.

Rodda, Kimberly. "Doubtful Forms: Uncertain Belief in Victorian Women's Writing." PhD dissertation, University of Toronto, 2020.

Romanow, Jacob. "Metafiction as Reality Effect: Trollope's Quixotism and Novel Theory." *ELH* 89, no. 4 (Winter 2022): 1077–1105.

Rosenberg, Aaron. "'Infinitesimal Lives': Thomas Hardy's Scale Effects." In *Ecological Form: System and Aesthetics in the Age of Empire*, edited by Nathan K. Hensley and Philip Steer, 182–202. New York: Fordham University Press, 2019.

Russell, Bertrand. "My Mental Development." In *Basic Writings of Bertrand Russell*, edited by Robert E. Egner and Lester E. Denonn, 9–22. New York: Routledge, 2009.

Ryan, Marie-Laure. "From Parallel Universes to Possible Worlds: Ontological Pluralism in Physics, Narratology, and Narrative." *Poetics Today* 27, no. 4 (Winter 2006): 633–74.

———. *Possible Worlds, Artificial Intelligence, and Narrative Theory*. Bloomington: Indiana University Press, 1991.

Saldívar, Ramón. "The Second Elevation of the Novel: Race, Form, and the Postrace Aesthetic in Contemporary Narrative." *Narrative* 21, no. 1 (January 2013): 1–18.

Scarry, Elaine. *Dreaming by the Book*. Princeton, NJ: Princeton University Press, 1999.

———. "Participial Acts: Working: Work and the Body in Hardy and Other Nineteenth-Century Novelists." In *Resisting Representation*, 49–90. New York: Oxford University Press, 1994.

Schaffer, Jonathan. "On What Grounds What." In *Metametaphys-*

ics: *New Essays on the Foundations of Ontology*, edited by David Manley, David J. Chalmers, and Ryan Wasserman, 347–83. Oxford: Oxford University Press, 2009.

Schmitt, Cannon. "The Evolution of Point of View." In *Nineteenth-Century Literature in Transition: The 1880s*, edited by Penny Fielding and Andrew Taylor, 98–116. Cambridge: Cambridge University Press, 2019.

———. "Tidal Conrad (Literally)." *Victorian Studies* 55, no. 1 (Autumn 2012): 7–29.

Schreiner, Olive. *From Man to Man, or Perhaps Only—*. Edited by S. C. Cronwright-Schreiner. New York: Grosset & Dunlap, 1927.

———. Letter, Olive Schreiner to Betty Molteno, May 24, 1895. In *Olive Schreiner Letters Online*. Edited by Liz Stanley. http://oliveschreiner.org.

———. *The Story of an African Farm*. Edited by Joseph Bristow. Oxford: Oxford University Press, 2009.

———. *Thoughts on South Africa*. London: Fisher Unwin, 1923.

———. *Undine*. New York: Harper, 1928.

Sedgwick, Eve Kosofsky. *Epistemology of the Closet*. 2nd ed. Berkeley: University of California Press, 2008.

———. *Touching Feeling: Affect, Pedagogy, Performativity*. Durham, NC: Duke University Press, 2003.

Sharpe, Christina. *In the Wake: On Blackness and Being*. Durham, NC: Duke University Press, 2016.

Shires, Linda M. "The Radical Aesthetic of *Tess of the d'Urbervilles*." In *The Cambridge Companion to Thomas Hardy*, edited by Dale Kramer, 145–63. Cambridge: Cambridge University Press, 1999.

Simplicius. *On Aristotle Physics 6*. Edited by Richard Sorabji. Translated by David Konstan. London: Bloomsbury, 1989.

Smith, Zadie. "The I Who Is Not Me." In *Feel Free: Essays*, 333–48. New York: Penguin, 2018.

———. "Notes on *NW*." In *Feel Free: Essays*, 248–50. New York: Penguin, 2018.

———. "Two Directions for the Novel." In *Changing My Mind: Occasional Essays*, 72–98. New York: Penguin, 2009.

Snorton, C. Riley. *Black on Both Sides: A Racial History of Trans Identity*. Minneapolis: University of Minnesota Press, 2017.

Souriau, Étienne. *The Different Modes of Existence*. Translated by Erik Beranek and Tim Howles. Minneapolis: University of Minnesota Press, 2015.

Spencer, Herbert. *First Principles*. 4th ed. New York: Appleton, 1898.

Spillman, Deborah Shapple. *British Colonial Realism: Inalienable Objects, Contested Domains*. New York: Palgrave Macmillan, 2012.

Stanley, Kate. *Practices of Surprise in American Literature after Emerson*. Cambridge: Cambridge University Press, 2018.

Steinberg, Leo. *Other Criteria: Confrontations with Twentieth-Century Art*. New York: Oxford University Press, 1972.

Steinlight, Emily. *Populating the Novel: Literary Form and the Politics of Surplus Life*. Ithaca, NY: Cornell University Press, 2018.

Stengers, Isabelle, and Bruno Latour. "The Sphinx of the Work." Introduction to *The Different Modes of Existence*, by Étienne Souriau, 11–90. Minneapolis: University of Minnesota Press, 2015.

Stryker, Susan. "(De)subjugated Knowledges: An Introduction to Transgender Studies." In *The Transgender Studies Reader*, edited by Susan Stryker and Stephen Whittle, 1–17. New York: Routledge, 2006.

Summers, Anne. "Visual Landscapes and Sensual Settings in Schreiner's *The Story of an African Farm*." *Nineteenth-Century Contexts* 41, no. 2 (May 2019): 141–55.

Tanaka, Shouhei. "Fossil Fuel Fiction and the Geologies of Race." *PMLA* 137, no. 1 (January 2022): 36–51.

Wampole, Christy. *Rootedness: The Ramifications of a Metaphor*. Chicago: University of Chicago Press, 2016.

Ward, Megan. "*The Woodlanders* and the Cultivation of Realism." *SEL: Studies in English Literature, 1500–1900* 51, no. 4 (Autumn 2011): 865–82.

Warren, Calvin L. *Ontological Terror: Blackness, Nihilism, and Emancipation*. Durham, NC: Duke University Press, 2018.

Whitehead, Colson. *The Underground Railroad*. New York: Anchor, 2018.

Williams, Carolyn. *Transfigured World: Walter Pater's Aesthetic Historicism.* Ithaca, NY: Cornell University Press, 1989.

Williams, Raymond. *Marxism and Literature.* Oxford: Oxford University Press, 2009.

Wittgenstein, Ludwig. *Philosophical Investigations.* 4th ed. Edited by P. M. S. Hacker and Joachim Schulte. Translated by G. E. M. Anscombe, P. M. S. Hacker, and Joachim Schulte. Chichester, UK: Blackwell, 2009.

Woloch, Alex. *The One vs. the Many: Minor Characters and the Space of the Protagonist in the Novel.* Princeton, NJ: Princeton University Press, 2003.

Woolf, Virginia. "*Jane Eyre* and *Wuthering Heights.*" In *Collected Essays,* vol. 1, 185–90. Edited by Leonard Woolf. London: Hogarth, 1966.

———. "Modern Fiction." In *The Essays of Virginia Woolf,* vol. 4, 157–63. Edited by Andrew McNeillie. London: Hogarth, 1984.

———. "On Re-reading Novels." In *Collected Essays,* vol. 2, 122–30. Edited by Leonard Woolf. London: Hogarth, 1966.

———. *To the Lighthouse.* Edited by David Bradshaw. Oxford: Oxford University Press, 2008.

Wright, Daniel. *Bad Logic: Reasoning about Desire in the Victorian Novel.* Baltimore: Johns Hopkins University Press, 2018.

Wynter, Sylvia. "Novel and History, Plot and Plantation." *Savacou* 5 (June 1971): 95–102.

Yamboliev, Irena. "Vernon Lee's Novel Construction." *Nineteenth-Century Literature* 75, no. 3 (December 2020): 346–71.

Zhang, Dora. *Strange Likeness: Description and the Modernist Novel.* Chicago: University of Chicago Press, 2020.

Zhang, Dora, and Hannah Freed-Thall. "Modernist Setting." *M/m Print Plus* 3, no. 1 (March 2018): n.p.

Zumhagen-Yekplé, Karen. *A Different Order of Difficulty: Literature after Wittgenstein.* Chicago: University of Chicago Press, 2020.

INDEX

Adorno, Theodor, 25–26, 141–143, 146, 160, 178
aesthetics, 141–142, 163–164
Ahmed, Sara, 10, 39, 80, 172–173, 183
allegory, 107, 168
Amin, Kadji, 171
Arata, Stephen, 83
Aristotle, 8, 52–53, 70, 74
Aslami, Zarena, 201n17
Austen, Jane, x-xii, 110
Austin, J.L., 23
Auyoung, Elaine, 41, 193n21

Balzac, Honoré de, 117
Banfield, Ann, 205n19
Barthes, Roland, 39, 146, 162
Beauvoir, Simone de, 15, 194n22
being. *See* fictionality; metaphysics; nonbeing

Bennett, Arnold, 145, 147
Berger, Shelia, 41
Bersani, Leo, 24, 62, 195n41
Best, Stephen, 100
Bewes, Timothy, 20
Blackness: and being, 75, 98, 101; in metaphysics (*see also* metaphysics), 10, 74–76, 93, 96, 109, 180, 185; as ontological signifier of absence, 54, 71, 83, 95, 97
Black studies, 11–12, 192n13
Bliss, Ricki, 193n19
Blumenberg, Hans, 13–14
Bolaño, Roberto, 193n14
Bosanquet, Theodora, 122
Boxall, Peter, 20, 164, 207n34
Bradley, F.H., 78–79, 89
Brilmyer, S. Pearl, 40–41
Brontë, Charlotte, 136, 145–146

Brontë, Emily, 136–138
Bullen, J.B., 41
Burdett, Carolyn, 93
Byrne, Rhonda, *The Secret*, 150

Carnap, Rudolph, 18, 21–24
Carson, Anne, 53
Casagrande, Peter, 36
Cather, Willa, x, 8
Chandler, Nahum, 11, 75
Christoff, Alicia Mireles, 41, 135
Clark, T. J., 197n3
close reading: 17, 29, 109, 112–113, 133–134, 141–142, 195n41, 206n22
Coetzee, J.M., 200n3
Cohen, Lara Langer, 203n40
Cohen, Margaret, 206n22
Cohen, William A., 41
Cohn, Elisha, 41, 199n23
colonialism, 76, 93, 168, 200n2, 202n24

Dancer, Thom, 163–164
deconstruction, 29, 44, 81, 114, 173
denotation, 27–28, 30, 37–39, 68
Dickens, Charles, 72, 161
Doležel, Lubomir, 195n41
Dostoevsky, Fydor, 162
Du, Angela, 198n17
Dubey, Madhu, 100
dreambody: 170–171, 185. *See also* embodiment
dysphoria. *See* metaphysics

Eliot, George: *Daniel Deronda*, vii; "The Natural History of German Life," 102, 161
Ellison, Ralph: *Invisible Man*, 12, 183
embodiment: 11, 41, 161, 169–176. *See also* dreambody
Emezi, Akwaeke: *Dear Senthuran*, 139–141, 149–150, 166–176; *Freshwater*, 140–141, 165–176, 179
empiricism: 21–23, 102, 142–143, 146.
ethics, 88, 161–164, 205n11
Esty, Jed, 202n24
existence, rights to: 25, 127, 178–180, 183.
existentialism, 16, 62, 194n22, 199n23

Fairchild, Maegan, 192n5
fictionality: fictional being, 3, 11, 24, 127, 194n26, 195n41; as distinct from lying, 6, 100; vis-à-vis actuality, 20, 27–28, 62, 101, 119, 127, 136–139, 143–144, 168, 172–173. *See also* metaphor; figuration
figuration: and metaphor, 133; and literary criticism, 110–111, 133; of metaphysical ground, 8, 15, 107, 133; as opposed to denotation and actuality, 28–29, 156
form, 29–30, 41–42, 62, 111, 142–143, 195n38, 199n30

INDEX

Foucault, Michel, 7
Freedgood, Elaine, 27, 68, 94, 100
Freed-Thall, Hannah, 26
Freeman, Hannah, 201n5
Freud, Sigmund, 114

Gallagher, Catherine, 6
Galsworthy, John, 145
Gao, Timothy, 193n21
Gaston, Kara 199n30
Genette, Gérard, 94
Gibson, Lindsay Gail, 198n22
ground: basement being, 178–180; grounding the ground, 27, 41, 70; ground gained, 120, 123–125, 127, 129, 134–135; groundwork, 36, 38, 41, 46, 49, 56, 62, 69, 83, 116, 133; meeting grounds, 143, 161, 176; of the novel, ix, xiii, 10, 28, 44, 65, 108–109, 110, 112, 115, 119, 129, 134–135, 138, 141, 143, 148, 157, 177; underground, 70–73, 85, 96, 125, 133, 138

Hardy, Thomas: on Hegel, 63, 132, 143; *Far From the Madding Crowd*, 32–35, 42, 49–57, 131; *Jude the Obscure*, 43; and metaphysical dysphoria, 63, 165; *Under the Greenwood Tree*, 42; *Tess of the d'Urbervilles*, 45–46; *The Return of the Native*, 36, 42, 46–49, 57–63, 105, 158

Hartman, Saidiya, 100
Hawthorne, John, 192n5
Hayot, Eric, 195n44
Hegel, Georg Wilhelm Friedrich, 63–64, 132, 143
Henchman, Anna, 41, 199n30
historicism, 38–40
Holmes, Chris, 164, 207n34
Houser, Heather, 164

immanence, 15, 41, 65, 67, 201n5
inception: 114–115, 125. *See also* Ohi, Kevin
Irwin, Michael, 40

Jackson, Zakiyyah Iman, 101
Jacobus, Mary, 40
Jaffe, Audrey, 26, 40–41
James, David, 204n45, 207n34
James, Henry: 9, 12, 160; preface to *Roderick Hudson*, 104; preface to *The Golden Bowl*, 126–127, 132; preface to *The American*, 116, 119; *The Art of the Novel*, 107, 127–130, 133; *The Portrait of a Lady*, 120, 122, 124, 132; *The Princess Casamassima*, 121
Jones, Charlotte, 196n48
Joyce, James, 149

Keegan, Cáel M., 11, 173, 207nn39–40
Kennedy, Duncan, 196n49
Kingston-Reese, Alexandra, 164

Kolb, Margaret, 199n28
Korman, Daniel Z., 192n5
Kornbluh, Anna, 41, 196n44, 203n36, 204n8
Kramnick, Jonathan, 23, 195n38
Krebs, Paula, 92–93
Kreilkamp, Ivan, 95, 200n2
Kurnick, David, 193n14

landscape, 9, 41, 43–46, 49, 54, 57, 60, 61, 69, 77, 83, 94, 108, 111, 131, 164, 198n19, 201n5
Latour, Bruno, 5
Lavery, Grace, 174, 208n40
Lee, Vernon, 196n44
Levinas, Emmanuel, xii, 83
literary criticism: 133. *See also* close reading; historicism; new criticism
Li, Stephanie, 203n35
Livingston, Paisley Nathan, 195n41
Lubbock, Percy, 121, 124
Lukács, György, 39, 65, 129–130, 159, 164, 206n22

Macpherson, Sandra, 29
Manley, David, 14–15
McCarthy, Tom, 159
McClintock, Anne, 92–93
McEwan, Ian, 119
McKittrick, Katherine, 95
McMurry, Andrew, 201n5
McWeeny, Gage, 200n4

Meinong, Alexius, 17–20, 150, 166, 178, 181, 194n26
metalepsis, 27, 94, 100, 196n49
metaphor: absolute metaphor, 13–15, 147; extended metaphor, and fictionality and actuality, 76, 89, 100–101, 177; and methodology, 29–30, 113, 123; multiple metaphors, 107–110, 119–120; and ontology, 133, 138; 155; racialized metaphor, 40, 180, 203n40. *See also* figuration, racialization
metaphysics: the absolute, 9, 14–17, 73, 132, 116–117, 134, 182; actuality and fantasy, 5–7, 10, 21, 24, 118, 120, 134–135, 139, 140, 144, 158, 163, 165; blackness, 40, 74, 94; Igbo cosmology and metaphysics, 140, 165; infinite regress, 27, 70, 79, 124, 200n3; metametaphysics, 14–15, 21, 37–38, 44; metaphysical dysphoria or confinement, 140–141, 143, 150–151, 165, 170; metaphysical syncretism, 169; ontological pragmatism, 6–7, 18; Plato viii-xii, 2, 87, 181–182; as system versus as activity, 16, 124; unknowability, 16, 18, 77–81, 109, 118. *See also* nescience
mimesis: 14, 24, 39, 41, 92, 101, 139, 157, 194n25. *See also* realism
Mill, John Stuart, 74

Miller, D. A., 208n3
Miller, J. Hillis, 40, 44, 61, 130, 205n11
Miller, J. T. M., 193n19
Moi, Toril, 30
Morgan, Benjamin, 199n32
Moten, Fred, 11, 40, 74–76, 95–96, 100

Nancy, Jean-Luc, 34–35, 54
narration, 26, 94, 126–127, 159
Nersessian, Anahid, 24, 195n38, 201n17
nescience, 80–81, 88, 91, 201n17
New Criticism, 29
Ngai, Sianne, 204n2
Nolan, Christopher, *Inception*, 196n49
nonbeing: realms of, 19, 176, 181; and the novel (see also fictionality), 28; and blackness, 75, 97; the energy of, 178.
novel theory: 8, 12, 20, 122, 133, 142, 154, 157, 159, 163–164, 165, 166, 167, 194n22. See also Lukács, György; novel writing; realism
novel writing, viii, 150

ọgbanje: 140. See also metaphysics: Igbo cosmology and metaphysics
Ohi, Kevin, 26, 113–114, 120, 125, 204n5

omniscience, 26, 33, 54, 70, 72, 73, 78, 89, 102
O'Neill, Joseph, 159
Ong, Yi-Ping, 194n22
ontology. See metaphysics
ontological conservatism: 192n5. See also metaphysics
ontological permissivism: 192n5. See also metaphysics
ontological pluralism: 17, 195n38. See also metaphysics
ordinary language philosophy, 23

paradox: 200n3. See also Zeno's paradox
Parent, Ted, 194n26
Pater, Walter: "Diaphaneitè," 178–181; influence on Olive Schreiner, 74; and Plato, viii–ix, xii; *Studies in the History of the Renaissance*, 181–183
perspective, 199n30
phenomenology, 44, 56, 80, 194n25, 201n5
Plato, viii–x, xii, 2, 63, 74, 87, 181–182
Plotz, John, 194n25
possible worlds: 25, 195n41.
psychoanalysis, 135
Puchner, Martin, 192n10

queerness, 2, 7, 10, 11, 39, 80, 178, 183

queer studies, 173
Quigley, Megan, 205n19
Quine, Willard Van Orman, 1–5, 17, 89–90, 127, 144, 178, 183

racialization: and metaphors of ontological grounding, 71–72, 74, 76, 83, 180, 200n2; and the metaphysics of fictional being, 11–12, 176, 178, 183; and Schreiner's views on race, 92–93
Rauschenberg, Robert, 33–35
realism: experimental realism, 76, 95–96, 203n35; and fictionality, 67; hyperrealism, 145; its limitations, 105, 140, 149, 164, 175; lyrical realism, 164, 175, 207n34; and mimesis, 26–28, 36–41, 101, 196n44; the realist novel, viii, x, 8, 64, 96, 118, 143–145, 175; and romance, 116–119, 120; speculative realism, 96; synthetic realism, 196n48; trans realism, 147; Victorian realism, 149
reality: actuality, 19, 63–34, 87, 120; epistemology, 78–79; as an object of fantasy, 26–28, 100, 128–129; Totality, 14, 39, 118. *See also* metaphysics *and* realism
reality effect: 146, 159, 192n14.

See also Barthes, Roland; realism
refraction, 142
rereading, 106–109, 112, 124–125, 141
responsibility, 128–130, 205n11
romance. *See* realism
Romanow, Jacob, 144
Rosenberg, Aaron, 199n32
Russell, Bertrand, 20, 205n19
Ryan, Marie-Laure, 195n41

Saldívar, Ramón, 96
Sauchelli, Andrea, 195n41
Scarry, Elaine, 40, 48
Schaffer, Jonathan, 7–9, 89, 125
Schmitt, Cannon, 27, 30, 68, 202n25, 206n22
Schreiner, Olive: *From Man to Man, or Perhaps Only—*, 84–86, 90–92; *Undine*, 81–83, 88, 179; *The Story of an African Farm*, 69–74, 77–78, 86–92, 154, 179; *Thoughts on South Africa*, 93
Scott, Walter, 96, 117
Sedgwick, Eve Kosofsky, 111, 126, 132, 204n5
Shakespeare, William, 137
Sharpe, Christina, 97
Shires, Linda, 40
Simplicius, 53
Smith, Zadie: "The I Who Is Not Me," 137–138, 159–164, 172;

Swing Time, 137; *White Teeth*, 138; *Changing My Mind*, "Two Directions for the Novel," 159
Snorton, C. Riley, 174
Spillman, Deborah Shapple, 200n2
Spencer, Herbert, 74, 80–81, 201n17
standpoint: as locatable space, xi-xii, 74–75, 77, 135; metaphors of, 97, 109–110, 123, 125, 153; and perspective, 88, 120, 129, 157, 164; and point of view, 128–129; and spatial orientation, 118
Stanley, Kate, 134
Steinberg, Leo, 33
Steinlight, Emily, 191n2
Souriau, Étienne, 5, 12, 95
Stryker, Susan, 175
Summers, Anne, 201n5

Tanaka, Shouhei, 201n17
theory of the novel. *See* novel theory
transcendence, 5, 78, 79, 183, 201n5
transness, 10, 140
trans* being, 171, 173, 174
trans studies, 11–12, 143, 165, 171–174, 176
theater history, 192n10
theology, 201n7
Trollope, Anthony, 144
Turgenev, Ivan, 125

underground. *See* ground
unreality: and the neutral zone of metaphysical existence, 18–20, 80, 149, 173, 194n25; and the novel, ix, 42, 50, 52, 54, 127, 135, 161; and the real, xii, 18, 94, 149, 165, 167, 170–171; unreal being, 2, 11, 28, 162, 166, 168, 173, 177, 193n21

Wampole, Christy, 193n15
Ward, Megan, 40, 43
Warren, Calvin, 75
Wells, H.G., 145
Whitehead, Colson: *The Underground Railroad*, 76, 95–105, 138
Williams, Carolyn, 180
Williams, Raymond, 64
Wittgenstein, Ludwig, 28, 114, 205n19
Woloch, Alex, 161–162
Woolf, Virginia, 9, 12, 136–139, 166; "On Re-Reading Novels," 144–145; "Modern Fiction," 145–149, 154; *To the Lighthouse*, 150–159
Wright, Daniel, 116
Wynter, Sylvia, 97

Zeno's paradox, 50, 52–54, 57, 59, 66–67, 154
Zhang, Dora, 26, 150
Zola, Émile, 30, 117
Zumhagen-Yekplé, Karen, 150

The authorized representative in the EU for product safety and compliance is:
Mare Nostrum Group
B.V Doelen 72
4831 GR Breda
The Netherlands

www.ingramcontent.com/pod-product-compliance
Lightning Source LLC
Chambersburg PA
CBHW032057230426
43662CB00035B/588